TRADE POLICY AND THE
NEW PROTECTIONISM

Trade Policy and the New Protectionism

David Greenaway

St. Martin's Press   New York

Printed in Hong Kong

First published in the United States of America in 1983

Published in the United Kingdom 1983 by
The Macmillan Press Ltd, London and Basingstoke,
under the title *International Trade Policy: from tariffs
to the new protectionism*

ISBN 0-312-81213-2

Library of Congress Cataloging in Publication Data

Greenaway, David.
   Trade policy and the new protectionism.

   Includes bibliographical references and index.
   1. Commercial policy.   2. Free trade and protection—
Protection.   I. Title.
HF1411.G695   1982   382.7′3   82–10621
ISBN 0-312-81213-2

To my Mother and Father

Contents

Preface

This book grew out of the author's experiences in teaching a final-year undergraduate course in International Economics at the University College at Buckingham; a substantial part of this course is devoted to trade policy, in particular the 'new protectionism'.

The text is written principally for the consumption of undergraduates following courses in International Economics and International Trade. It therefore presumes familiarity with the principles of basic microeconomics and (although mathematical exposition is used sparingly) basic mathematics.

In this text an attempt is made to review and, where possible, synthesise theoretical and empirical aspects of tariff and non-tariff interventions, while emphasising the institutional framework within which tariffs have been gradually replaced by non-tariff instruments as the principal tools of commercial policy. There are therefore chapters which deal with the economic effects of tariff and non-tariff instruments as well as chapters outlining the methodological difficulties of quantifying their effects. In addition, there are chapters dealing with the emergence and operation of GATT and recent threats to the credibility of that organisation. Finally, for completeness, there are chapters which identify the forces which result in international specialisation and exchange, and adjustment difficulties which may be associated with the process.

Deciding how best to organise this material proved a little difficult. The obvious way would perhaps have been to group together theory chapters, empirical chapters and institutional chapters. From the reader's point of view, such an approach would have had advantages in facilitating immediate comparison between tariff and non-tariff instruments. Instead, however, the material has been ordered in such a way that theoretical, empirical and institutional aspects of tariff barriers are grouped together, and similarly with non-tariff barriers. It was felt that not only did this provide the opportunity for the reader to be presented with a fairly complete and integrated review of economic aspects of each type of instrument, but also that it lent some loose chronological ordering to the material.

The text does not cover every aspect of commercial policy, the most obvious exclusion being a consideration of customs-union theory. The exclusion clauses in the GATT articles dealing with customs

unions have undoubtedly influenced economic integration in Western
Europe quite significantly. We simply allude to such issues *en passant*,
however, in part to give due emphasis to the new protectionism, in
part because economic integration is an issue which is already given
adequate coverage in the textbook literature.

A great many people have assisted, whether knowingly or otherwise, in the preparation of this volume. Chris Milner (University of
Loughborough) read the entire draft manuscript and made a great
many helpful suggestions. In addition, one or more chapters were
perused by Hugh Corbet (Trade Policy Research Centre), Andrew
Mason (University College at Buckingham), David Sapsford (University
of East Anglia) and Ron Shone (University of Stirling). All of the
chapters in question underwent improvement as a result of comments
from these individuals. Some of the policy chapters were prepared
while I was a Visiting Scholar at the Graduate Institute of International Studies in Geneva and these benefited from conversations
with Gerard Curzon. Despite such extensive advice, errors of commission and omission no doubt remain for which I alone am, of course,
responsible.

The draft chapters and subsequent revisions were conscientiously
and expeditiously typed by Linda Waterman, who as well as compiling
the manuscript drew my attention to many grammatical errors.

Finally, my wife Susan and my children Stuart and Daniel deserve
my warmest thanks for their encouragement and forbearance. Much
of the time expended on this text should perhaps have been leisure
time, a substantial share in which would have been theirs.

Buckingham, England   DAVID GREENAWAY
April 1982

List of Tables

Introduction

INTERNATIONAL TRADE: SOME ORDERS OF MAGNITUDE

It is generally accepted that the depression years of the 1930s were the most overtly protectionist era of the twentieth century. Depressionary pressures induced most trading nations to become more inward-looking. By contrast, the post-war era, certainly until the oil shock of 1973, has been a period of sustained growth of output and trade. In part this can be directly attributed to the dismantling of protective barriers erected during the inter-war years, while in part it is attributable to the unprecedented technological development which has taken place.

Table I.1 gives some indication of the extent to which trade increased over the two decades 1955-76. From this we can see that, in value terms, exports increased tenfold. In absolute terms, the value of world exports in 1976 was some ten times the value of UK GNP. Of course, increases by value may merely reflect inflationary forces.[1] When, however, we examine quantum figures, or when we take constant price valuations, a similar picture of a quite remarkable increase in trade still emerges. For instance, either measure suggests that world trade more than doubled in the decade 1963-73.

Taking such aggregate figures may not, however, be very revealing. It gives us some idea of the monetary flows which are likely to be associated with international exchange, but it tells us little about the importance of traded goods *relative* to non-traded goods. How, for example, does the rate of growth of trade compare with the rate of growth of GNP over this period? Still taking all countries together, we find that the annual average rate of growth of exports exceeds the annual average growth of GNP. For the period 1948-73, these figures are 7 per cent and 5 per cent p.a. respectively. This has at least two important implications. First, international specialisation has been steadily increasing. Second, as a direct consequence of the first trend, the welfare of most countries is becoming increasingly and more inextricably linked to the foreign trade sector. In short, countries have in general become more 'open'. The extent to which income and employment in many countries has become 'dependent' on foreign trade can be gauged from Table I.2. This provides indices

1

TABLE I.1 Networks of world trade, 1955, 1968 and 1976

Origin → / Destination →	Industrial areas			Developing areas			Eastern trading areas			World		
	1955	1968	1976	1955	1968	1976	1955	1968	1976	1955	1968	1976
Industrial areas	35.7	117.7	435.7	15.8	31.1	138.2	1.3	6.3	33.1	56.7	160.7	622.8
Developing areas	16.5	31.5	180.2	5.9	8.9	57.4	0.6	2.2	10.2	23.7	43.6	253.1
Eastern trading area	1.7	6.1	27.2	0.7	4.0	14.6	6.9	16.7	52.1	9.4	27.0	94.0
World	56.7	99.6	657.4	22.9	45.2	214.5	8.9	25.5	96.5	93.3	237.8	991.0

Note: Figures refer to value of exports (f.o.b) in billions of US dollars.

Source: Compiled from *Networks of World Trade by Areas and Commodity Classes 1955–76*, GATT Studies in International Trade No. 7 (Geneva, 1978) table A.1.

of 'openness' for some fifty-one developed market and less developed economies.[2]

As we can see from Table I.2, activity in the foreign sector accounts for over 10 per cent of GNP in almost all of the countries in the sample. In almost three-quarters of the countries, the index exceeds 20 per cent. If we assume a tendency to balanced trade this amounts to saying that 20 per cent of national income is generated in the foreign trade sector. There are therefore very few countries which could even contemplate withdrawal from the international trading system. It is probable that only a few (physically) large countries would have a sufficiently broad resource base to consider such a step (e.g. the USA, India, the USSR or China). Even these countries would be likely to pay a high cost. Given, however, the interdependencies which trade generates, a great many other nations would pay an even higher cost. In summary, increased specialisation and increased openness have resulted in increased dependence on the traded goods sector, and, through this, increased interdependence. Policy actions which any given country takes affecting its overseas sector have implications for other countries.

The broad pattern of specialisation is also worthy of brief comment at this point. This is summarised by Table I.3. Very broadly speaking

TABLE I.2   Indices of 'openness'

Country	Z	Country	Z	Country	Z
Liberia	78.1	Nicaragua	35.2	Thailand	22.0
Gabon	64.1	Austria	34.5	Sri Lanka	20.0
Swaziland	64.0	Nigeria	32.0	Greece	19.4
Mauritius	60.0	Venezuela	32.0	France	18.6
Botswana	54.5	Korea	32.0	Peru	16.1
Israel	51.2	Sierra Leone	29.1	Colombia	15.0
Singapore	50.0	Sweden	28.6	Sudan	15.0
Netherlands	49.9	Finland	28.0	Australia	15.0
Belgium	48.6	United Kingdom	27.0	Ethiopia	14.0
Denmark	47.7	New Zealand	27.0	Spain	13.4
Ireland	47.1	South Africa	27.0	Japan	12.8
Norway	45.5	Ecuador	27.0	Turkey	9.8
Zambia	45.0	Morocco	25.0	Brazil	9.0
Malaysia	45.0	W. Germany	24.4	Mexico	9.0
Zaire	42.0	Canada	24.0	United States	7.2
Costa Rica	36.0	Italy	22.4	Burma	6.3
Honduras	36.0	Philippines	22.0	India	5.9

Note: $Z = \frac{1}{2} \left[\frac{X + M}{GNP} \right] \times 100$, average for years 1972–7.

TABLE I.3   Structure of merchandise exports

Developing areas	Trading countries' % share of					
	Fuels, minerals and metals		Other primary commodities		Manufactures	
	1960	1977	1960	1977	1960	1977
Low income countries	13	37	70	44	17	19
Middle income countries	25	33	61	30	14	37
Oil exporting developing countries	95	99	4	0	1	1
Eastern trading area	n.a.	24	n.a.	16	n.a.	60
Industrialised countries	11	9	23	15	59	71

Note: n.a. = not available.

Source: Compiled from the World Bank's *World Development Report 1980*, table 9, pp.126–7 (the countries included in each category can be found in this table).

we can see that the merchandise exports of less developed countries are dominated by primary products (fuels, raw materials and food-stuffs), while exports of the industrialised countries are dominated by manufactured goods. Although there have been some changes over the past two decades, as a number of less developed countries have successfully industrialised, the pattern remains of exports of manu-factures being dominated by industrial countries and primary products by less developed countries.

Outline of text

In these introductory paragraphs we have discussed certain general features of international trade, and in so doing we have no doubt masked a large number of distinctive differences. We have, however, only been concerned with gaining some idea of the importance of international trade in the economies of the world, and even an over-view as *simpliste* as this begs a number of fundamental questions. For instance, why does international exchange play such an important part in the economic well-being of so many countries? What are the benefits associated with trade? What determines the commodity composition of international trade flows? What are the implications of policy designed to restrict or reduce the amount of trade which takes place?

These are basically the questions we will be seeking to answer in this volume. Initially we will examine the factors which are likely to result in goods (and services) being exchanged across international frontiers. This in turn will permit us to comment on what determines the commodity composition of trade. Following this we will examine the gains and losses associated with unrestricted international exchange. This will then put us in a position to explore the issues to which this text is predominantly addressed, namely what policy instruments are aimed at influencing foreign trade flows? What are the implications of using these instruments, and what institutional arrangements exist at present and may exist in the future to encourage co-ordinated actions on trade policy?

Our view of trade policy is necessarily restricted. Our central aim is to comment on the forces behind the changing orientation of commercial policies away from tariff interventions towards non-tariff interventions. Perforce this requires a comparison of the economic effects of a variety of instruments, and where possible empirical investigations. It is important to note that one significant aspect of commercial policy is largely ignored, namely the economic effects of discriminatory trade policies associated with economic integration. This is not intended to imply that this aspect of policy is unimportant. Clearly this is not so. Economic integration and the explicit use of discriminatory trade policy has shaped post-war economic development in a significant way, most obviously in Western Europe.

On occasions we shall refer to the impact of economic integration, for example on the GATT system, but it will really only enter our analysis tangentially. A thorough review of thought on the economics of international integration would require a text on its own. Within the context of our analysis of tariff and non-tariff intervention, its role will only be considered *en passant*.

The text is ordered as follows. Part I reviews a number of explanations of the emergence of foreign trade flows and examines the welfare economics of foreign trade. Part II focuses on tariff interventions. Some economic analysis of the 'positive' effects of tariffs is followed by a review of some of the arguments for tariff interventions. This is followed by a more formal analysis of the concept of effective protection. After a review of the GATT system which has 'supervised' the progressive reduction of tariff barriers during the post-war period, we conclude this part with a chapter which focuses on empirical analyses of tariff liberalisation. Part III opens with a chapter aimed at explaining the reorientation of commercial policy away from tariff towards non-tariff interventions in the late 1960s and 1970s. This is followed by an analysis of the economic effects of non-tariff barriers using partial equilibrium techniques.

We then review the difficulties faced by researchers in establishing the extent to which non-tariff interventions are used and report the results of some empirical work. Part IV briefly considers the context for a possible reduction in reliance on non-tariff barriers. The first chapter in this section looks at the economics of adjustment policy and considers to what extent adjustment assistance can be regarded as a substitute for protection from import competition. Finally, we conclude the text with a few speculative comments on the institutional changes which may be necessary to cope with the 'new protectionism'.

PART I

Causes and Consequences of International Exchange and Specialisation

1 An Overview of the Determinants of Exchange and Specialisation

In this introductory chapter, our interest lies in exploring the circumstances under which trade will open. If we are to comprehend fully the implications of restricting trade, whether by tariff or non-tariff interventions, in particular if we wish to have a clear perception of the gains and losses associated with these interventions, then we must also be clear on the forces which are being suppressed.

We will review in this chapter a selection of possible influences which may result in trade opening. The chapter is not intended as any kind of authoritative survey on the sources of trade, but rather a genuine review which can serve as a revision of basic trade theory for those readers familiar with the determinants of trade, while still being comprehensible to those meeting these concepts for the first time. Consequently we do not explore all implications of every model outlined, nor do we comment on empirical studies of the determinants of exchange. Instead we concentrate on emphasising the proximate determinants and the circumstances in which certain influences are likely to be important.

PRECONDITIONS FOR EXCHANGE

The principle of exchange on which a market-based economy is founded is well established. The principle is very simple: if two individuals have different goods, and the valuations which they place on these goods (or services) differs, then a necessary condition for exchange prevails. If both individuals can gain from exchange, a transaction will actually take place. The rate of exchange (or price) at which the exchange is transacted is determined by the relative strength of the two valuations.

Now this may seem intuitively obvious, so obvious perhaps that the necessity of spelling it out might be questioned. Obvious it may be, but it is worth noting that not only is orthodox trade theory founded on this principle, but also the entire edifice of general equilibrium analysis has its roots in it. Most problems in economics revolve around an analysis of the circumstances under which efficient exchange will take place, and the consequences of these conditions not being met.

Our concern is with exchange in one particular type of market, the market for tradeable goods, i.e. those commodities which are exchanged internationally. Basically, the same fundamental principle applies to nations as applies to individuals. If different nations (or more accurately individuals within those nations) have different marginal valuations across different commodities, then exchange will take place. Although the actual process of exchange may be more complicated than an international transaction (because individual countries are politically independent units with individual currencies), the fundamental principle is the same: differences in marginal valuations result in exchange.

SUPPLY-SIDE DETERMINANTS OF EXCHANGE

Labour productivity

One of the first authoritative statements on the emergence of trade was contained in Adam Smith's notion of absolute advantage. Smith proceeded from a fundamental tenet of classical economic thought, the labour theory of value, to the proposition that relative production costs and relative prices are entirely determined by relative labour inputs. In order to outline the principle, it is helpful to make a number of assumptions:

(i)   There are only two countries (A and B), both of which are capable of producing two commodities (x and y).

(ii)   Labour is homogeneous and perfectly mobile, both geographically and occupationally.

(iii) Product and factor markets are competitive, so commodity prices reflect production costs.

(iv)   Production functions exhibit constant returns to scale.

(v)   Demand conditions are given.

(vi)   There are no impediments to exchange (such as transport costs, tariffs, non-tariff barriers).

(vii) Factors of production are immobile internationally.

If these assumptions hold, the long run costs of producing x and y would amount to:

$$x = wl_x \qquad\qquad (1.1)$$

$$y = wl_y \qquad\qquad (1.2)$$

where w refers to wage costs per unit of labour and l_x (l_y) to the number of units of labour per unit of output. Given competitive conditions, wages would of course be equalised across industries and production costs would be reflected in product prices. It follows therefore that relative prices are entirely determined by relative labour requirements, i.e.

$$\frac{P_x}{P_y} = \frac{l_x}{l_y} \tag{1.3}$$

Smith proceeded from here to assert the importance of absolute advantage. Thus, if in country A, one unit of x can be produced with 10 man hours of labour whereas one unit of y requires 20 man hours, then A enjoys an absolute advantage in the production of x. Likewise if in B a unit of x requires 20 man hours while a unit of y requires 10 man hours, B would enjoy an absolute advantage in the production of y. In these circumstances it is in the interest of both countries to specialise in that commodity in which they enjoy an absolute advantage, A in x and B in y. Smith himself summarised the principle by stating:

> it is a maxim of every prudent master of a family never to make at home what it will cost him more to make than to buy. . . What is prudence in the conduct of every private family, can scarce be folly in that of a great kingdom. (Smith, 1776, p.424)

This is a plausible enough statement. It does however lead us to question the outcome of a situation where labour productivity is higher in *both* activities in one of the countries. If, for instance, as above one unit of x and y could be produced with 10 and 20 man hours respectively, while in B the respective inputs were 15 and 25 hours, would A specialise in both commodities? This is an issue to which Ricardo addressed himself. It is worthwhile quoting Ricardo's thoughts on the matter in full:

> England may be so circumscribed that to produce . . . cloth may require the labour of 100 men for one year; and if she attempted to make . . . wine, it might require the labour of 120 men for the same time.
> To produce the wine in Portugal might require the labour of only 80 men for one year, and to produce the cloth in the same country might require the labour of 90 men for the same time. It would therefore be advantageous for her to export wine in exchange for cloth. This exchange might even take place notwithstanding that the commodity imported by Portugal could be produced

there with less labour than in England. Though she could make the cloth with the labour of 90 men, she would import it from a country where it required the labour of 100 men to produce it, because it would be advantageous to her rather to employ her capital in the production of wine, for which she would obtain more cloth from England, than she could produce by diverting a portion of her capital from the cultivation of vines to the manufacture of cloth. (Ricardo, 1817, p.82)

In other words, although labour productivity is higher in both activities in Portugal such that she enjoys an absolute advantage in both cloth and wine, she still finds it advantageous to trade. This follows because what is relevant is not labour productivity per activity *per se* but relative productivity compared with other countries. Put another way, it is not absolute advantage which determines whether or not exchange will take place, but rather *comparative advantage*. Although Portugal enjoys an absolute advantage in both activities, she enjoys a comparative advantage in only one, wine. This can be further elaborated if we take Ricardo's example and actually compute relative prices of wine for cloth in both countries, as follows:

Portugal	1 wine = 0.88 cloth, or 1 cloth = 1.125 wine
England	1 wine = 1.2 cloth, or 1 cloth = 0.83 wine

It is clear that Portugal enjoys a comparative advantage in wine, while England enjoys a comparative advantage in cloth. As long as Portugal can obtain cloth for less than 1.125 units of wine, while England can obtain wine for less than 1.2 units of cloth, then both countries can gain by specialising in the activity in which they enjoy a comparative advantage and exchanging.

Factor proportions

In *The Principles of Political Economy and Taxation*, Ricardo comments:

It is quite as important to the happiness of mankind that our enjoyments should be increased by the better distribution of labour, by each country producing those commodities for which *by its situation, its climate and its other natural or artificial advantages it is adapted*. (Ricardo, 1817, p.80)

Ricardo himself did not elaborate on these 'natural or artificial advantages'. Analysis of these factors more than a century or so later did however provide the basis for the most influential of all theorems dealing with the genesis of trade, the Heckscher-Ohlin-Samuelson theorem. This is the so-called neoclassical analysis of trade (a description applied to describe the mode of analysis rather than period of development) and is founded on the work of Eli Heckscher (1919), Bertil Ohlin (1933) and Paul Samuelson (1948 and 1949). The central question which the H-O-S theorem addresses is, can trade emerge even if factor productivity is identical across countries? The central proposition is again more easily analysed if we make a number of preliminary assumptions:

(i)   We continue with our assumption of two countries (A and B) and two goods (x and y).
(ii) When considering labour productivity we assumed only one variable factor of production (labour). We will now assume that two variable factors can be combined in the production process, labour and capital (L and K).
(iii) Production functions are similar across countries, but differ between commodities. Specifically we will assume that commodity x is relatively labour intensive, while production of y is relatively capital intensive.
(iv) The two countries have different initial endowments of the two factors of production. Specifically we will assume that country B is relatively better endowed with labour, while country A is relatively better endowed with capital. Thus, the price of labour will be relatively low in B, the price of capital relatively low in A.
(v)   Competitive conditions prevail in all product and factor markets.
(vi) Demand conditions are given.

The only difference between the two economies, therefore, is that initial factor endowments differ. From these assumptions we can make the following deductions:

$$\left(\frac{L}{K}\right)_B > \left(\frac{L}{K}\right)_A \Rightarrow \left(\frac{P_L}{P_K}\right)_B < \left(\frac{P_L}{P_K}\right)_A \qquad (1.4)$$

Because initial factor endowment ratios differ between A and B, pre-trade factor price ratios will also differ. Furthermore, given (1.4),

$$\left(\frac{l}{k}\right)_x > \left(\frac{l}{k}\right)_y \Rightarrow \left(\frac{P_y}{P_x}\right)_B > \left(\frac{P_y}{P_x}\right)_A \qquad (1.5)$$

Given different factor intensities in the production of x and y, and different pre-trade factor prices, it follows that pre-trade product price ratios will differ. In our case, x will be relatively cheap in country B and y will be relatively cheap in country A. In other words, the commodity which uses the relatively abundant (scarce) factor intensively in each country is relatively cheap (expensive). We have therefore the precondition for exchange, i.e. a difference in marginal valuations, which results from the fact that our two countries have differing initial endowments of factor inputs. From this the H–O–S postulate logically follows, i.e. each country will specialise in and export that commodity which uses its relatively abundant factor more intensively.

The analysis is easily analysed geometrically. In Figure 1.1 production and consumption of y and x are plotted on the vertical and horizontal axes respectively. AA' and BB' trace out each country's production possibility curve (PPC). Given initial factor endowments these curves trace out those combinations of y and x that can be produced when all factors of production are fully employed. Both PPCs are concave to the origin, reflecting the fact that factor intensities differ between the two commodities. If factor intensities were identical, factors could be transferred from one activity to another without any loss in aggregate output. Because factor intensities differ, there are increasing costs associated with moving from one activity to another. Since the slope of the PPC at any point tells us the marginal rate of transformation of one commodity into another, concavity of the PPC implies a diminishing marginal rate of transformation.

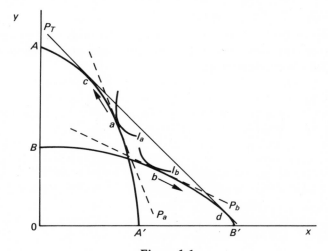

Figure 1.1

The other notable feature of Figure 1.1 is that AA' and BB' have different configurations, which reflects our assumption about differences in initial factor endowments. Since A is relatively well endowed with capital, and since y is relatively capital intensive, A's production frontier suggests that complete specialisation in y would yield a greater total output than complete specialisation in x. The reverse holds true for country B.

Which of the infinity of possible output mixes is actually produced in A and B in the pre-trade situation depends on the strength of consumer demand for each commodity. If we assume that this can be represented by the community indifference curves I_a and I_b then pre-trade equilibrium in each country will be established at points a and b.[1] Finally, the relative prices of the two commodities are given by the relative price ratios P_a and P_b. The steeper slope of P_a indicates that y is relatively cheap in A, while x is relatively cheap in B. It should now be apparent why a and b are equilibrium points. The tangency of the production frontier, the price ratio and the indifference curve implies on the one hand that the marginal rate of transformation in production and the price ratio are equated (yielding a production equilibrium), while on the other hand the equality of the price ratio and the marginal rate of substitution guarantees a consumption equilibrium.

The difference in P_a and P_b, as we noted above in (1.5), creates the basis for exchange. A demands x from B and B demands y from A in exchange. A specialises in the production of y. In order to obtain the resources to do so, her import substitute sector has to contract. Again the opposite process occurs in B. The production mix in both countries moves in the direction indicated by the arrows in Figure 1.1. Specialisation will continue until such time as the incentive to exchange is removed. This will occur when A can no longer obtain x from B cheaper than it can be produced at home, and likewise for B with respect to y. This will only occur when product prices in the two countries are equalised.

Consider further what happens to relative product prices once trade actually opens. Import penetration in A reduces the relative price of x. This is perhaps obvious. What is less obvious however is the change which takes place in the price of y at home. The increased (overseas) demand for y puts upward pressure on prices. More significantly, however, producers of y can only increase output by employing resources which are released from the import substitute sector, i.e. from the rundown of production of x. We know, however, that x is a relatively labour-intensive activity while y is relatively capital intensive. The proportions in which capital and labour are released from production of x are not suited to production of y. The excess supply of labour is manifested in a fall in its relative price, while pressure of demand pushes up the reward to capital. This induces producers of *y* to economise on capital and use more labour-intensive methods – this must follow to maintain full employment.[2] Given greater amounts of labour to work with raises the marginal product of capital and puts further upward pressure on its price. Thus both demand and supply forces serve to raise the relative price of the exportable in *A*. A similar process of adjustment occurs in *B*.

In *A*, therefore, following the opening of trade, the relative price of *y* rises, while in *B* the relative price of *x* rises. The very difference which created the incentive to exchange in the first instance is being eroded. When these tendencies have reached the point where product prices are equalised, further specialisation and exchange will cease. In Figure 1.1 this point is reached when *A* and *B* produce at *c* and *d* respectively. At these points they both face the same international price ratio, *PT*, and they are both incompletely specialised. When product prices are equalised, factor prices will also be equalised. Factor price equalisation implies that the two factors of production gain to a different extent from international specialisation and exchange. Specifically, rewards to the abundant factor increase while rewards to the scarce factor fall.[3] As long as full employment prevails before and after the specialisation process in both countries, then both countries gain from exchange. Although we have not included post-trade indifference curves in Figure 1.1, it should be obvious that in shifting from *a* and *b* to a point on the international price ratio between *c* and *d*, both countries are moving further out into commodity space, and on to higher indifference curves.

Technological changes

The celebrated unsuccessful attempt by Leontief (1953, 1956) to provide some empirical validation for the H–O–S postulate stimulated a considerable amount of rethinking of the proximate determinants of exchange in the 1950s and 1960s.[4]

Important papers by Posner (1961) and Vernon (1966) explicitly introduced technological change as a proximate determinant of trade. The so-called technology gap theorem, due to Posner, examined the influence of technological change on trade between countries with similar factor endowments. Vernon's product cycle model, on the other hand, viewed the commodity composition and direction of trade as the outcome of the interaction of the various stages of development through which a product may proceed and differential factor endowments.

To illustrate the principles of Posner's analysis, assume we have two countries with similar factor endowments, similar demand conditions, and therefore similar pre-trade factor price ratios. In such a world the H-O-S theorem would predict that no trade would take place.

If we admit the possibility of dynamic influences, in particular technological change, the situation is entirely different. For example, suppose due to initial factor endowments that both countries produce commodities x and y. Furthermore, suppose that in industry x in country A there is process innovation which changes the production function and allows x to be produced to the same specification but at a lower unit cost, or leaves unit costs unchanged but results in a new variety of x being produced. In the latter case process innovation results in product innovation.[5] In such circumstances the preconditions for exchange now exist. Whether, and for how long, any trade takes place depends on how consumers and producers in country B respond to innovation in A, or as Posner puts it, the 'demand' and 'imitation' lags. The former derives from the fact that although x in A and B may be substitutes for each other, consumers in B may take time to react to the fall in the price of x in A, or the change in specification. (Presumably the lag will prove longer in the case of the latter.) The foreign produced product may, for a variety of reasons, not be regarded as a perfect substitute for the domestic variety.

On the supply side, producers in B have to decide whether to respond to the technological development in A. This will depend on certain institutional arrangements (such as whether or not A has patent protection) and it will depend on the nature of the innovations. The more complicated the development, the longer the learning period is likely to be. The net effect of the demand lag and imitation lag determines whether or not trade takes place. A number of possibilities exist. For example, the demand lag could be longer than the imitation lag. In this case, producers of x in B would react to innovation in A before any import penetration takes place. Assuming away the purely pathological case of simultaneous coincidental development in both countries, this would be feasible where the innovation is relatively simple and/or where competition takes the form of regular new product development. It would also be the case where consumers are slow to respond, perhaps because of imperfect information flows. In these circumstances no trade would take place, although interestingly one might argue that the potential for trade exerts competitive pressures and stimulates more rapid technological change than might otherwise occur.

In the more usual case where the demand lag is shorter than the imitation lag, trade is generated, and a few possible scenarios are outlined in Figure 1.2. In all three panels country A's trade balance

18

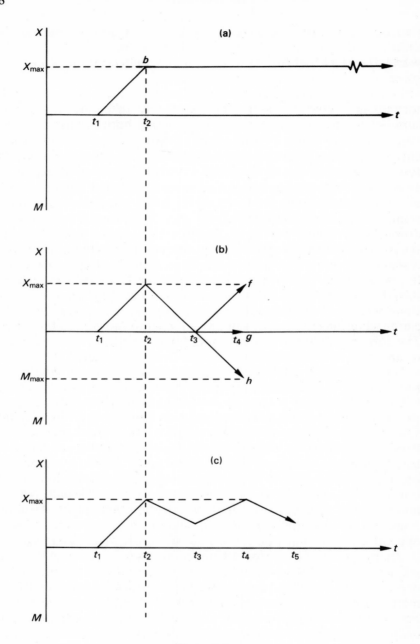

Figure 1.2

for commodity x is plotted against time. Up to t_1 we are in the autarky (i.e. pre-trade) situation. At t_1 innovation takes place. The demand lag in B will determine how quickly exports initially build up, and will therefore determine the slope of t_1b. The imitation lag will determine the height of the export function, that is to say whether or not exports reach a maximum (as set by effective demand in B and capacity constraints in A); and it will also determine for how long country B imports the commodity from A. In panel (a) we take the extreme case of an infinite imitation lag, due either to indefinite patent protection or an inability of B producers to replicate the innovation. Exports from A rise to X max by t_2 and remain at that level indefinitely.

A more plausible possibility is outlined in panel (b). Here we assume that the imitation lag amounts to t_1t_2. B producers are marketing their improved product from time t_2, and country A's export surplus is eroded. If producers in A fail to counterreact, then the surplus may be completely removed, conceivably trade could cease and we could proceed towards point g by t_4. B's improvement could be such, however, that she actually penetrates A's market, in which case we would move towards h by t_4. Alternatively, A producers could counterreact at t_3, pushing the export function towards point f. This final possibility is taken a stage further in panel (c), where it is assumed that A producers counterreact sufficiently quickly to prevent the export surplus ever being wholly eroded.

To conclude the analysis at this point is of course to leave unanswered the most fundamental question: what in the first instance generates the innovation in country A, or the succession of innovations implicit in the case outlined in panel (c), or the competitive pattern of innovations of panel (b)? These are stimulating and interesting issues related to market structure. Even to attempt the most superficial analysis of the innovation process would take us beyond the brief of this present volume. We have however said enough to clarify the manner in which a further supply side influence may stimulate trade, namely 'temporary' differences in industry specific knowledge.

In so far as the Vernon model focuses on the implications of a given product cycle for trade, and thereby focuses on the development of a particular innovation, it can be viewed as a subcase of the technology gap theorem. In other respects, however, the model is qualitatively distinct. Unlike the Posner analysis, for example, it does rely to some extent on differential factor endowments across trading countries. Furthermore, it is also a theory of international investment as well as a theory of international trade.

As with the technology gap model, the starting point of the Vernon analysis is the development of a new product. In a world where some countries are relatively labour abundant, some relatively land abundant and some relatively capital abundant, Vernon argues that new products are more likely to be developed initially in capital-rich countries.

In their early stages of development such new products will be manufactured close to the market. As the product matures, however, and a certain amount of standardisation takes place, an increasing amount of total production may be exported. At this stage of the product's life-cycle, however, relative production costs may become increasingly important. Recall that the product was introduced in a capital-rich, labour-scarce economy (in Vernon's example this is the United States). As the product becomes standardised and the knowledge which stimulated the innovation becomes more freely available, potential competition may threaten in export markets. In the case where the original producer obtains patents for exports markets, this threat may be delayed. Upon expiry of the patent it could be translated into actual competition. The point is that the potential competition is most likely to be translated into actual competition in other capital-rich countries. If in these countries unit labour costs are lower than in the originating country, the comparative advantage will shift.

Once the technological know-how becomes freely available, it is inevitable that comparative advantage will shift to lower wage economies. The originators of the innovation need not accept this with equanimity – they could shift with comparative advantage. In other words they could set up production facilities in the importing countries. Whether this occurs, or whether production comes predominantly from local producers, the implication for trade is the same: exports from the originating country decline.

The final stage of the product cycle occurs when standardisation takes place. Assuming that the knowledge inherent in the production process is still relatively freely available, it is conceivable that the location of production could shift yet again, in this case to labour-abundant economies where unit labour costs are relatively low. Production could be from local indigenous producers or from multinational firms, with the parent company setting up a production facility in the low wage economy. Again, from the point of view of trade, it does not really matter (at this level of generality, anyway). Imports into the low wage economy will decrease and production will increase to such an extent that some output is exported. Thus exports from the high wage and medium wage economies decline, and may indeed even be converted into imports. Figure 1.3 outlines the process.

As with the technology gap theorem we have only presented a

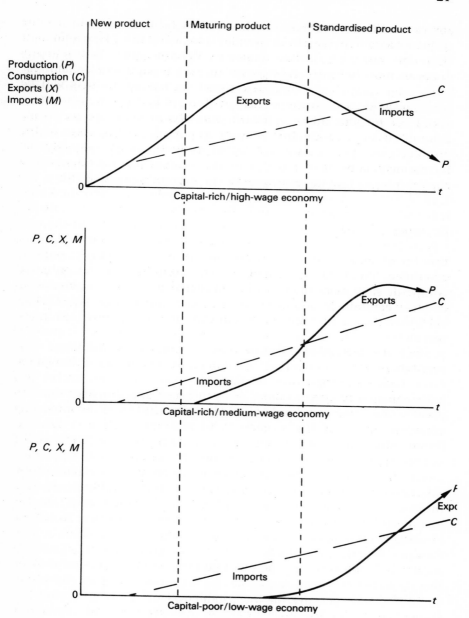

Figure 1.3

rather superficial treatment of the product cycle model and it must be emphasised that many important aspects of the model have not been developed. The most interesting insight developed in this model is the manner in which comparative advantage can shift through time. As we shall see when we examine the forces behind the proliferation of the new protectionism in Chapter 8, there are many commodities which seem to fit quite well into the framework developed by the product cycle - commodities such as textiles, transistor radios, cutlery, sports equipment and so on. It is the pressures generated by the decline of production in these sectors which has been one of the most important determinants of the new protectionism.

Economies of scale

Empirical studies of cost functions in many developed market economies have found widespread evidence of decreasing costs. Although such evidence has been available for some years, the inconvenience which scale economies cause for general equilibrium analysis has meant that their integration into mainstream trade theory has been rather slow in occurring. Even recent theorising which has explicitly assumed decreasing costs has tended to take the simplest possible production functions (see, for instance, Krugman, 1979; Lancaster, 1980).

To see how scale economies can generate trade, consider the situation of two countries, each with identical initial factor endowments and each capable of producing two commodities which have identical factor input ratios. According to the H-O-S theorem, trade would not open. Furthermore, if we assume zero opportunities for new product development, we can eliminate the possibility of technology gap trade. Mutually beneficial exchange is still possible however if there are decreasing costs associated with the production of x and y. In Figure 1.4 we construct a production frontier which is convex to the origin rather than concave, reflecting the fact that there are decreasing costs in the production of both goods. In a pre-trade situation countries A and B could produce at points a and b respectively. Given the opportunity to exchange at the world price ratio ced either country could specialise in the production of *either* good. For the sake of argument we assume that A specialises in x and shifts production from a to d, while B specialises in y, shifting production from b to c. If we stay with the two-country model, a feasible equilibrium would be point c, with trade triangles of ceg and edf. However, the analysis is easily generalised to the case where A and B are two small open economies facing a given international terms of trade of ced.

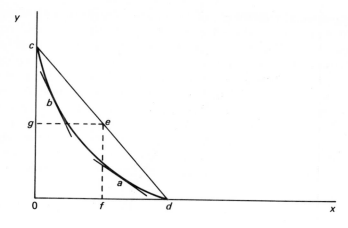

Figure 1.4

Thus the possibility of increasing returns in the production function provides us with yet another supply-side stimulant to exchange. This is an important factor in explaining the significant volume of trade which takes place between developed market economies with very similar factor endowments (such as the Western European industrialised economies).

DEMAND-SIDE DETERMINANTS OF EXCHANGE

In considering the classical (labour productivity) and neoclassical (factor endowment) explanations of trade we assumed away the influence of demand. This should not be taken to imply that the role of demand in establishing relative prices was ignored. Indeed, it was the explicit recognition of demand factors in the work of Mill and Marshall in particular which facilitated the development of the trade offer curve, or reciprocal demand curve. Although we shall not employ that particular medium for exposition in this volume, students of trade theory will be familiar with its ubiquitous presence.

Analysis at this stage has been confined to the most general considerations. Thus, in a given situation with given supply conditions, differing demand pressures might result in differences in autarkic price ratios, and thereby create the necessary preconditions for exchange. This general case can be easily illustrated, as in Figure 1.5.

Both countries are assumed to have a common production frontier of *PR*. In autarky, however, different preferences could result in different relative price ratios. In Figure 1.5 we have not included

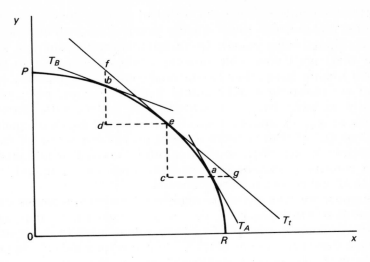

Figure 1.5

either country's indifference set in order to keep the diagram clear. One could easily imagine, however, indifference curves for *A* and *B* which are tangential to the production frontier at *a* and *b* respectively, thereby generating relative prices of T_A and T_B respectively. Clearly the preconditions for trade exist. Both countries would specialise, their production equilibria converging on *e*, and their consumption equilibria shifting towards points *f* and *g* on the international price ratio. Balanced trade would be consistent with trade triangles of *fed* and *egc*.

This is a straightforward enough piece of analysis. All it tells us, though, is that differences in pressure of demand can also create differences in marginal valuations; it says nothing about whether such differences emerge in any systematic manner.

Overlapping demands

Linder (1961) was concerned with trying to explain the large volume of trade that took place between Western European industrial economies which appeared to differ little in terms of initial factor endowments. The key, according to Linder, lay in overlapping demand patterns. Countries would export to other countries having a similar pattern of demand as on the home market. Thus, when one observes overlapping demand, one will observe trade taking place.

Linder argued that within any given country consumers at different levels of income will demand different quality goods. Low-income groups will demand lower quality goods than high-income groups (other things being equal). In an international setting one will also find that, on average, high-income countries will tend to demand higher quality goods than low-income countries. In Figure 1.6, therefore, we can posit a relationship between income per capita and quality as given by OZ. Countries A, B and C, with incomes per capita of Y_a, Y_b and Y_c respectively, demand goods of quality Q_a, Q_b and Q_c. If income were equally distributed across all members of society in each of these three countries, no trade would take place, each country producing the one commodity of a standard 'quality' which all indigenous residents demand.

Suppose we take the more realistic case where income is unevenly distributed within each of the three countries such that within a particular country a range of qualities is demanded. In A, for example, income distribution may result in demands for goods in the range fg, while in B the range might be hj. Taking these two countries together, we clearly have taste overlap of hk. Even if both countries were to produce only one commodity to suit 'average' tastes, as long as these differed between countries there would be scope for exchange.

As we can see from Figure 1.6, a more limited range of overlap between the tastes of countries B and C exists, specifically the range

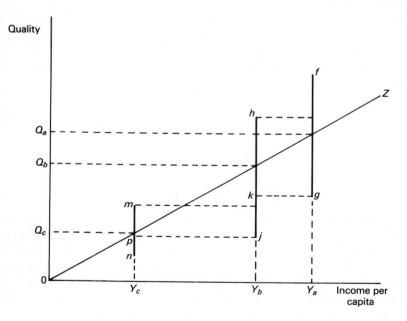

Figure 1.6

mp. This may nevertheless be enough to generate trade with 'low' quality products being exported from the lower income per capita country to cater for the demands of 'low' income consumers in the high income per capita economy. In the reverse direction 'high' quality products are exported from the high income per capita country to the low income per capita country to cater for the demands of consumers at the top end of the income distribution in the latter.

From the Linder model, therefore, we obtain the (testable) prediction that the more similar economies are in terms of income per capita, and the more similar the spread of incomes within both countries, the greater the likelihood of overlapping tastes, and the greater the potential for trade. We must note two points, however. First, we are dealing with countries which have similar factor endowments. Clearly if factor endowments differ we would expect this to exert an influence on exchange – even when income per capita is similar (compare Kuwait with Switzerland!). Second, the Linder analysis still leaves a couple of fundamental issues unresolved. What, for example, do we mean by 'quality' and, if we can identify such a dimension, can we measure it? Equally important, is 'quality' the only factor which will systematically vary with income per capita and have a bearing on trade? Finally, and most significantly, if we accept all of the above reasoning, why, if two countries demand very similar ranges of goods, do they engage in trade rather than producing the full range themselves? To answer this latter question we simply re-introduce non-factor proportions supply-side influences, like technology gaps and economies of scale. The existence of the latter in particular ensures that even when *identical* ranges of goods are demanded, mutually beneficial trade is still possible.

Attribute differentiation

Neoclassical trade theory assumed that all commodities were homogeneous. The implications of such an assumption are first that the cross elasticity of demand between A's and B's x is infinite – small price differentials stimulate substitution. Second, it implies that only one 'variety' of good x will be marketed in both countries. Given the increasing volume of trade in differentiated commodities which takes place, this assumption is becoming ever more restrictive. Linder relaxed the assumption somewhat by permitting variations in quality, while an integral aspect of Posner's technology gap theorem was the emergence of 'new' versions of existing products – new in the sense that they are differentiated in some respect from existing or 'old' products.

This line of enquiry has been pursued to an increasing extent in recent years. An expanding volume of empirical studies has suggested that trade in differentiated goods produced using similar production methods may account for a significant proportion of total trade – in the case of European developed market economies, over half of their total trade. Recent efforts have therefore focused on explaining why such trade may emerge.

A useful starting point for such an analysis is the Lancastrian 'characteristics' approach to consumer behaviour. Lancaster (1966) contended that goods should be regarded as combinations of characteristics, or attributes. Clearly there is a large number of commodities which are likely to exhibit some scope for attribute differentiation – whether this takes the form of genuine physical differences in style and quality, or whether it has more to do with image differentiation. For us, the point of interest is that where such potential for differentiation exists, there is a further possible basis for exchange.

The fundamentals of the analysis can be grasped by reference to Figure 1.7. Here we assume that we are dealing with a commodity with two identifiable attributes, a_1 and a_2. For example, the commodity could be automobiles, attribute a_1 being average miles per gallon, attribute a_2 being overall size. Assume we are still dealing with a two-country case. Both countries have similar size markets (measured in terms of effective demand), and production functions for all 'varieties' are similar. In country B, the majority of consumers may

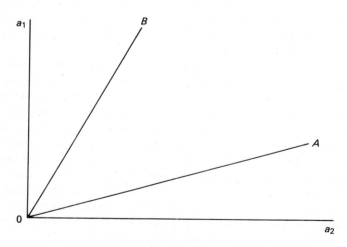

Figure 1.7

have a distinct preference for small, economy cars, while in country A majority preferences are for large cars, miles per gallon being a relatively unimportant consideration. In order to cater for majority tastes, producers in A and B produce along the rays OA and OB respectively. In B, for example, the ray OB indicates the proportions in which attributes a_1 and a_2 are combined. Linearity indicates that these proportions remain unchanged as production expands.

It should be clear that a basis for exchange exists – minority consumers in A and B could find their demands better satisfied by the opening of trade. Thus, if minority consumers in A can obtain small cars from B, and minority consumers in B could obtain large cars from A, then exchange could take place. In this case, differences in tastes across countries is the proximate determinant of trade. This is not to assert that relative prices need be entirely unimportant. If there are decreasing costs in production, then any attempt to manufacture small cars in A or large cars in B would presumably be associated with relatively high unit costs. Although large cars could be produced in B, they are not, because length of production run would be relatively short and unit costs of production relatively high, compared with unit costs for the equivalent product produced in A.

If we confine ourselves to this case, where preferences are clustered around a particular combination of attributes such that it is possible to identify 'minority' and 'majority' tastes, we are adding very little to Linder's overlapping tastes case. In the latter, majority tastes were clustered around high quality or low quality goods, depending on income per capita. The present framework, however, is capable of much wider generalisation. Suppose, for example, tastes are evenly spread over attribute space in Figure 1.7. There would then be a much greater potential for attribute differentiation, increased scope for a greater number of varieties and, other things being equal, greater potential for exchange.

There are a wide range of influences which can affect the volume of trade which is transacted in commodities differentiated by attributes. Income per capita is relevant since it seems that the demand for variety increases with rising income per capita (see Barker, 1977); as we have noted, the degree of taste overlap is relevant (see Lancaster, 1980); relative market size is important because this influences the number of autarkic varieties which can be produced (see Lancaster, 1980); and the nature of the commodity in question is of obvious relevance – specifically manufactured finished commodities appear to offer greater scope for attribute differentiation than primary and intermediate goods. (Further analysis of the interaction of the various explanatory factors can be found in Greenaway, 1982b.)

CONCLUDING COMMENTS

This concludes our overview of the determinants of exchange. Enough has been said by now to indicate that at any point in time, trade may be the outcome of a number of interacting influences.

The necessary prerequisite for exchange is that marginal valuations differ between the residents of different countries. Fundamentally, differences in marginal valuations can be traced to differences in market structure. There are therefore a number of supply-based and demand-based hypotheses which have been advanced to explain the emergence of trade, some of which are competing, some of which are complementary. Our overview of these theorems should provide us with a reference point against which we can examine pressures which shape trade policy, as well as the implications of trade policy.

POSTSCRIPT: INTER-INDUSTRY TRADE AND INTRA-INDUSTRY TRADE

Before we comment on the welfare implications of specialisation and exchange, we ought briefly to comment on the distinction between intra- and inter-industry trade, since the explanations which we adumbrated above are frequently classified into these categories. As we shall see in Chapter 2, the distinction is also relevant because the welfare implications of inter-industry trade and intra-industry trade may differ somewhat.

The terms inter-industry trade and intra-industry trade are to some extent self-explanatory. Inter-industry trade refers to a situation where products from one industry are exchanged for the products of a different industry. In the case of intra-industry exchange, products from a particular industry are exchanged for the output of its foreign counterpart. If, therefore, we were to look at the trade balance of a representative industry, j, using the ratio

$$B_j = 1 - \frac{|X_j - M_j|}{(X_j + M_j)} \cdot 100 \tag{1.6}$$

where $0 \leqslant B_j \leqslant 100$, we can identify the extent to which inter- and intra-industry trade takes place. Thus, when B_j tends towards zero, trade comprises either exports or imports only, indicating that inter-industry trade is taking place. When B_j tends towards 100, exports are matched by imports, and the proportion of exchange which is of an intra-industry type tends towards its maximum.

The significance of the distinction is the implication that different determinants are at work in generating trade. In the case of inter-industry exchange, differences in factor proportions might be antici-pated as being relevant; in the case of intra-industry exchange, attribute differentiation could reasonably be expected to be an influence. The seriousness with which we treat the distinction depends on our ability to define the term 'industry' in an economically meaningful way. Were the term 'industry' an unambiguous concept, this would present few problems. Even when we find seemingly acceptable criteria for separating activities into industries, practical application can be diffi-cult. For example, it may be agreed that substitutability in production (i.e. the ease with which inputs can be transferred from one activity to another) is an acceptable basis for distinguishing between activities. This may be proxied by reference to similarity of factor inputs. This is not, however, a straightforward matter. One might also argue that substitutability in consumption is relevant, as proxied perhaps by cross elasticity of demand.

In principle, the term industry could be meaningfully applied to a group of activities where there was both a high degree of substi-tutability in production and consumption. In practice, however, indices of inter- and intra-industry trade are computed for 'industries' as defined by official statistical classifications, like the Standard International Trade Classification (SITC) or the UK Standard Industrial Classification (SIC).

In the SITC,[6] trade data are classified in a systematic manner. Any activity belongs to a 'division', of which there are ten. At this level activities are fairly broadly defined, for example 'chemicals and related products', 'machinery and transport equipment', and so on. Each division has a number of sections. For example, within Division 5 we have 51 organic chemicals, 54 medicinal and pharmaceutical products, and so on. There are in total sixty sections. In turn these are broken down into 139 groups, which spawn some 453 subgroups, and so on. As the data become more disaggregated, the description of activities becomes ever more specific.

The purpose of this brief outline of the SITC is simply this: as there is no level of disaggregation in the SITC which can generally be regarded as being consistent with the concept of an industry, one should regard indices of inter- and intra-industry trade with some caution – particularly studies which report levels of intra- and inter-industry trade at the economy-wide, division or section level. Data here are so highly aggregated that, in general, indices of intra- and inter-industry trade are of limited value. Many commentators have argued that the 'group' level is by and large an appropriate level of disaggregation for empirical analysis. Indeed, the bulk of empirical studies take this level of disaggregation as approximating an 'industry' (see, for example, Grubel and Lloyd, 1975; Greenaway and Milner, 1982). Although Finger (1975) warns against uncritical use of this level of disaggregation, Greenaway (1982a) and Greenaway and Milner (1982) have argued that it is possible to make certain adjustments to improve the credibility of one's results.

The terms inter-industry trade and intra-industry trade will be used at various points in this volume. When referred to, no further comment will be made on the problems of operationalising the concepts. This brief postscript should stand as a recognition of empirical difficulties.

NOTES ON FURTHER READING

The seminal contributions for the various theorems which we reviewed are all referred to in the text itself. A useful survey of classical, neoclassical and technology theorems of the genesis of trade can be found in Bhagwati (1971). Extensions of the basic neoclassical model are provided in the volumes of readings edited by Caves and Johnson (1968) and Bhagwati (1981). The latter is particularly useful since it includes recent readings covering, for instance, scale economies.

The role of scale economies, and to a lesser extent technology gaps and product cycles, tends to be included with preference diversity and analysed in the context of intra-industry trade. The standard reference for the measurement and sources of intra-industry trade is Grubel and Lloyd (1975). In addition, however, the readings edited by Giersch (1979) are especially useful.

Surveys of empirical work on the classical and neoclassical theorems can be found in Stern (1975) and Baldwin (1971) – the latter is particularly concerned with explaining the Leontief paradox. Empirical studies of intra-industry trade are rather more scarce. An econometric analysis for the UK is given in Greenaway and Milner (1982), while an international comparison can be found in Caves (1981).

2 Welfare Implications of Specialisation and Exchange

Almost all of Chapter 1 was concerned with identifying underlying forces of supply and demand which could stimulate exchange. Exchange is, as we emphasised at the outset, a two-way process, and implicit in all we have said so far has been the presumption that exchange is mutually beneficial. After all, if it is not mutually beneficial, it suggests that one of the parties to the transaction ends up worse off after the exchange than before. Although there may be special circumstances under which this may occur, as a general rule it seems highly implausible. Our task now, therefore, is to make the gains from specialisation and exchange more explicit. Not only is this necessary to round off our review of the determinants of exchange, but it is also clearly a prerequisite to any assessment of the net benefits or costs associated with reducing the opportunities for exchange, and resisting the specialisation process.

INTER-INDUSTRY EXCHANGE

Gains from trade in a small open economy

Consider again Figure 1.1. It will be recalled that here we examined the movement from autarky to unrestricted exchange for both countries simultaneously. Figure 2.1 takes the case of country A only. On this occasion, however, we include A's indifference curves. We may note that in moving from a pre-trade production and consumption equilibrium at a to a post-trade consumption equilibrium at e and production equilibrium at b, A moves from indifference curve I_1 to indifference curve I_2. From the country's point of view this appears to represent an unambiguous improvement in welfare. The movement from a point on I_1 to a point on I_2 can in fact be broken down into two conceptually distinct elements. The gain in welfare has followed from the fact that (i) A has been able to take advantage of a more favourable price ratio, specifically a higher price

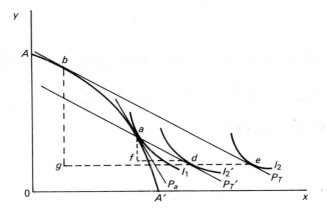

Figure 2.1

of *y* and a lower priced *x* than prevailed under autarky; and that
(ii) a certain amount of resource reallocation took place in response
to the exchange and specialisation elements. These two elements can
be conceptually separated. In order to do so, confine *A* to her
autarkic production point (*a*) and permit her to face the more
favourable international price ratio of P_T' (which is parallel to P_T).
Faced with these prices *A* would be willing to exchange *af* of *y* for
fd of *x*. The movement from *a* on I_1 to *d* on I_2' is therefore the pure
gain from exchange. If, however, *A* specialises in production of *y* to
take further advantage of changed international prices by shifting to
production at *b*, then *bg* of *y* could be exchanged for *ge* of *x*. Thus,
the movement from *d* on I_2' to *e* on I_2 is the pure *gain from specialisation*. This only follows if resources are reallocated from the import
substitute sector to the export sector.

Another way of looking at this is presented in Figure 2.2. In the
right-hand segment, demand and supply conditions in the *y* sector
are depicted, while supply and demand in the *x* sector are presented
in the left-hand segment. Note that since we have the *relative* price
ratio plotted on the vertical axis, rather than the absolute price of *x*
or *y*, D_x is positively sloped and S_x negatively sloped. In autarky a
price ratio of P_a prevails, and at this price ratio both markets are
cleared. When trade opens, however, the relative price ratio rises to
P_T. The change in relative prices causes *A* to specialise in *y*, increasing
supply from OQ_1 to OQ_2. As the price ratio rises from P_a towards
the world price level of P_T, domestic demand contracts, and ultimately at P_T, Q_3Q_2 units are exported. If we commenced (by
assumption) from a situation of full employment, expansion of the

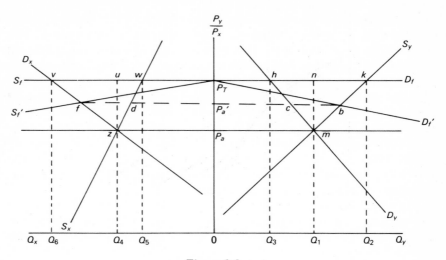

Figure 2.2

export sector can only be achieved by contraction of the import substitute sector. If we look to the left-hand quadrant, we observe that as the relative price of y rises and therefore the relative price of x falls, domestic producers leave the market, being replaced by imports. The portion of the market supplied falls from OQ_4 to OQ_5. Simultaneously, however, the total market expands, as consumers purchase relatively cheaper imports. Demand expands from OQ_4 to OQ_6, and the difference between domestic supply and demand is met from imports Q_5Q_6.

The welfare implications of these changes can be assessed by reference to the changes that take place in consumer and producer surplus. In the import substitute sector consumer surplus increases by an amount equivalent to the area $P_a zv P_T$. Producer surplus, on the other hand, falls by $P_a zw P_T$. The net change therefore amounts to zvw. The triangle zvu is the pure gain from exchange. This accrues as a consequence of market expansion. The area zuw is the pure gain from specialisation, or more accurately in this case, from de-specialisation. This results from the replacement of relatively inefficient domestic producers by relatively efficient overseas producers. The gain effectively accrues to consumers who were in the market prior to the opening of trade. (Note that one could obtain the gain from exchange without de-specialising, for instance by paying a production subsidy to domestic producers to permit them to supply OQ_4 at OP_T.)

Analogous gains are realised in the export sector. Producer surplus increases by P_a m k P_T. This is partly offset by a reduction in consumer surplus of P_a m h P_T, leaving a net gain of mkh. Again this can be broken down into an exchange and specialisation element. The area mnh represents the exchange element which could be realised without specialising and producing more than OQ_1. The triangle mkn results following specialisation, and the expansion of supply from OQ_1 to OQ_2.

From Figures 2.1 and 2.2 we can derive a number of important propositions:

(1) The opening of trade unambiguously results in a welfare improvement for both trading countries.

(2) Although both countries gain overall, there appear to be redistributions between groups. In the import competing sector, consumers gain and producers lose, while in the export sector consumers lose and producers gain.

(3) In order that net gains are realised, full adjustment must take place. That is to say, resources that are displaced in the import competing sector have to be re-employed in the export sector, and consumers in the export sector are able to obtain relatively cheap imports. If adjustments are frustrated, then the gains from trade will be lower. (We will consider the implications of less than full adjustment taking place in Chapter 10.)

(4) Since the relative price of exportables tends to rise, there is also a redistribution between factors of production. In particular, the factor which is employed relatively intensively in the export sector finds its relative rewards rising. If the basis to trade is differential factor endowments, then we can conclude from this that free trade tends to raise the real reward of the abundant factor.

Gains from trade in a large open economy

Figure 2.1 is constructed on the assumption that the country concerned is a small open economy, i.e. the prices at which it trades are given. The act of trading cannot affect product prices in any way. Thus country A can supply as much of commodity y on the world market as she wishes without affecting world prices. Likewise she can purchase as much x as she pleases without affecting the relative price of x. In terms of Figure 2.1, this amounts to assuming that country A faces an infinitely elastic demand curve for her exports (D_f) and an infinitely elastic foreign supply curve for imports (S_f). Such an assumption is undoubtedly reasonable for many countries. Few countries supply such a large share of the total world market in particular commodities that they can influence price by variations in supply. Likewise, few countries consume a sufficiently large share of total supply of a particular commodity to be able to influence price through variations in demand. Although this may generally be true for finished manufactures, one can think of certain commodity markets where it is inapplicable: Brazilian supply of coffee, or US consumption of coffee, for instance. Furthermore, there are many instances of bilateral exchange where variations in supply and demand on the part of one trading partner can influence significantly the terms at which trade takes place. It is reasonable to ponder, therefore, whether similar gains from trade can be realised in the case of a large open economy as in the case of a small open economy.

This case can be conveniently dealt with in Figure 2.2 also. Domestic supply and demand conditions can remain unaltered. Foreign demand and supply conditions have to be changed, however, to reflect the fact that country A can now affect world prices. In the export market D_f becomes D_f', i.e. a downward sloping demand for commodity x implying that country A has some monopoly power in the supply of x. Thus as she expands supply, she lowers price relative to what would prevail in a competitive market. In the import substitute sector, the possession of any monopsony power means that S_f' rather than S_f is the appropriate foreign supply curve.

If either of these states prevail it should be obvious that, *ceteris paribus*, the gains from trade are lower than in the case of the small open economy. This follows because, once trade opens, exchange does not take place to the same extent. In our example, we have constructed the diagram such that D_f' and S_f' are symmetrical, simply in order to simplify the analysis. In that event exports and imports would only expand to bc and df respectively. Thus the net gains from trade are the smaller triangles mbc and zdf.

Although it would be most unusual to find a case where a country has both monopoly *and* monopsony power such that it can influence *both* export and import prices, it is less unusual to find that either monopoly or monopsony power is possessed. In terms of Figure 2.2 this would be depicted by either S_f or D_f being applicable. Our conclusion nevertheless holds, i.e. that the gains from trade are lower than in the case of the small open economy. There is one final remark we can make here. Clearly, if a country can influence world prices by engaging in international exchange, it can also influence world prices by restricting trade. When we examine the economic effects of tariffs this important possibility will re-emerge.

INTRA-INDUSTRY EXCHANGE

It has been argued that the gains associated with a given volume of trade are likely to be greater when that trade is of an inter-industry type than when it is of an intra-industry type (see, for instance, Aquino, 1978). The rationale for this is that relative price ratios are likely to differ to a greater extent when there are differences in factor endowments, which results in trade, than when the exchange takes the form of an import and export of differentiated goods. Here, it is argued, attribute differentiation will be more important, and the gains from exchange are primarily benefits which consumers reap from greater product variety.

This may or may not be the case. Clearly consumer surplus is likely to be higher as a result of greater product variety. This need not be the only gain from exchange, however. The exchange of scale economies cannot be disregarded, nor can benefits from the reduction of X-inefficiency which would presumably be associated with increased competitive pressures. No generally applicable propositions can be reached about the relative gains of intra- and inter-industry trade. We can assume, however, that, as with inter-industry exchange, if full adjustment takes place, both countries unambiguously gain. One interesting contrast which can be drawn is that where trade is of an intra-industry type, and takes place between countries with similar factor endowments, both factors of production gain from trade. This is an important result, and differs from that associated with Heckscher-Ohlin trade. It follows because factor input ratios are similar in both the export and import substitute sectors, and relative factor prices do not therefore have to alter to the same extent to maintain full employment once trade opens (see Krugman, 1981). This is the basis to the argument that adjustment to trade expansion is relatively easier when trade is of an intra-industry type than when it is of an inter-industry type.

A relatively simple model can be developed to illustrate the nature of the gains to be reaped from exchanging scale economies, and from greater product diversity.

Take, for instance, the Lancastrian framework introduced in Figure 1.7. Instead of placing attributes along a horizontal and vertical axis, we could plot relative attribute proportions along a horizontal plane, as in Figure 2.3. As we move further to the left we have a greater relative proportion of a_1, while as we move to the right we have a greater relative proportion of a_2. If we assume that consumer preferences are diverse, but are evenly distributed in characteristics space, then it follows that there will be a potential demand for every con-

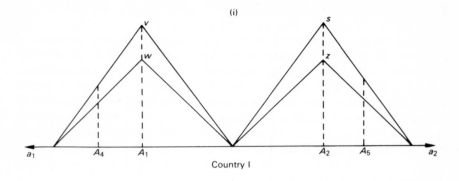

Country I

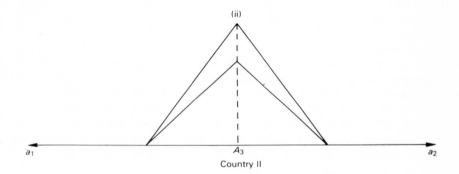

Country II

Figure 2.3

ceivable combination of a_1 and a_2. If production technologies were such that constant costs prevailed whatever variety of commodity A was produced, then presumably a variety would be produced to suit all tastes. In practice, of course, decreasing costs (at least over some range of output) will prevail. Therefore only a limited number of varieties will be produced – the actual number being determined by the minimum efficient scale of production.

Assume that production conditions are such that two varieties are initially produced in country I, namely A_1 and A_2. It seems reasonable to suppose that those consumers whose preferred attribute mix as given by A_1 and A_2 will buy more of these commodities than those who prefer different combinations of a_1 and a_2. Therefore one can expect higher levels of producer and consumer surplus to be associated with production and consumption of A_1 and A_2. In fact, if we assume equal intensity of preferences and equal prices for A_1 and A_2,[1] both producer and consumer surplus will reach local maxima above A_1 and A_2. This is depicted in panel (i) of Figure 2.3, with producer surplus reaching maxima of w and z, while consumer surplus reaches maxima of v and s. Since consumers who would prefer a different combination of a_1 and a_2 will be unable to purchase their preferred variety, less will be consumed and lower values of producer and consumer surplus will be generated. This will apply for instance to those consumers who would prefer A_4 and A_5.

In panel (ii) of Figure 2.3 we depict the situation in country *II*, where only one variety of this same commodity is produced, namely A_3.

Assume that the opportunity to trade opens, perhaps because of the elimination of tariff barriers, such that A_1 and A_2 can be marketed in country *II*, while A_3 can be marketed in country *I*. We can identify some of the gains that could be associated with exchange in Figure 2.4.

Consider the effects of introducing variety A_3 into country *I*. Other things being equal, the introduction of the new variety will result in a further peak in our surplus contours. If for the moment we assume that the new variety sells at the same price as existing varieties, then the peak will be of the same height as those associated with A_1 and A_2. The emergence of the new peak results in a gain in consumer surplus of area f, and a gross gain in producer surplus for foreign producers of areas $a + b + c + d + e$. Included in the latter, however, are certain transfers. Areas a and e are transfers from producers of A_1 and A_3 respectively. Areas b and d are transfers from consumers of A_1 and A_2 respectively. These transfers result because the introduction of A_3 encroaches on the markets for A_1 and A_2. Area c is a net gain, therefore.

All we have focused on so far is imports of A_3 into country *I*. The

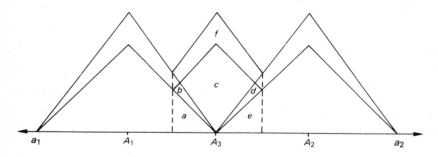

Figure 2.4

outcome appears to be (as with inter-industry exchange) a gain for domestic consumers, while domestic producers lose. The essence of intra-industry exchange, however, is *simultaneous* import and export. Thus country *I* would be exporting quantities of A_1 and A_3 to country *II* and similar transfers and gains would arise as in the case of exports from country *II* to country *I*. The net result is that both producers and consumers gain from exchange.

We have focused on effects of the exchange of existing varieties, assuming that relative prices play an unimportant role. It is of course possible, likely in fact, that relative prices will have a part to play. The lengthening of production runs which would be the corollary of this exchange might result in reductions in unit costs. If these reductions are reflected in final prices, then presumably market expansion will follow and further gains will be realised.

The object of this simple piece of analysis is to demonstrate that there will be gains associated with intra-industry exchange, gains which derive from preference diversity and economies of scale. It is not possible *a priori* to say whether the gains from a given volume of trade expansion will be greater with intra-industry exchange than with inter-industry exchange. Although pre-trade differences in relative prices may be greater with the latter than the former, the fact that adjustment costs can be lower with intra-industry exchange makes generalisation difficult.

CONCLUDING COMMENTS

This relatively short chapter serves to outline the gains associated with international exchange and specialisation. Our analysis seems to indicate that where inter-industry and intra-industry trade is concerned, unrestricted exchange unambiguously results in a welfare improvement, assuming that full adjustment takes place. *A priori* we cannot say whether the gains from intra-industry exchange will be less than, greater than or equal to the gains from inter-industry exchange. There is a *prima facie* case for feeling that pre-trade relative price differentials will be greater in the case of inter-industry trade. On the other hand, adjustment costs of intra-industry trade are likely to be lower.

The framework developed in this chapter can now be extended to consider the implications of trade interventions and tariff barriers in Part II and non-tariff barriers in Part III.

NOTES ON FURTHER READING

There is a well established literature on the gains from trade. Samuelson's classic papers are an obvious reference (Samuelson, 1939, 1962) as is Haberler's (1950) paper and Baldwin's (1952) paper. Most introductory texts on international economics cover the subject matter, for example chapter 1 of Milner and Greenaway (1979).

Little work has been done so far on the welfare implications of intra-industry trade. One notable exception is Krugman (1981). The framework used in this chapter is based on Scherer's (1979) analysis of product variety and social welfare. The use of this framework in the context of intra-industry exchange is elaborated fully in Greenaway (1982b).

PART II

The Old Protectionism:
Aspects of Tariff Interventions

3 Economic Effects of Tariff Interventions

In Part I we examined the forces which result in a tendency to international specialisation and exchange, and the benefits which might accrue if exchange and specialisation are permitted to take place. The latter were in turn contingent on market structure conforming to certain conditions.

We are now ready to consider the economic effects of tariff and non-tariff interventions. In addition, however, we are interested in the efficacy of arguments used to justify recourse to interventionist policies. In Part II our interest will be focused on tariff interventions, while in Part III we will examine non-tariff interventions.

FORMS OF TARIFF INTERVENTION

The tariff is an indirect tax on tradable goods. By indirect tax we mean a tax which is levied on a commodity in contrast to a direct tax which is levied on a factor of production.[1] By tradable goods we mean those commodities which are actually or potentially exchanged internationally.

Since tariffs are levied on tradable commodities, we can identify both an import tariff and an export tariff. The former tend to be far more common than the latter. In fact, export tariffs tend principally to be levied for revenue purposes rather than protective purposes. As such their use is more common in less developed countries (LDCs) than developed market economies (DMEs). Although LDCs also exhibit a dependence on import tariffs for revenue purposes, this instrument is widely used for protective purposes in both LDCs and DMEs (see Greenaway, 1980). Throughout this chapter we will use the import tariff for illustrative purposes. This can be justified not only because the instrument is more common than the export tariff, but because, as Lerner (1936) demonstrated some years ago, the effects of the two interventions are symmetrical.

Tariffs may be specific or *ad valorem*, and they may be single-

45

stage or multi-stage. If a tariff is specific, the post-tariff domestic price of an import would amount to:

$$P_D = P_m + t_s \tag{3.1}$$

where P_m refers to the world price of the import and t_s the specific tariff. This may be levied at so much per pound, or a given amount per litre: in other words by reference to some physically identifiable dimension. *Ad valorem* tariffs on the other hand are levied at some percentage of the value of the import. Here the post tariff price would be:

$$P_D = P_m \, (l + t_a) \tag{3.2}$$

where t_a is the rate of tax.

Ad valorem tariffs have the advantage that they are self-adjusting in inflationary periods. Because one is levying the tariff at a given rate, the real value of the tax is fixed – it guarantees in effect that the tax revenue is index-linked. This does not apply to specific duties. Clearly, as long as the commodity's physical characteristics remain unchanged in an inflationary period, the nominal value of revenue from the specific duty will remain unchanged but its real value will fall.[2] One major advantage of specific duties, however, is that tax evasion through under-invoicing becomes extremely difficult. Where *ad valorem* tariffs are concerned, tax liability can be reduced by under-declaring the value of the commodity imported. In the case of specific duties it is clearly more difficult to reduce liability by under-declaring weight or volume. One has a more objective basis for measurement. It is primarily for this reason that LDCs rely on specific duties to a greater degree than DMEs.

Single-stage tariffs occur when one rate of duty applies to all imports, multi-stage when the rate varies with volume. For instance, 10 per cent duty on the first 10,000 units, 20 per cent duty on the next 10,000 units, and so on.

ECONOMIC EFFECTS OF TARIFF IMPOSITION

Let us then examine the economic effects of a given *ad valorem* import tariff.[3] To do so we shall re-apply the partial equilibrium framework developed in Chapters 1 and 2. We are therefore dealing with a system where there are only two countries, two factors of production and two commodities. All markets are competitive and therefore adjust smoothly and quickly to changes in basic structural conditions. We shall examine two general cases. First, the situation where the country which imposes an import tariff is unable to influence its terms of trade. This is the case of the 'small' open economy. Second, the situation where the tariff imposing country can influence the prices at which it trades, the 'large' open economy.

Tariff imposition in a small open economy

The economic effects of an import tariff in a small open economy can be outlined by reference to Figure 3.1.

Where the tariff-imposing country is a small open economy, world prices are a given datum. In effect, therefore, it can purchase any volume of imports it chooses at a given price. In the case of Figure 3.1, this price is P_w. Thus, where trade is unrestricted, imports amount to AB. If a tariff of t_1 is imposed on all imports, then a wedge is driven between the world price of the import and its domestic price. In fact, the domestic price increases to $P_w(1 + t_1)$. Given domestic demand and supply conditions as represented by D_h and S_h, demand for importables contracts, while supply of import substitutes expands. The extent to which domestic demand and supply respond to the price increase clearly depends on domestic price elasticity of demand for importables, and domestic price elasticity of supply of import substitutes (over the relevant range).

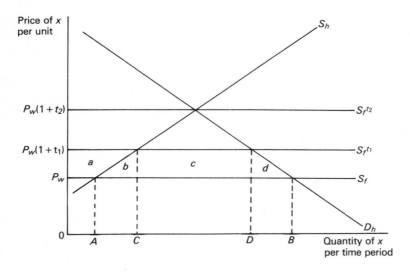

Figure 3.1

In Figure 3.1, demand contracts by DB, supply expands by AC and the post-tariff volume of imports amounts to CD. The tariff is therefore non-prohibitive in that some imports remain. Had the tariff been set at t_2, it would have been prohibitive.

The static welfare effects of this tariff can be evaluated by reference to changes in producer and consumer surplus. The higher price and consequent contraction of demand generates a fall in consumer surplus equivalent to $a + b + c + d$. However, this is not the *net* change associated with the tariff. Part of this reduction amounts to a redistribution from consumers to other economic agents. For instance, area a represents an increase in producer surplus which results because domestic producers are able to supply more, at a higher price. Area c is a redistribution to the government agency. This is the revenue which the tariff yields. The net changes in welfare are therefore the triangles d and b. The former represents a consumption loss associated with DB consumers leaving the market; the latter represents a production loss (or efficiency loss) which emerges because AC units are now provided by relatively inefficient domestic producers.

These losses are the analogue of the gains from trade. Thus area b can be thought of as a loss from de-specialisation, and area d as a loss from being unable to exchange. In the case of the former, resources which could be more productively employed in the export sector are channelled into the import substitute sector. In the case of the latter, expenditure which would formerly have been used on imports is instead channelled to the exportable.

Clearly, given competitive factor as well as product markets, these changes in price must have implications for relative factor rewards. As the classic article by Stolper and Samuelson (1941) demonstrated, the real reward of the factor of production employed intensively in the import substitute sector will rise at the expense of the factor used less intensively. In a two-factor Heckscher-Ohlin-Samuelson world this implies that tariff imposition raises the real return to the tariff-imposing country's scarce factor, while lowering the real reward to the country's abundant factor. Tariff imposition therefore reverses the effect of unrestricted trade on factor rewards.

The overall effect on welfare can be seen in Figure 3.2. Under conditions of unrestricted trade, production and consumption equilibria are at a and c respectively. When a tariff is imposed, the domestic price ratio changes from P_w to P_D. Production of the import substitute (x) expands, while production of y contracts, with equilibrium being established at point b. Although domestic producers and consumers now allocate their expenditures on the basis of P_D, trade does of course continue at the international price ratio P_w'. Thus bf of y now exchanges for fd of x internationally. Dom-

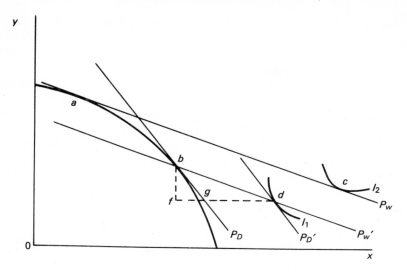

Figure 3.2

estically, however, the same amount of y only exchanges for fg of x - the difference, gd, constitutes the tariff revenue. It seems therefore that the non-prohibitive tariff lowers welfare from I_2 to I_1. If the tariff had been prohibitive, consumption possibilities would have been constrained to the production frontier and welfare would have been reduced even further.

From this analysis we can conclude that, when the assumptions of the H–O–S model hold, unrestricted trade results in a higher level of welfare than restricted trade. Furthermore, less restricted trade is consistent with a higher level of welfare than more restricted trade. Thus, given the assumptions of the above analysis, a small open economy appears to be worse off as a consequence of tariff imposition.

Tariff imposition in a large open economy

Whereas the small open economy cannot affect its terms of trade by tariff imposition, the large open economy can. It is therefore either a sufficiently important purchaser of an importable to affect its terms of trade by levying an import tariff, or alternatively a sufficiently important seller to change prices by imposing an export tariff (in a two-commodity world these amount to the same thing, of course). The tariff-imposing country therefore enjoys some element of market power.

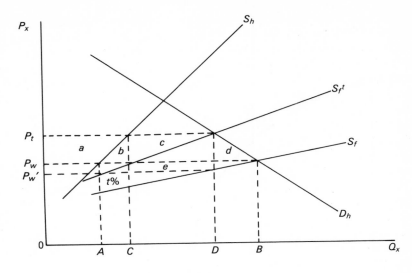

Figure 3.3

Figure 3.3 examines the case of a tariff on imports in a large open economy. Because the tariff-imposing country is a 'significant' purchaser of x, it faces a less than perfectly elastic foreign supply curve, S_f. Following the imposition of a given *ad valorem* tariff of $t\%$, the foreign supply curve shifts from S_f to S_f^t. The crucial difference between this case and that of the small open economy is that the price of the importable on the domestic market does not increase by the full amount of the tariff. In fact, part of the tariff is borne by overseas producers. Their price falls from P_w to P_w' as they absorb a portion of the tariff.

Reapplying our surplus analysis of Figure 3.1, we observe a fall in consumers' surplus of $a + b + c + d$, the net reduction in welfare again being $b + d$. On this occasion, however, there is an additional area to take into account, namely area e. This accrues because foreign producers bear part of the tariff, thus constituting a redistribution of income from overseas producers to the tariff-imposing authority. The less elastic the foreign supply curve (over the relevant range) the greater the proportion of the tariff they will bear and the greater the redistribution.

If one is considering the change in welfare of the tariff-imposing country only, then clearly this redistribution of income must be viewed as a welfare gain, to be weighed against the welfare losses $b + d$. If it is the case that $e > |b + d|$, then the country is actually better off as a consequence of levying an import tariff. If on the other hand

$e < |b + d|$ then clearly the deadweight losses outweigh the redistribution effect and the country is worse off. The extent of the gain, as we have noted, depends on how much of the tariff is absorbed by the foreign producer. This is the same as saying that it depends on the terms of trade change. Other things being equal, the greater the favourable shift in the terms of trade, the greater the welfare gain.

Again, the net welfare implications can be established by using indifference curves, as in Figure 3.4. We commence at production and consumption points a and c. The imposition of an import tariff raises the domestic price of the importable, and domestic producers and consumers take their expenditure decisions on the basis of the relative price ratio P_D. Production settles at b. Because the country is a 'large' country, there is a favourable shift in the terms of trade, to the price ratio P_w''. This raises consumers' real income and therefore their real expenditure such that they are in a position to settle at a point such as d on I_2. Because of the favourable movement in the terms of trade, post-tariff equilibrium is consistent with a higher level of welfare than the pre-tariff situation.

The possibility that a country can raise its welfare by turning the terms of trade in its favour has been recognised for a very long time (see Bickerdike, 1906). The circumstances under which this can occur have been subject to close scrutiny, and it is clear that when a country enjoys some degree of bargaining power, restricted trade may be superior to free trade. This does not mean that the tariff-imposing

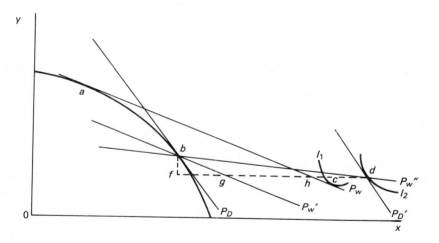

Figure 3.4

country can raise tariff levels successively in order to appropriate greater and greater welfare gains. It is possible over a certain range of tariff values to make gains. Further tariff increases beyond this 'range' result in the deadweight losses outweighing any terms of trade gains. There is in fact a unique tariff level which is consistent with maximum welfare. This unique level is referred to as the *optimum tariff*. The value of the optimum tariff for any given country is dependent on its trading partner's elasticity of supply of its exportable, and its elasticity of demand for the tariff-imposing country's exportable.[4]

In conclusion, therefore, we can state that when the tariff-imposing country can influence world prices it can raise its level of welfare by imposing a tariff. There is, however, an upper constraint on the extent to which welfare can be raised which is set by the optimum tariff. It must be emphasised that our remarks refer to the welfare of the tariff-imposing country only. Were we to adopt a global perspective we would be forced to conclude that restricted trade is still inferior to unrestricted trade. Furthermore, our analysis takes no account of the fact that the tariff-facing country may be in a position to retaliate. Although there are circumstances when a country which has imposed an optimum tariff and faced retaliation may nevertheless still be better off than under free trade (see Johnson, 1965a), this is the exception rather than the rule. In general it is likely that retaliatory action leaves both countries worse off compared to unrestricted trade.

TRADE RESTRICTION AND THE THEORY OF OPTIMAL INTERVENTIONS

Tariffs, or indeed any instrument of trade restriction, are methods for intervening in the free flow of goods and services. We have already seen, however, that unless a country can levy an optimum tariff, unrestricted trade appears to be consistent with a higher level of economic welfare than restricted trade. The process by which we deduced this conclusion is analogous to the manner in which we reach conclusions about the efficiency of perfect competition, i.e. we make a great many assumptions which ensure that static equilibrium is consistent with the conditions for Pareto optimality. This also applies to the foregoing comparison of the welfare implications of unrestricted and restricted trade. Here equilibrium in our small open economy model was also consistent with the conditions for Pareto optimality, namely:

$$DRS_{xy} = DRT_{xy} = FRT_{xy} = FRS_{xy} \qquad (3.3)$$

In other words the marginal rate of substitution in consumption at home (DRS) was equal to the domestic marginal rate of transformation in production (DRT). Through foreign trade this is equated with the foreign marginal rate of transformation (FRT) which in turn is equal to the foreign marginal rate of substitution (FRS). Resources are therefore optimally allocated from each individual country's, and from the global, viewpoint.

When discussing the welfare economics of Pareto optimality in the closed economy, it is readily admitted that the conditions for optimal resource allocation may not be fully met due to the presence of market imperfections. These imperfections might be present in product or factor markets. In the case of the former, monopoly supply or external economies could prevent the free market from reaching an optimum. In the case of the latter, factor price rigidity or factor immobility might be a constraint. It is widely accepted that in such circumstances, an *a priori* case for intervention exists to correct the distortion and permit the market to perform its allocative function more efficiently.

Although, as we saw earlier, unrestricted trade may appear preferable to restricted trade when all of our underlying assumptions hold, it might be necessary to amend our conclusions in the presence of market distortions. This would again constitute an *a priori* justification for some form of intervention to move the system towards an optimum. What is of interest from our viewpoint is whether tariffs are particularly suited or unsuited to correcting market distortions. In other words, if a specific distortion exists which prevents the attainment of some production, consumption, or income distribution objective, is the tariff the most efficient instrument for attaining that objective?

Domestic product market distortions

The kind of distortions which could be present in domestic product markets are production or consumption externalities, monopoly elements in production, or production functions which exhibit increasing returns to scale. For illustrative purposes let us take the case of a production externality in the importable sector.

In Figure 3.5 we have two domestic supply curves for importables which are labelled MPC_1 and MSC. The former is based on marginal private costs, the latter on marginal social costs. For every level of output MSC lies below MPC, indicating the presence of an external

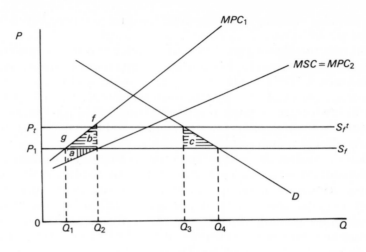

Figure 3.5

production economy. This could be present for a variety of reasons. For instance, the social costs of employing factors of production could be less than private costs. This would be so in the case of the so-called 'surplus labour model' (see Lewis, 1954). In this model employers in the import substitute sector (manufacturing) have to pay labour the value of its marginal product, which is positive. The labour, however, is drawn from the agricultural sector where its marginal product is frequently zero. Here the marginal private cost of employment exceeds its marginal social cost. In the absence of intervention, manufacturing employment would be less than the social optimum.

Another possibility is that the marginal social benefits of production exceed marginal private benefits. This could be the case with certain infant industries which generate production linkages. Again, producers will base their production decision on marginal private benefits, and output will be less than the socially desired level.

Either of these cases could be represented by Figure 3.5, where an output level of OQ_1 rather than OQ_2 is produced. We have an *a priori* case for intervention to raise output to OQ_2.

Clearly, a tariff of P_tP_1/OP_1 could stimulate the required production change. Such a tariff would raise the price faced by domestic producers from OP_1 to OP_t, thereby stimulating an expansion of output from OQ_1 to OQ_2. Because output has increased to the socially desired level, society gains area a – a gain in social surplus which follows from the replacement of Q_1Q_2 imports with domestically produced import substitutes. (The increased price which producers face has the effect of shifting the value of marginal product curve, which generates a higher level of employment and output.)

We know, however, that when we impose a tariff, the price of the importable rises not only to domestic producers but also to domestic consumers.

As a result, demand contracts from OQ_4 to OQ_3 and a consumption loss of c is inflicted. This has to be set against the gain of a. Whether a social gain or loss results depends on the relative magnitudes of a and c. *A priori* we can say nothing about this since it is dependent on demand and supply elasticities over the relevant range. The point is that in attempting to remove the original (production) distortion we have ended up replacing it with another (consumption) distortion. This has occurred because the tariff is not the most efficacious instrument for removing the original distortion; it is not the 'first best' policy response.

Suppose that instead of using a tariff we had given a production subsidy of the same rate. This would have the effect of displacing the *MPC* curve until it coincided with *MSC* ($= MPC_2$). Faced with MPC_2, domestic producers expand their output to OQ_2. They receive a price of OP_t (OP_1 plus the subsidy) and consumers continue to face a market price of OP_1. Because there is no 'by-product' consumption cost, the net result is that society gains all of area a. By relying on a production subsidy rather than on an import tariff we have avoided any distortion costs and we can therefore say that the policy is 'first best'. The conclusion of the analysis seems to be that if we wish to correct for a distortion without generating further distortions, we should treat the original distortion at source.

In terms of our more concrete 'surplus labour' and 'infant industry' examples, what is implied is that a tariff is an inappropriate instrument of intervention in both cases. In the surplus labour model a direct wage subsidy would be 'first best', since lowering the private costs of employment removes the distortion at source. In the infant industry case, if the argument for intervention is founded on production externalities, then it is more efficient to give a production subsidy than tariff protection.[5]

This deceptively simple yet powerful piece of analysis can be generalised to a whole host of cases. For each distortion/problem, we can trace out what Corden (1974) calls 'a hierarchy of policies', the hierarchy being based on the number of subsidiary distortions created by the instruments employed. Thus in the case of other product market distortions, a consumption tax would be preferable to an import tariff to remove a consumption diseconomy; while a production subsidy would be preferable to an import tariff as a means of increasing output where scale economies are present.

Domestic factor market distortions

The theory of optimal intervention is also applicable to distortions which may be present in domestic factor markets. For illustrative purposes we can again take a common case, namely real rewards which are inflexible downwards and which prevent the attainment of full employment following trade expansion.

We know from the Stolper-Samuelson theorem that trade expansion reduces the real rewards to the scarce factor, both in relative and absolute terms.[6] Assume that labour is the scarce factor, and that any reduction in real wages is resisted, with the result that unemployment emerges. The level of employment is now below its socially optimal level, and the export sector is prevented from expanding. According to the Stolper-Samuelson theorem, an import tariff would raise the real rewards of the scarce factor, or, in this case, facilitate the maintenance of employment at the initial real wage. There would, however, be by-product consumption costs, the magnitude of these costs depending on the degree of import restriction. The theory of optimal intervention tells us that 'first best' policy would be to tackle the distortion at source.

In this instance one would first have to enquire as to the source of real wage rigidity. This could be the result of market imperfection, for instance labour unions which resist any reduction in real wages, or legislation which permits real wages to fall to some minimum level.[7] First best policy would be to remove or ameliorate the market imperfection. This could be regarded, however, as politically unfeasible and/or socially undesirable. Given this constraint, second best policy would be a wage subsidy. From employers' point of view this would lower the real wage to the 'shadow level', i.e. the level which would generate full employment.

In an ideal world the subsidy would be financed by some non-distortionary, lump-sum method of taxation. In practice, of course, the subsidy would be financed by distortionary taxes.[8] This therefore would be a third best policy, since the method of taxation is adding another distortion. Employment would still increase, but not to the same extent as in the second best case, due to the disincentive effects of taxation. Fourth best policy would be a production subsidy. This too would have the effect of increasing employment, but not by as much as the third best policy since one is lowering the effective price of all factors, not just labour. After this perhaps comes an import tariff. This would have an effect analogous to a production subsidy, but becomes fifth best by virtue of imposing a tax on consumers and generating a concomitant consumption loss. According to the theory of optimal intervention, therefore, the tariff should only be used as a fifth best option if for some reason none of the superior options is feasible.

Again, as with product market distortions, the analysis can be readily applied to a number of imperfections. If we take the capital market rather than the labour market, we might observe 'under-investment' in the import substitute sector due to the fact that private rates of discount are higher than social rates of discount. This again tends to be a common argument for tariff restriction as it can be an aspect of the infant industry argument. Tariff imposition could possibly raise the level of investment, but again at the cost of a consumption distortion. A first best policy would be an interest rate subsidy at a rate just sufficient to equate private and social rates of discount. Second best policy would be a production subsidy. Since, however, this is a general subsidy it would impose the by-product distortion of stimulating more labour-intensive production techniques than an interest rate subsidy. Third best policy would be an import tariff which, as we have seen, is analogous to a production subsidy and consumption tax and imposes an additional consumption distortion.

Income distribution

In examining the way in which various trade policies can be used to correct for product market or factor market distortions, our concern is with resource allocation criteria: this is the essence of our Pareto efficiency criterion. Arguably, however, most decisions to levy import tariffs (and indeed other non-tariff restrictions) have rather more to do with income distribution than resource allocation objectives. It is therefore worth considering income distribution separately.

Refer again to Figure 3.5. Suppose our objective had been to raise the incomes of factors employed in the import substitute sector by $P_1 P_t fg$, rather than to raise domestic output from OQ_1 to OQ_2. Clearly our original tariff of t could accomplish such a transfer. In the process, however, we would generate our now familiar consumption distortion cost of c. In addition, we would also generate a production distortion cost of b. This arises because our objective is simply income redistribution, yet the instrument which we are employing has unavoidable resource allocation effects. As before, a production subsidy of $P_t P_1 / OP_1$ could achieve the desired result. By using a production subsidy we avoid the consumption distortion, but we still incur a production cost, again because a by-product of the subsidy is to raise the level of domestic production.

Thus reliance on the tariff redistributes income from consumers of the import substitute to producers, and generates two distortions. Reliance on a production subsidy redistributes income from the Exchequer and generates one distortion. These are third and second best policies respectively. First best policy would be to redistribute $P_1 P_t fg$ direct from the Exchequer in the form of an income transfer. In this way the income distribution objective is met without any adverse implications for resource allocation.[9]

It would seem, then, that intervention in the market for traded goods is a rather blunt instrument for income redistribution, direct income transfers being more efficient (in the resource allocation sense).

Foreign market distortions

The principle which seems to emerge from the theory of optimal intervention is that if one wishes to correct for a distortion, one should employ an instrument which affects the distortion at source. What about when the distortion affects international rather than domestic markets?

In the small open economy model the question has no significance, since international prices are taken as given. In the large open economy context, however, the issue is of relevance. We have already noted that if a country faces a less than infinitely elastic demand for its exports, it can raise foreign prices of exports by restricting export supply. Similarly, if it faces an import supply function which is less than infinitely elastic, it can lower the world price of imports by restricting import supply. This is of course tantamount to saying that the country can affect its terms of trade – it has some degree of market power.

We have already considered this case earlier in the chapter and established that when a country is in such a position it can increase its real income by imposing an import tariff. We referred to the tariff which will actually maximise real income as the optimum tariff. This is the rate of tax which serves to equate the marginal gain from any terms of trade improvement with the marginal loss from resource misallocation.

The optimum tariff is the widely accepted exception to the general rule that unrestricted trade generates a higher level of welfare than restricted trade, there being some optimal degree of restriction which is dependent on foreign elasticity of demand for home exports and foreign elasticity of supply of imports. This is a case which has been examined in some detail in the literature (see Johnson, 1958). Its importance in the present context is that it provides a first best case for tariff intervention in order to exploit an imperfection in foreign markets.

RELIANCE ON TARIFFS FOR COMMERCIAL POLICY

We have not covered all possible motives for tariff interventions in this brief introduction to the theory of optimal intervention. That is simply not possible in a book of this length. However, we have covered a sufficient number of cases to gain some idea of the principles underlying the analysis. In particular we would emphasise the central postulate of optimal intervention analysis that, in general terms, tariffs are second (or third, or fourth, etc.) best instruments for intervention. In general there will always be more efficient instruments available. The only generally applicable exception to this rule is the optimum tariff argument, and this rests on some rather severe assumptions, not least that trading partners would not take retaliatory action.

Were we to conclude the analysis at this point it would leave a great many important questions unanswered. There is widespread use of tariff interventions by many countries in many product markets. Although tariff levels have been systematically reduced over the post-war period (see Chapter 5), they remain important barriers to trade in many markets. Does this suggest that the optimum tariff case is more common than intuition would imply? The most casual inspection of the country and commodity range of interventions indicates that this is hardly likely to be the case. How, therefore, are we to explain the widespread reliance on tariff interventions which are explicitly imposed to influence the composition of domestic production and consumption or to influence domestic income distribution, rather than to affect the tariff-levying country's terms of trade?

Second best intervention in a second best world

The first point we can make, of course, is that the theory of optimal intervention analysis prescribes a hierarchy of policy instruments which have certain consequences, given first best assumptions. The theory suggests that in general when one faces a domestic market distortion, some form of subsidy is preferable to a tariff. An assumption which has been implicit in this analysis, however, and which ought now to be made explicit is that subsidies can be financed in some non-distorting manner. For a genuine first best solution, any subsidies should be financed by lump-sum taxes. In an ideal world this might be possible. In practice, however, lump-sum taxes tend to be regressive, and therefore greater reliance is placed on income and expenditure taxes. Although there are likely to be distortions associated with these taxes, in general they are less than those associated with trade taxes. Thus subsidies financed by income or expenditure taxes are preferable to tariffs. This assumes, however, that such taxes can be collected relatively costlessly. In a developed market economy where income per capita is relatively high and administrative expertise is readily available, this is a reasonable assumption to make. In a less developed country, however, where administrative expertise is lacking, subsistence production important, barter common and income per capita low, the revenue yield of income and expenditure taxes can be relatively low. This would follow from a combination of a restricted tax base and high collection costs.

Thus where there appears to be a case for infant industry protection and where the first best recommendation in a first best world would be a production subsidy financed from general Exchequer funds, the authorities may be unable to raise the necessary revenue from domestic sources. In such circumstances the traded goods sector may have attractions as a source of revenue. The objects of taxation (either imports or exports) are relatively clearly defined, they invariably enter or leave the country concerned through a relatively small number of 'ports of entry' (legal trade, at least) and an administrative framework does exist – most countries have import/export licensing procedures. These conditions often mean that the cost/yield ratio for trade taxes is somewhat lower than the cost/yield ratio for domestic income or expenditure-based taxes (see Greenaway, 1981).

Although a production subsidy is first best, in principle collection costs might serve to make a self-financing subsidy the 'feasible first best' policy. We examine this case in Figure 3.6. S_f again refers to the foreign supply of imports whilst *MPC* and *MSC* denote marginal private and marginal social costs respectively. The latter lies below the former due to external economies, indicating a socially optimal rate of output of OQ_2. First best policy would be a production subsidy of $P_3 P_1/OP_1$ financed from general taxation. Revenue constraints make this infeasible, and second best policy becomes a self-financing subsidy. A tariff of $P_2 P_1/OP_1$ is levied which raises the home price of the importable to OP_2. The revenue from the tariff is used to finance a production subsidy of $P_3 P_2/OP_2$, which raises the price faced by producers to OP_3 and stimulates an expansion of output to OQ_2. Thus the socially desired level of domestic output is attained. A consumption distortion cost is incurred in the process, but this is less

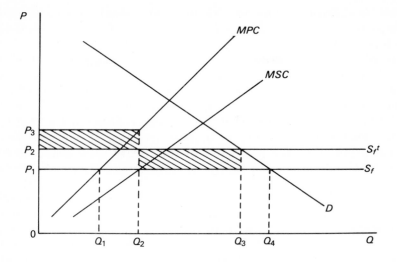

Figure 3.6

than the cost which would have been incurred had a tariff been used in isolation. This would have raised the domestic price to producers *and* consumers to OP_3, restricted import volume further, and generated higher distortion costs.

If collection costs of non-trade taxes are prohibitively high, tariffs may be used not just to facilitate subsidy intervention, but for purposes of raising revenue *per se*. The central authorities may require tax revenue to finance the provision of public goods, and in certain circumstances the foreign trade sector may be the most convenient tax handle. A good deal of empirical evidence exists to suggest that many LDCs rely quite heavily on such revenue tariffs (see Greenaway, 1980) and some effort has been expended in identifying maximum revenue tariffs (see Johnson, 1950-1) and optimal revenue tariffs (see Vanek, 1971; Greenaway, 1982c).

Non-Paretian social welfare criteria

The theory of optimal intervention is founded on the Paretian principle of welfare improvement, i.e. if a given change results in one person being made better off while no one else is made worse off, the change can be thought of as desirable. Of course most (if not all) economic policies result in some agents being made better off while others are made worse off; therefore the compensation principle is invoked. This requires that any gainers from a particular change benefit to such an extent that they are able to compensate the losers from the change.

Since the compensation need not actually take place, we are implicitly evaluating the implications of various changes for potential welfare. Ostensibly the Paretian criterion ignores the effects of trade policy on income distribution since it presumes that some mechanism is available to effect any necessary income redistribution, that is to ensure that potential gains become actual gains. If one accepts this presumption, then the postulates of the theory of optimal intervention hold and tariffs will invariably turn out to be second best (or worse).

But, of course, one might find the Paretian welfare criterion objectionable. Even if actual compensation takes place, the criterion is consistent with an unequal distribution of income becoming more unequal. Instead, the Pigovian welfare criterion might be adopted. This explicitly assumes a diminishing marginal utility of money income, and therefore explicitly favours policies which redistribute income from 'rich' groups in society to 'poor' groups. Adoption of such a welfare criterion by the authorities could result in trade policy being regarded as a necessary instrument of redistribution, with zero tariffs being levied on necessities and high tariffs on luxuries, the revenue from the latter being used for income support schemes.

Another possibility is that the authorities may implicitly follow policies designed to maximise what Corden (1974) describes as a 'conservative social welfare function'. A principal argument in such a function would be 'income maintenance'. The authorities aim to ensure that the income of any particular group does not change suddenly and significantly, and are willing to stand ready to take the requisite policy action to avoid this. Obvious policies such as social security benefits would be recommended. So too would tariff protection of specific markets when those markets are threatened by a sudden increase in import penetration. One could argue that the GATT Charter recognises the importance of this consideration in the provisions of Article XIX, which permits member countries to take temporary action to restrict imports when market disruption threatens (see Chapter 5 below).

Thus the existence of non-Paretian welfare conceptions can also assist in explaining reliance on tariff interventions.

Taxation without representation

Milton Friedman has frequently referred to the fiscal implications of inflation as taxation without representation. With non-indexation of tax allowances and tax bands, total tax yields rise with inflation.

There is an analogue here with the use of tariffs as instruments of intervention. Frequently there is a 'free lunch' illusion associated with the use of tariffs. Superficially it seems as if the 'foreigner' is paying to maintain the income of a particular group, or paying to maintain employment in a particular activity. As we have seen, however; this is illusory. The costs are borne by domestic consumers of the importable product. Furthermore, if the import in question is an input into exportables, the price of exportables rises. As we shall see in Chapter 4, this is a common source of negative effective protection in exportable activities.

Despite the fact that the costs are very real and indeed invariably greater than those associated with an income transfer from general Exchequer funds, commercial policy can have very great attractions for vote-maximising governments. Many of the costs are hidden. Even those which are evident tend to be spread thinly across a disparate and disorganised group of voters, and psychologically the impact is not the same as, say, an increase in the rate of income tax. By contrast, the benefits to the recipients are very much more explicit. This can be an influential consideration where an activity is geographically concentrated. Furthermore, import protection is itself more evident than a production subsidy and does not have the same aura of a 'hand-out'.

These are persuasive considerations from the viewpoint of a vote-maximising government and should not be underestimated. Producer lobbies are traditionally influential, and it tends to be extremely easy to relate employment loss and import penetration, the implication being that increases in the latter result in increases in the former. As we shall see in Chapter 11, the relationship between the two is not quite so straightforward. Nevertheless, the appearance of a costless panacea in the guise of import controls can be extremely appealing.

Non-economic objectives

The final area we might focus on is that of non-economic objectives, objectives which are socio-political rather than economic. Income distribution objectives are frequently classed as non-economic, but we have already considered these. Here we are concerned more with objectives that relate to self-sufficiency.

Such targets might range from the maintenance of an arms production capability to self-sufficiency in agriculture, to a resistance to de-industrialisation, perhaps for strategic reasons. We could still apply optimal intervention analysis to these objectives and recommend, for instance, subsidies rather than tariffs. It may be felt, however, that prohibitive tariffs are a more effective guarantee of maintaining domestic production than subsidisation.

CONCLUDING COMMENTS

In this chapter we have examined the economic effects of tariffs and considered the circumstances under which the tariff can be viewed as an efficient instrument of intervention. If we follow the Paretian efficiency criterion, such circumstances are few in number. Thus, if we are to understand the widespread use of tariff interventions we have to look beyond narrow economic criteria.

In the next chapter we shall consider the economic effects in rather more detail in order to elaborate on the concept of the effective rate of protection, and in Chapter 5 we shall examine the institutional framework for dismantling tariff barriers.

NOTES ON FURTHER READING

Most introductory texts on international economics provide chapters on the economic effects of tariffs. Chapter 2 of Milner and Greenaway (1979) looks at the issue using both partial techniques (as we have done here) and offer curve analysis. The theory of optimal intervention has developed over the last twenty years or so and two early classic articles are Bhagwati and Ramaswami (1963) and Johnson (1965b). For a thorough review of the principles and a clear and detailed analysis of their application to a wide range of problems, the student can do no better than read Corden (1974). This remains the classic textbook reference on the subject. Worthwhile collected readings are Johnson (1971) and Bhagwati (1981). Both contain papers germane to the analysis of this chapter. section II in Johnson (1971) contains a number of well known articles, while section III of the Bhagwati volume contains some relevant papers.

4 Nominal and Effective Protection

In examining some of the welfare effects of tariffs in Chapter 3, we emphasised throughout that our initial concern was with the welfare effects of nominal tariffs. Although we separated consumption effects from production effects, we clearly assumed that a given nominal tariff had the same effect on the prices faced by both consumers and producers. In practice this amounts to assuming that the production process is single-stage. It should be obvious, however, that this is rarely the case. In fact, most production processes are multi-stage. Thus we may well ask ourselves, what is the situation when a given producer is only the final link in the chain of production? In order to assemble a given product he has to purchase intermediate inputs, some of which may be imported. By definition, therefore, his value added is less than 100 per cent. Will a given nominal tariff have the same effect on prices faced by consumers and producers in these circumstances?

THE CONCEPT OF EFFECTIVE PROTECTION

In responding to a given change in the level of tariffs, consumers are influenced by the effect which any alteration has on final prices. In a small open economy the proportionate change in price would reflect exactly the proportionate change in tariff on the final good. Thus, in the case of a tariff increase, consumer behaviour is influenced by the ultimate change in the final price of imports relative to import substitutes.

The extent to which production of import substitutes changes depends, however, not on the nominal tariff which is applied to a particular product, but rather on the degree of protection which a given nominal tariff confers. This may appear a little convoluted at first sight. After all, if a tariff of 10 per cent is levied on imports, their price will rise by 10 per cent. The price of import substitutes can therefore rise by up to 10 per cent. The links which run from a change in the nominal tariff on the firm's output through to a decision as to whether or not to employ more productive factors are a little more complex, however. The producer of any particular final good is the last stage in the production process. Typically he purchases inputs which are subsequently assembled into units of output; or he purchases a semi-finished article for finishing. In the process, value is added to the intermediate inputs. Thus the *effective* protection which is given to this producer is dependent not on the nominal tariff *per se*, but on the extent to which a nominal tariff on the firm's outputs affects its value added. This in turn determines whether or not the firm will expand output and employ additional factors of production.

In order to elucidate the effective protection concept, we will initially continue with our two-country case. As before, competitive markets are assumed. Thus factors are paid the value of their marginal product, and price flexibility ensures that markets clear without adjustment problems. All goods which are produced are traded. In earlier chapters we simply distinguished between importables and exportables. Now, however, we shall also make a distinction between intermediate inputs and final goods. Intermediate inputs are produced inputs, and are combined with primary factors of production to produce final goods. The difference between the value of intermediate inputs and the value of final goods is value added. We will also assume that there are fixed relationships in production between inputs and outputs; in other words, input coefficients remain fixed and are the same for all firms. Finally we will impose the usual assumption that the tariff-imposing country is a small open economy. and any tariff which it imposes is non-prohibitive.

The effective protective rate

Proceeding from the above assumptions, we can define the *effective rate of protection* which a given import substitute activity receives (e_j) as follows:

$$e_j = \frac{V_j^* - V_j}{V_j} \tag{4.1}$$

where V_j = value added per unit of final good j, at free trade prices, and V_j^* = value added per unit of final good j, at tariff distorted prices.

Thus the effective rate of protection is measured by the extent to which value added in the import substitute sector can be raised, as a consequence of the imposition of tariffs (while still leaving domestic producers of import substitutes in a position to compete with imports).

Consider the parameters on the right hand side of this equation further:

$$V_j = P_j (1 - z_{ij}) \tag{4.2}$$

$$V_j^* = P_j [(1 + t_j) - z_{ij} (1 + t_i)] \tag{4.3}$$

where P_j = free trade price of commodity j, z_{ij} = share of inputs in the production process of j, t_j = nominal rate of tariff on imports of j (final good), and t_i = nominal rate of tariff on imports of i (intermediate input).

If we substitute (4.2) and (4.3) into (4.1) and simplify, we can write

$$e_j = \frac{t_j - z_{ij}t_i}{1 - z_{ij}} \tag{4.4}$$

All we have done is to alter the simple case of Chapter 3 to allow for the possibility that the import substitute sector may require imported inputs, and this makes a striking difference to the determinants of the effective rate of protection. The import substitute sector of Chapter 3 was implicitly a single-stage production process, with a value added of 100 per cent. In terms of equation (4.4) this would result in $e_j = t_j/1$, i.e. the effective rate is equal to the nominal rate on the final good. However, as soon as we allow for an imported input, effective protection is a function of three variables:

1. The nominal rate of tariff on the final good. Other things being equal, a rise in the nominal tariff will raise effective protection.
2. The nominal rate of tariff on the imported input. Other things being equal, a rise in this nominal tariff will raise intermediate costs, reduce value added, and therefore effective protection.
3. The share of imported inputs in final value. For a given level of nominal tariffs, a higher z_{ij} will be associated with a higher rate of effective protection. This follows because as z_{ij} rises, value added falls (in absolute terms) and a given nominal tariff will have a greater proportionate effect on value added.

In a classic work on the subject, one of the pioneers of the study of effective protection summarises the above implications as follows (Corden, 1971):

$$t_j = t_i \quad \Rightarrow \quad e_j = t_j = t_i \tag{4.5}$$

$$t_j > t_i \quad \Rightarrow \quad e_j > t_j > t_i \tag{4.6}$$

$$t_j < t_i \quad \Rightarrow \quad e_j < t_j < t_i \tag{4.7}$$

$$\left. \begin{array}{l} t_j < z_{ij}t_i \quad \Rightarrow \quad e_j < 0 \\ \text{or} \quad 1 < z_{ij} \end{array} \right\} \tag{4.8}$$

Implications (4.5), (4.6) and (4.7) are self-evident. They follow because an import tariff on the final good j affects producers of the import substitute in the same way as a production subsidy, while tariffs on imported inputs have an effect akin to a production tax. Thus when the tax and subsidy elements are identical, the effective rate will be the same as the nominal rates. When the subsidy element outweighs the tax element, the effective rate of protection will exceed the nominal rate. The same applies *mutatis mutandis* for the case where the tax element exceeds the subsidy element. This is an important point to grasp, and it follows because we are looking at the protective effects of the *entire* tariff structure rather than simply at nominal tariffs on final goods. By taking account of the full range of tariffs we can calculate their impact on value added in the import substitute sector. Ultimately it is the extent to which this can rise as a consequence of the protective structure, rather than the extent of any rise in the price of imports, which influences resource movement into the import substitute sector.

The point can be reinforced by the use of a simple example. Assume that $P_j = 100$, $P_i = 50$ and therefore $V_j = 50$. If one assumes that V_j remains fixed at 50, and z is fixed, one can compute e_j for a variety of combinations of t_j and t_i, as in Table 4.1 where various rates of nominal tariff on inputs are ranked horizontally, while rates on final goods are ranked vertically. The cells in the matrix record the e_j which are associated with different combinations of t_i and t_j. Along the diagonal which runs from left to right we find that $t_j = t_i = e_j$. Below the diagonal, $t_j > t_i$, therefore $e_j > t_j > t_i$. Above and to the right, however, $t_i > t_j$, and we find that $e_j < t_j$.

TABLE 4.1   Nominal rates of tariff on inputs and outputs, and effective rates

t_j \ t_i	0	10	20	50	100
0	0	−10	−20	−50	−100
10	20	10	0	−30	−80
20	40	30	20	−10	−40
50	100	90	80	50	0
100	200	190	180	150	100

Negative effective protection

Implication (4.8) outlines the condition for negative effective protection. In these circumstances, tariff-distorted value added is *less* than free-trade value added. Intuition may suggest that this is no more than a pathological case. It is, however, far from uncommon. We suggest in inequality (4.8) that negative effective protection can result either as a consequence of $t_j < z_{ij}t_i$ or $z_{ij} > 1$. These are conceptually distinct cases. The former could arise as a result of an *ad hoc* and essentially unplanned regime of import tariffs, import quotas and multiple exchange rates.[1] Even when the tariff structure is 'planned' in some sense, one often finds negative effective rates emerging. For example, different tariffs may have differing objectives. A protective tariff may be applied to final goods. Because of fiscal constraints, however, a revenue tariff may simultaneously be applied on intermediate inputs, the combined effect of the two being that $z_{ij}t_i > t_j$ and therefore a negative effective rate on the final good (see Greenaway, 1981). It is not unusual to find negative effective rates in exportables as the outcome of $z_{ij}t_i > t_j$. Typically this arises because the exportable activities use imported inputs which are subject to tariffs, but receive no offsetting subsidy on their final good. (A glance forward to Table 4.4 gives details of negative protection of exportables in the United Kingdom.)

It may be objected that such a situation is only sustainable in the short run – in the longer run firms become cognisant of the fact that the protective structure is conferring negative effective protection and press for rationalisation. It is far from clear that this is the case, however. There is a great deal of evidence of highly complicated protective structures generating negative protection, especially (though not exclusively) in less developed countries, and negative protection of exportables is frequently found. The point about negative protection is simply that value added would be higher under free trade – individual firms may not be aware of the alternative![2] (Even if they are, they may prefer the more relaxed atmosphere of a protected home market to more competitive conditions.)

The second possibility (i.e. $z_{ij} > 1$) is conceptually different. Here negative effective protection results because the value of imported inputs exceeds the world value of the finished product. Again, one's initial reaction might be that this is only a theoretical possibility, as it implies producing something which will be sold for less than it cost to produce. A moment's thought, however, tells us otherwise. The denominator in equation (4.4) is negative, but the numerator is positive. In other words, the final good is sold on the home market behind high nominal tariffs. This is a situation which commonly accompanies infant industry protection as part of an import substitution programme. It is in fact a common source of negative effective rates emerging for import substitute activities in less developed countries (see Balassa, 1971).

ELABORATIONS OF THE SIMPLE EFFECTIVE PROTECTION CONCEPT

The foregoing has analysed, in partial equilibrium terms, the simplest possible notion of effective protection, where we have only one intermediate input into the production process, and only one instrument which distorts trade, namely the tariff. Even if we confine ourselves to partial equilibrium analysis, elaborations of these have to be allowed for. In addition to these, more ambitious general equilibrium analysis calls for further refinement and development of the basic concept.

(1) *Many inputs.* The case where a production process uses a number of traded inputs is, in principle anyway, the easiest complication to accommodate. More information is clearly required to calculate the effective rate, since we would wish to know not only the number of imported inputs but also their individual shares in final value, and the nominal rates of tariff which apply to each. Given this information, we would simply rewrite equation (4.4) for the multi-input case as:

$$e_j = \frac{t_j - \sum_{i=1}^{n} z_{ij} t_i^*}{1 - \sum_{i=1}^{n} z_{ij}} \qquad (4.4a)$$

where Σz_{ij} refers to the sum of the input shares, and t_i^* is a weighted average of input tariffs (with weights applied according to input share).

(2) *Non-tariff protection.* Clearly tariffs are not the only instrument to affect the protective structure. Strictly speaking any instrument (whether applied to traded goods specifically or to all goods) which affects value added will affect the effective protective rate. Thus an effective protective rate could only be said to be 'true' if it took account of all such influences. Some influences are more obvious and easier to take account of than others. For example, a net production subsidy (i.e. a production subsidy which exceeds any production taxes) will raise effective protection, *ceteris paribus*. Thus

if a production subsidy were given, (4.4a) would have to be rewritten as:

$$e_j^T = \frac{t_j + s_j (1 + t_j) - \sum\limits_{i=1}^{n} z_{ij} t_i}{1 - \sum\limits_{i=1}^{n} z_{ij}}$$

(4.4b)

where s_j refers to the net subsidy.

The problem of incorporating the effect of quantitative restrictions is more intractable. One has to compute the tariff equivalent of a particular quota, then incorporate this into the effective rate. As tariffs become less important as instruments of commercial policy, and non-tariff interventions more common, problems of estimating effective rates of protection intensify. Indeed, often researchers simply work from (4.4a) and estimate what really only amounts to an effective tariff rate, rather than an effective protective rate. We shall spend a good deal of time examining non-tariff barriers in Part III, and this is an issue to which we shall return for closer consideration in due course.

(3) *Production functions.* Of the assumptions which were made at the outset, a number related to production relationships. Specifically we assumed that input–output coefficients were fixed, and were identical for all firms in the relevant sector. Furthermore we assumed that there were no possibilities for substitution between traded inputs, or between intermediate inputs and primary inputs.

Fixing input–output coefficients is not a problem *per se*; what is more problematic is the assumption that they are identical across firms. The implication of this is that all firms enjoy the same degree of effective protection from a given set of nominal tariffs. Clearly it is probable that intra-industry differences will exist and, as Corden points out, it is probable that differences will either be exaggerated or narrowed as firms respond in different ways to a given tariff structure. When this is the case, there will clearly be differing output responses across firms. Highly disaggregated data would be necessary to adjust fully for this problem. In practice a uniform coefficient is imposed.

The constancy or otherwise of the input–output coefficient is also related to the scope for substitution between inputs, and the extent to which substitution takes place in response to the tariff structure. Suppose, for example, that substitution were possible. A tariff on an imported input, which would be expected to lower effective protection, may stimulate substitution of the taxed input for an untaxed input. Measured effective protection would then understate actual effective protection.

(4) *Exportables*. Our analysis so far has been concerned only with effective protection of the import substitute sector, as will most of our subsequent analysis. It must be pointed out, however, that the theory of effective protection is equally applicable to the export sector. In order to gauge the extent of effective protection, one would again be interested in the overall impact of the fiscal system. As we would expect, subsidies on the final good would tend to raise effective protection, as would subsidised use of imported inputs. Taxes which are applied to both inputs and outputs would tend to lower effective protection – except for the case where the input itself is an exportable and is subject to an export tax. As we have noted, a situation which is not uncommon arises when the output of the export sector is subject to neither taxes nor subsidies, but it uses in the production process an imported input which is subject to a tariff (or quota). This is one of the more common sources of negative effective protection of the export sector.

(5) *General equilibrium analysis*. The point about substitution possibilities in the production function brings us conveniently to the final 'technical' issue which we will examine, namely general equilibrium considerations. The most important implication which can be drawn from our analysis so far is a warning against drawing conclusions about production effects of tariffs from information on nominal rates which apply to the finished good. Rather one has to look to the outcome of the entire protective structure. Precisely the same point can be made with respect to multi-sector analysis: one has to examine the implications of the protective structure for one activity *relative* to another. In a simple two-sector model this is not necessary – protection given to the import substitute sector unequivocally results in resources being drawn into that sector. As one moves into a general equilibrium framework, this conclusion no longer remains valid. The direction and extent of resource shift depends on *relative* rates of effective protection. Thus, even when positive effective protection is conferred by the protective structure, it is still possible for resources to move from that activity towards a sector with a higher degree of effective protection.[3] This is an extremely important point which has far-reaching implications for policy formulation – an issue we will return to shortly.

General equilibrium analysis also means that the non-traded goods sector cannot be ignored, or assumed away.[4] This is an issue of some importance, as a secular tendency for the non-traded sector to grow is evident in most developed market economies. (This trend has been variously labelled 'de-industrialisation', 'tertiarisation', 'post-industrialisation'.) The effects of protection on traded good activities for the non-traded sector depend on whether non-traded goods compete for inputs with traded goods, and on whether non-traded goods are substitutes for traded goods in consumption or not. If a non-traded good competes for inputs with an activity which enjoys a high degree of effective protection, then this activity will tend to contract as the protected activity expands. This would be the case, for instance, where the protected activity is a relatively labour-intensive import substitute, the non-traded 'good' being relatively labour-intensive services. On the consumption side, however, if the non-traded good is a close substitute for the protected activity, its output will tend to expand. In any particular case, the ultimate effect depends on the relative magnitude of production and consumption effects, which depends upon elasticities of substitution. The point is that we can no longer ignore the non-traded sector. Protection of tradables will affect output and employment in non-tradables. The issue is a complex one which, as we shall see, creates difficulties for empirical researchers. We can do little more than recognise the problem here, suggesting that the interested reader look to Corden (1971) for more detailed analysis.

MEASUREMENT OF EFFECTIVE PROTECTION

In this section we shall shift emphasis from the conceptual to the practical. Assuming that we regard accurate estimates of effective rates of protection as being more clearly indicative of relative resource 'pulls' from the tariff structure, how do we actually translate the concept discussed above into a measure?

Our development of the effective protective rate resulted in the derivation of equations (4.4a) and (4.4b). The former referred to the effective tariff rate, which when estimated gives an indication of the proportionate change in value added resulting from the tariff structure. The latter referred to the effective protective rate. When estimated this gives an indication of the proportionate change in value added which results from the entire protective structure. A number of studies have estimated both of these rates. In general, however, empirical analysis concentrates on the latter. The difference between the two is the net subsidy conferred by non-tariff interventions, i.e.

$$e_j^T - e_j = n_j = \frac{s_j}{1 - \sum_{i=1}^{n} z_{ij}} \qquad (4.4c)$$

Since s_j is invariably defined to include only domestically applied taxes and subsidies, and exclude an allowance for quantitative restrictions, data for this can be relatively easily acquired.

Supposing we are therefore using (4.4b) as a basis for estimation:

$$e_j^T = \frac{t_j + s_j(1 + t_j) - \sum_{i=1}^{n} z_{ij}t_i}{1 - \sum_{i=1}^{n} z_{ij}} \tag{4.4b}$$

What difficulties would we expect to confront? If we recall again equation (4.1):

$$e_j = \frac{V_j^* - V_j}{V_j}$$

it will be remembered that effective protection was defined as the proportionate difference between free-trade value added and tariff-distorted value added. In attempting to estimate equation (4.4b), however, we would be working from tariff-distorted data – we are not in a position to observe free-trade prices! Our first problem, therefore, is to adjust our parameters z_{ij} and s_j in some way to convert them from tariff-distorted to free-trade levels. In the case of the former, for example, we would be working from published input-output tables which give us the information to calculate the *ex post* situation, i.e. V_j^* in the presence of tariffs, but not the *ex ante* V_j.

Basically, two techniques have been employed by researchers. One method involves taking a country with very low tariffs as being representative of free-trade conditions and then using z_{ij}s from its input-output tables to calculate V_j^* for the home country (e.g. Balassa, 1965). The major drawback with this procedure is that it assumes input coefficients are identical between countries. The alternative is to try to estimate the tariff-distorting effect directly, as follows.

We know that in the input-output tables a unit of input is valued not at free-trade prices, but at local tariff-distorted prices, i.e. $P_i(1 + t_i)$, in the same way as a unit of output is valued at $P_j(1 + t_j)$. We can thus write the tariff-distorted input coefficient as:

$$z'_{ij} = \frac{P_i(1 + t_i)}{1 + t_j} \tag{4.9}$$

Since under conditions of free trade $z_{ij} = P_i$, we can write:

$$z_{ij} = \frac{z'_{ij}(1 + t_i)}{1 + t_j} \tag{4.10}$$

Substitution of (4.10) into (4.4b) yields

$$
e_j^T = \frac{t_j + s_j(1 + t_j) - \sum_{i=1}^{n} z'_{ij}\left(\dfrac{1 + t_i}{1 + t_j}\right) t_i}{1 - \sum_{i=1}^{n} z'_{ij}\left(\dfrac{1 + t_i}{1 + t_j}\right)}
\tag{4.11}
$$

To complete the exercise, allowance must also be made for the fact that net subsidies are valued at tariff-distorted, rather than free-trade prices:

$$
s_j = s'_j(1 + t_j)
\tag{4.12}
$$

Substitution into (4.11) gives us our final estimating equation:

$$
e_j^T = \frac{t_j + s'_j(1 + t_j)^2 - \sum_{i=1}^{n} z'_{ij}\left(\dfrac{1 + t_i}{1 + t_j}\right) t_i}{1 - \sum_{i=1}^{n} z'_{ij}\left(\dfrac{1 + t_i}{1 + t_j}\right)}
\tag{4.13}
$$

Thus data from the *ex post* protected situation only can be used to estimate e_j^T. This procedure has been used in a number of studies (see, for instance, Barker and Han, 1971; or Oulton, 1976).

Obtaining a figure for nominal tariffs can also create difficulties. As we have noted, data on z_{ij} are usually obtained from input-output tables.[5] This limits the sample size to perhaps a maximum of 100 activities. Tariff lines invariably run to thousands of items! Furthermore, the classification principles for both are likely to differ - the classification of input-output data being based on production characteristics, tariff classifications according to commodity characteristics. Thus one either has to estimate an average nominal tariff for the input-output classification from details of tariff revenue, or one has to reclassify tariff data according to input-output classifications, and then average actual rates. Both approaches have their problems.

In the case of the former one simply divides tariff revenue raised by total imports to obtain an 'average' tariff. There may be problems due to timing differences here. More significantly, however, this procedure groups together all imports in the category and imposes an average, when in fact differential rates may apply to different commodities in the group and differential rates may apply to different sources of supply (due to tariff preferences). These problems can to some extent be avoided by working from the more disaggregated tariff data and reclassifying according to input-output groupings.

When the data are regrouped, however, one is still faced with the problem of averaging. Does one simply average all rates, or does one compute some kind of weighted average (with, for example, weights applied by imports)? As Tumlir and Till (1971) show, the estimate of effective protection is sensitive to the method of averaging.

In practice the former procedure, of deriving an average from revenue data, is most frequently adopted – one presumes primarily for pragmatic reasons, i.e. it is a much less costly method than re-classifying. It is generally agreed, however, that this procedure does tend to bias estimates of nominal tariffs in a downward direction.

Estimating the extent of non-tariff protection can also create some practical problems. Obtaining data on taxes and subsidies is relatively straightforward. Indeed, UK input-output tables actually provide a net subsidy figure.[6] The more important problem here is placing a figure on quantitative restrictions. Many studies have simply ignored this element. However, given the widespread use of quantitative restrictions in trade in agricultural commodities and textiles, and given the increasing use of voluntary export restraints and orderly marketing agreements,[7] such an omission must be considered increasingly unsatisfactory.

The final point that we might make in connection with empirical problems is to return to the subject of non-traded goods. How does one treat non-traded inputs? Corden (1966) suggests that value added in non-traded inputs could be aggregated with all other value added. Although this may be a straightforward method of dealing with the problem, as Oulton (1976) points out, the resultant effective protective rate which is estimated applies now to a number of distinct production activities rather than one. An equally simple procedure, followed by Balassa (1965), is to assume that the price of non-traded goods is insensitive to protection. In practice this means that they can be treated as if they were a traded input, but one to which a zero tariff applies. As we saw earlier, no general presumptions can be made about whether prices will rise or fall in the non-traded goods sector. The extent to which one regards this procedure as valid depends on the extent to which one feels that upward pressures and downward pressures on prices in the non-traded sector cancel each other out.

EMPIRICAL RESULTS

Having outlined some of the problems which researchers in this area face, let us now turn to a review of their findings.

Since the development of the effective protection concept in the 1960s, an exhaustive literature has emerged examining the pattern of effective protection for a variety of countries at widely differing stages of development. Representative contributions to this literature are Basevi, 1966 (United States); Balassa, 1971 (a number of developing countries); Barker and Han, 1971 (United Kingdom); Gamir, 1971 (Spain); Guisinger, 1971 (Pakistan); Oulton, 1976 (United Kingdom); Hiemenz and Von Rabenau, 1976 (West Germany); Yeats, 1979 (developing countries) and MacAleese, 1971 (Ireland). (This list is meant to be illustrative rather than exhaustive.) Exercising a certain amount of poetic licence in summarising this literature, a consensus seems to have been reached on a number of findings:

(1) The rank correlation between nominal and effective rates of protection turns out to be consistently high. Table 4.2 summarises some of the evidence on this. The interesting implication of this finding is that some idea of relative resource pulls of the tariff structure (which are dependent on effective rates) can be gained from the structure of nominal rates.

(2) As we would expect from point (1), there is a clear pattern of escalation in effective rates as well as in nominal rates. Table 4.3 gives some indication of this for the United Kingdom, with a clear

TABLE 4.2 Rank correlation coefficients between nominal and effective rates of protection

	Country	Number of industries*	r	Number of industries*	r
(1)	Norway	10	0.96	56	0.82
	Philippines	10	0.93	56	0.83
	Mexico	10	0.95	53	0.82
	Pakistan	9	0.93	54	0.90
	Chile	10	0.90	40	0.88
	Malaysia	9	0.79	56	0.88
	Brazil	10	0.96	56	0.94
(2)	Korea	34	0.89	218	0.92
(3)	United Kingdom			70	0.94
(4)	United Kingdom			90	0.94

* The larger sample of 'Number of industries' applies to more disaggregated data.

Sources: (1) Balassa (1971), (2) Korean Development Association (1967), (3) Barker and Han (1971), (4) Oulton (1976).

TABLE 4.3   Average nominal and effective rates of protection by industrial
category in the United Kingdom, 1968

Commodity group	Nominal tariff on imports %	Effective tariff on importables %	Total effective protection for importables %
Primary products	1.5	3.6	9.1
Intermediate goods I	6.7	14.9	8.9
Intermediate goods II	5.6	12.5	9.5
investment goods	10.4	18.9	16.8
Consumer goods	8.4	17.0	12.8
Construction and services	0.0	-1.3	-7.9
Total manufacturing	7.8	15.8	12.2
Total industries	2.8	4.9	0.6

Note: Intermediate goods are divided by stage of production.

Source: Taken from Oulton (1976) table 3.7, p.62.

TABLE 4.4   Nominal and effective rates of protection in the United
Kingdom, 1968

Commodity	Nominal tariff on imports	Effective tariff on importables	Total effective protection of importables	Effective tariff on exportables
	%	%	%	%
Agriculture	2.1	3.4	28.4	- 2.6
Grain milling	14.9	171.2	156.0	-15.1
Sugar	0.1	-2.2	-7.7	- 2.8
Tobacco	0.0	-4.0	- 6.9	- 4.0
Toilet preparations	13.2	41.1	37.2	- 9.6
Fertilisers	6.8	23.2	14.7	-17.2
Iron castings	23.9	57.3	53.5	- 9.9
Textile machinery	21.9	48.5	46.2	- 8.7
Electrical machinery	22.6	46.1	44.3	- 9.7
Insulated wires and cables	18.1	217.2	205.1	-12.4
Motor vehicles	17.8	41.5	36.3	- 30.0
Cans and metal boxes	0.0	-12.4	-15.1	-12.4
Cotton spinning and weaving	5.6	6.0	4.3	-14.3
Hosiery and knitted goods	8.7	15.8	14.0	- 8.9
Textile finishing	0.0	- 2.9	-7.1	- 2.9
Leather, leather goods and fur	4.4	8.6	3.6	-7.1
Footwear	6.6	9.1	4.7	- 6.0
Construction	0.0	- 3.1	-11.3	- 3.1
Electricity	0.0	-1.1	-6.8	-1.1
Railways	0.0	- 2.6	36.8	- 2.6
Distributive trades	0.0	- 0.6	-9.4	- 0.6

Source: Adapted from Oulton (1976) table 3.7, pp.78-80.

pattern of escalation of both nominal and effective rates towards investment goods and consumer goods.

(3) There appears consistently to be a wider dispersion of effective rates than nominal rates. This is entirely predictable since the effective rate is influenced by the share of value added in final value. An interesting implication of this is that, whereas we might be able to predict ranking of effective rates from nominal rates, and therefore comment on relative resource pulls, we cannot comment on the static production costs of tariff imposition from nominal rates. These are dependent on the effective rate, and the latter has to be calculated before the deadweight loss can be estimated.

(4) Total effective protection frequently emerges as lower than effective tariff protection. This, however, is more a reflection of the fact that estimates of the effect of non-tariff instruments on value added tend to confine themselves to taxes and subsidies, rather than a reflection of the relative unimportance of quantitative restrictions. Table 4.4 illustrates this point.

(5) When explicit account is taken of exportables, effective protection tends to emerge as being negative. This is often due to the fact that exportables use imported inputs which are subject to an import tariff. Again Table 4.4 gives some details of this for the United Kingdom.

EFFECTIVE PROTECTION AND TRADE POLICY

Having developed the concept of effective protection and considered some of the difficulties faced in empirical analysis, what remarks can we make about the implications which the concept has for commercial policy?

The first point we might make is that the development of the theory of effective protection has undoubtedly had an impact in shifting attention in tariff negotiations from a narrow focus on nominal rates to the somewhat wider perspective of effective rates. Negotiators no longer look simply at concessions being offered on final goods, but approach negotiations with an eye to the entire protective structure. As Balassa (1968) has observed in connection with the Kennedy Round of trade negotiations, there have been occasions when tariff concessions have actually increased effective protection. An awareness of the concept of effective protection enables negotiators to make a more accurate appraisal of concessions offered.

This brings us to a related point, namely the development of the concept. The increasing volume of empirical work which has followed its conception has facilitated a more thorough appraisal of tariff structures in general. In particular the role which tariff escalation in developed market economies may play in frustrating industrial development in LDCs has been widely debated. As a group the latter have consistently claimed that tariff escalation perpetuates LDC dependence on primary production, and has arrested progress on the processing of primary commodities. Although there is some controversy over the extent of this problem, a recent report has reaffirmed its importance (Brandt, 1980).

A third implication is that the possibility of negative effective protection has been recognised. In particular this has resulted in a closer scrutiny of the implications of the tariff structure for exportables. This is no doubt one of the reasons for the recent reappraisal of the role of import substitution policies in LDCs. It is now widely accepted that the success or failure of import substitution is paid for, at least in part, by the export sector.

A further aspect of import substitution that has been examined more closely through effective protection theory is the linkage mechanism. We will recall from Chapter 3 that one of the arguments for infant industry protection aimed at import substitution is the creation of backward linkages. It is now often argued that many import substitution programmes have failed to create backward linkages because high effective rates on final goods have simply served to attract resources away from intermediate activities, rather than inducing resources into those activities.

Finally, assessing implications for resource allocation by reference to effective protection rather than nominal protection has heightened awareness of the protective impact of non-tariff barriers.

CONCLUDING COMMENTS

Although the consumption effects of tariff imposition can be assessed by reference to any change in nominal tariffs, production effects have to be evaluated by reference to the impact which any change in nominal tariffs and non-tariff barriers have for value added. Despite the conceptual and practical difficulties of estimating effective rates of protection, the concept has been operationalised and has been seen to influence trade policy. At the very least, the concept should warn against simplistic recommendations about uniform increases in nominal tariffs on final goods. This is an idea which has been given wide currency in recent years, with its protagonists contending that such a uniform tariff would ensure non-differential inter-industry protection (see Cripps and Godley, 1978). Clearly, if the theory of effective protection has any substance, such a proposition is question-able, to say the least.

NOTES ON FURTHER READING

The seminal theoretical contributions to the development of the concept of effective protection were made by Johnson (1965c) and Corden (1966). Corden (1969) subsequently developed a general equilibrium model of effective protec-tion. Johnson's 1965 paper, together with a number of other important con-tributions which he made to the literature, can be found in Johnson (1971). Although it is always advisable to refer to original sources, Corden (1971) develops many of the ideas from the two papers referred to above. Corden (1971) remains the most comprehensive and most thorough textbook treatment of effective protection available.

One further very important source of reference is the volume of readings edited by Grubel and Johnson (1971). The papers included in this volume cover most theoretical and empirical aspects of effective protection, as well as two country-specific studies. The additional references on empirical work which were cited in the text above should be sufficient to keep the interested reader occupied.

5 Dismantling the Old Protectionism: Tariff Liberalisation and GATT

In Chapter 4 we saw that, as a general rule, tariff imposition resulted in a reduced volume of trade and a reduction in the welfare of the countries concerned. Under certain circumstances, however, most notably where a country was in a position to influence its terms of trade, individual countries could gain from unilateral tariff imposition. Gains only materialised in the absence of retaliation, and since gains which are made by some countries are invariably at the expense of losses incurred by others, unilateral action is generally followed by retaliation. The example *par excellence* of competitive commercial policies occurred in the depression years of the 1930s. A direct outcome of this era of protectionism was increased awareness of the interdependent nature of commercial policy, an increased awareness which found expression in the development of a multilateral institutional framework aimed at fostering more liberal trade policies.

The institution which emerged in the period after the Second World War to deal with this question was the General Agreement on Tariffs and Trade (GATT). This chapter will be devoted to examining a variety of aspects of GATT and its impact on commercial policies. Our first efforts will be directed at exploring the origins of GATT. Following this we will examine its structure and functions, and finally we will investigate the mechanism of tariff liberalisation, the 'Rounds' system.

THE ORIGINS OF ORGANISED LIBERALISATION

One does not have to be an avid student of economic history to be aware of the fact that the period between the two world wars was one of generalised surplus capacity - 'the Great Depression', as it became known. Although the intensity and actual period of depression varied from country to country, all major trading countries felt its repercussions. Faced with unprecedented levels of unemployment, often accompanied by acute balance of payments difficulties, many countries attempted to insulate themselves by imposing protective import tariffs, protective quotas and exchange controls. Rather predictably such a battery of protective instruments failed to provide a remedy to the problems created by depression.

The experiences associated with the economic chaos of the 1930s had a salutary effect. Even before the end of the Second World War, the Allies were planning a co-ordinated response to provide a framework within which international monetary and trade relations could be conducted in an orderly fashion. It was quite obvious that when protective policies, which may appear attractive to individual countries acting in isolation, were applied by all countries (with a competitive fervour worthy of a market system) the outcome would be generally self-destructive. Industrial production in the leading OECD countries (excluding Japan) was still below its 1929 levels by 1937, the year when recovery from depression reached its peak. A measure of the extent to which world trade was depressed can be gauged by the fact that in 1933, the value of exports from the main industrial countries stood at only 25 per cent of its 1929 value.

The foundations for restoring order to international monetary relations, and simultaneously providing a basis for post-war reconstruction in Western Europe, were laid at the Bretton Woods Conference of 1947, with the creation of the International Monetary Fund (IMF) and the International Bank for Reconstruction and Development (IBRD). A sister organisation, the International Trade Organisation (ITO), was envisaged which would provide the medium for permitting orderly trading relations to develop in the post-war world, while providing a framework for reducing and eventually eliminating the protective barriers erected in the 1930s. The draft charter for the ITO (the Havana Charter) was prepared for ratification by 1948. The organisation was never actually created, however. Differences between the USA and the United Kingdom over the extent to which an international organisation should proscribe the authority of autonomous governments prevented ratification ever actually taking place.

GATT then assumed responsibility for providing a framework for trade relations – one could almost say by default. Deliberations on a document on a general agreement on tariffs and trade prepared by the US authorities in 1946 were taking place between a number of countries concurrently with discussions on the ITO. The outcome of these discussions was that the agreement, which was simply intended as a stepping stone and which incorporated many of the commitments of the Havana Charter, was initialled by some twenty-three nations in 1947. Thus the failure to agree on the more far-reaching ITO left GATT as the only instrument relating to trade relations. From the adoption of this initial charter, GATT has now grown into an organisation with a permanent secretariat in Geneva to which, by March 1981, there were eighty-five 'contracting parties', two other countries which had provisionally acceded to the Agreement, and some thirty countries which were 'applicants' - *de facto* members awaiting ratification of the Agreement by their legislatures, and which benefited from the Agreement pending ratification.

GATT: STRUCTURE AND FUNCTIONS

Objectives

There appear to be three fundamental objectives to the creation of the GATT:

1. To provide some kind of orderly framework for the conduct of trading relations. This could reasonably be regarded as a short-term objective, in the sense that the presence of a charter would ensure that trade relations did not take up from where they left off in the 1930s.
2. To provide a system of rules and codes of conduct which would make it more difficult for individual nations to take unilateral action and which would therefore minimise the risks of a repetition of the 1930s.
3. To provide a framework for the progressive elimination of trade barriers.

Implicit in these objectives is a judgement about economic efficiency and equity. The former is embodied in the recognition that the interests of the system are best served by freer rather than more restricted trade, and a movement towards this implies that resources will be more efficiently allocated and participating countries will enjoy real income gains from exchange. It could be argued that, where considerations of equity are concerned, the provision of a set of rules and regulations could be expected to benefit the 'weak' relative to the 'strong', in so far as it reduces the risk of unilateral action on the part of the latter. It is also reasonable to argue that more overtly political objectives were important, the feeling that if the probability of economic warfare can be reduced, the probability of open military conflict is correspondingly reduced.

Structure

The Articles of GATT deal with most aspects of trade relations. The Agreement falls into four parts. Part I (Articles I and II) relate to the basic obligations of all contracting parties (i.e. those countries which adopt the Agreement). Part II (Articles III to XXIII) is in essence a code for fair trade, and lays down the general rules for customs valuation procedures, marks of origin and so on; it also sets out the conditions under which anti-dumping duties, duties to protect the balance of payments, or duties to safeguard domestic industry can be used. Part III (Articles XXIV to XXXV) deals with procedures for application and conditions for the amendment of Articles. As we shall see, there have been a number of amendments since the original Agreement, most significantly the adoption of a new Part IV in 1965, and the addition of new codes of conduct in 1980. Part IV (Articles XXXVI to XXXVIII) deals principally with the trade of less developed countries. Details of the individual Articles are given in Table 5.1.

Underlying principles

We could not possibly hope to comment on each and every article in detail. It is clear, however, that a number of principles underpin the Agreement:

1. Non-discrimination. Article 1 of GATT outlines the most favoured nation principle (MFN). This is the most important principle of the GATT system, the aim of which is to ensure that any alterations in tariff rates or any quotas imposed (through one of the exception clauses) are applied in a non-discriminatory manner. Thus if countries *A* and *B* agree on a bilateral reduction in tariffs in a given line of goods, this tariff concession should immediately be extended to all other contracting parties on an MFN basis, i.e. all parties benefit to the same extent as the most favoured nation.[1] Likewise, if quantitative restrictions were imposed to safeguard domestic industry (under Article XIX) the restriction had to apply to all importing countries, rather than any particular group.

The MFN principle is undoubtedly a keystone in the agreement. The clause is central to encouraging nations to participate in the process of tariff liberalisation, safe in the knowledge that any bargain which they may strike will not be undermined by a subsequent agreement between other contracting parties which does not apply to them. Furthermore, since tariff reductions are 'bound' against

TABLE 5.1   **GATT articles of agreement**

I	Objectives
II	General most favoured nation treatment
III	Schedules of concessions
IV	National treatment and internal taxation and regulation
V	Freedom of transit
VI	Anti-dumping and contervailing duties
VII	Valuation for customs purposes
VIII	Fees and formalities connected with importation and exportation
IX	Marks of origin
X	Publication and administration of trade regulations
XI	General elimination of quantitative restrictions
XII	Restrictions to safeguard the balance of payments
XIII	Non-discriminatory administration of quantitative restrictions
XIV	Exceptions to the rule of non-discrimination
XV	Exchange arrangements
XVI	Subsidies
XVII	State trading enterprises
XVIII	Governmental assistance to economic development
XIX	Emergency action on imports of particular products
XX	General exceptions
XXI	Security exceptions
XXII	Consultation
XXIII	Nullification or impairment
XXIV	Customs unions and free trade areas
XXV	The organisation for trade co-operation
XXVI	Acceptance, entry into force and registration
XXVII	Withholding or withdrawal of concessions
XXVIII	Modification of schedules
XXIX	Tariff negotiations
XXX	Amendments
XXXI	Withdrawal
XXXII	Contracting parties
XXXIII	Accession
XXXIV	Annexes
XXXV	Non-application of the agreement between particular contracting parties
XXXVI	Trade and development: principles and objectives
XXXVII	Undertaking relating to commodities of special export interest to LDCs
XXXVIII	Outline of joint action on trade and development

further arbitrary increase under GATT, parties can be confident that any tariff concession gained can reasonably be expected to be permanent. In principle, of course, non-discrimination should result in a tendency towards imports being supplied from least cost sources, other things being equal. 'Other things' are, however, rarely equal and, as we shall see in Chapter 7, the proliferation of hidden barriers to trade in the 1970s has in large measure represented a deliberate attempt to circumvent the non-discrimination principle.

Although the MFN principle has been integral to the process of tariff liberalisation in the post-war period, there have been a number of departures from the principle. The most significant departure perhaps is the panoply of controls which have regulated trade in textiles and clothing since 1961. We shall consider the question of trade in textiles in rather more detail in Chapter 9. For the moment, however, we might note that experience in textiles is illustrative of what can happen when discrimination is explicitly permitted. In the case of textiles, a temporary short-term arrangement became a long-term arrangement which became the multi-fibre arrangement. As the system has developed, controls have become more restrictive and have been extended to an ever-widening product coverage. The same process may at present be in evidence with the hardening of many 'voluntary export restraints' into 'orderly marketing agreements' (see Chapters 7 and 9).

2. Reciprocity. The embodiment of a reciprocity obligation represents a recognition that there are 'free rider' problems associated with trade liberalisation. Specifically, certain parties may be content to benefit from lower tariffs in their export markets without offering concessions on imports to the home market. As well as ensuring that consumers on the home market do not share in the gains from trade liberalisation, this may also frustrate the liberalisation process itself. Suppose, for example, that the country which reduces tariffs finds that it faces balance of payments difficulties, or an adverse movement in its terms of trade, when it takes unilateral action. The principle of reciprocity, which lays down that countries which accept tariff concessions should offer comparable concessions in return, is designed to encourage genuine multilateral trade liberalisation and therefore increased global benefits from less restricted trade. Furthermore, the presence of a reciprocity obligation serves to help defuse domestic political resistance to tariff liberalisation. The fact that the authorities can point to improved access to overseas markets helps emphasise that domestic producers as well as consumers benefit from the liberalisation process. This is likely to be especially important in the case of intra-industry trade.

The reciprocity obligations to some extent compromises the MFN principles. However, since the strict application of unconditional MFN treatment would permit 'free riders' and might thereby reduce the incentives to liberalisation, the compromise is justified. The obligation is not rigidly enforced, anyway, which makes allowance for obvious asymmetries in 'ability to offer', in particular between developed market economies and less developed countries.

3. Transparency. Article XI forbids the use of direct controls on trade, in particular quantitative restrictions, except under certain designated circumstances, e.g. balance of payments crisis (Article XII). It is generally agreed that a quota is an inferior instrument to a tariff as a means of intervention, for reasons which we shall explore in Chapter 8. One of the problems with a quota is that its economic effects are less clearly visible than those of a tariff. Where this is the case, uncertainty is generated, which is itself an extremely effective non-tariff barrier. One of the reasons, therefore, for proscribing the use of direct controls was a desire for greater transparency in trade restrictions. (When we examine the economic effects of quotas in Chapter 8, we will see that this is not the only reason, nor indeed even the most important reason, for the prohibition of direct controls.)

4. Exceptions. There are permitted exceptions to each of the principles adumbrated above, exceptions that derive from a recognition that short-term exigencies may require exceptional measures, or that political constraints may impose limits on the freedom of individual governments to act. Thus, as we noted when discussing the desire to concentrate protective action on the tariff, clauses outlining circumstances under which direct controls could be employed were included. Temporary balance of payments difficulties, and the need temporarily to protect domestic industry from market disruption, were the most significant exceptions here. It was also recognised that there may be circumstances when departures from the MFN principle are permissible. Thus, under Article VI discriminatory action against goods which are dumped by a particular country is permitted via the imposition of countervailing duties.

The most important exception to tariff liberalisation according to the MFN criterion is contained in Article XXIV, which lays down rules for the establishment of free trade areas and customs unions, within which preferential treatment may be accorded to co-partners.

The principal exception with respect to reciprocity is that the obligation is effectively waived with respect to less developed countries. LDCs which are contracting parties may benefit from MFN tariff concessions without the necessity of reciprocating. It has been argued by many that this represents no more than *de facto* recognition of the power structure inherent in GATT, with the principal industrial nations conducting any negotiations, agreeing on a package of tariff cuts which benefits them to the greatest extent, and imposing that package on the smaller countries. Interestingly, the waiver has been questioned in recent years, with many industrial countries complaining that some of the newly industrialising countries (NICs) have developed their industrial bases to a sufficient degree to honour the principle of reciprocity. The issue of when an NIC is no longer in need of 'preferential' treatment relative to industrialised countries is bound up with the so-called 'graduation' question.

TARIFF LIBERALISATION UNDER GATT

Since from the inception of GATT quotas were illegal except in certain circumstances, GATT was primarily concerned with day-to-day information and conciliation services, and with reducing tariff rates inherited from the 1930s. The process of continuous consultation is, of course, fundamental to the very notion of GATT as an arbiter in disputes. Articles XXII and XXIII outline the procedures for complaints to be made, and any aggrieved parties can take their complaint to GATT, where it could be heard by a Panel of Conciliation. In addition to this conciliation function and to monitoring trade flows on a regular basis, the Secretariat has an active research department which investigates current trade problems.

These 'day-to-day' activities of GATT are undoubtedly an important (one might even argue the most important) aspect of its work. Indeed, it is this function which goes some way to fulfilling the objectives, relating to an orderly framework for trade, which were noted above. The 'results' of these activities, however, are less tangible than the outcome of periodic 'Rounds' of trade liberalisation conducted under the aegis of GATT, which is a much more widely publicised aspect of the organisation's work, and which is aimed directly at fulfilling the third of our objectives, namely the progressive elimination of trade barriers.

For purposes of analysis, the tariff liberalisation which has taken place can be conveniently separated into three phases: the period 1947-61, or the pre-Kennedy Rounds; the Kennedy Round itself; and the most recent negotiations, the Tokyo Round.

The pre-Kennedy Rounds 1947-61

The process of tariff liberalisation commenced, quite literally, at the inception of GATT. The twenty-three nations which gathered in Geneva in 1947 to initial the GATT Articles agreed to make tariff concessions on some 45,000 individual items, which together comprised about half of world trade at the time. The results were achieved largely as a consequence of US anxiety to get the liberalisation process under way, an anxiety founded on the belief that trade liberalisation had an integral part to play in the reconstruction of Western Europe. Such US willingness meant that this Round was relatively one-sided in that although European nations nominally reciprocated, there was a great deal of tariff redundancy in Western Europe, and their markets remained protected by quotas imposed in the pre-war and wartime period which remained in existence for balance-of-payments purposes. Nevertheless, this proved an important first step.

The momentum generated by the initial Geneva Round was maintained by subsequent Rounds held in Annecy in 1949 and Torquay in 1951. By the completion of the Torquay Round bargains had been struck resulting in tariff concessions being made on over 58,000 individual items. Between 1951 and 1964, however, progress within GATT was rather limited. There were two further Rounds in this period, one in 1956 in Geneva, and one in 1960–1 (the Dillon Round), but relatively little was accomplished by way of further liberalisation.

This loss of impetus can be traced to a number of interrelated factors. It seems that the item-by-item approach probably outlived its usefulness rather quickly, even by the early 1950s. In part this was due to the cumbersome nature of item-by-item bargaining on a multilateral basis. More important, however, was the fact that the process was meeting genuine political resistance. In the early Rounds, item-by-item bargaining proved acceptable because it permitted negotiators to select items for concessions – selection of items with a degree of tariff redundancy amounted to liberalisation with the minimum potential for adjustment. Even by the early 1950s, such items were becoming increasingly difficult to find. Furthermore, those countries which had relatively low tariffs were concerned that a continuation of the item-by-item process would eventually leave them in an exposed position relative to those countries with high tariffs. There was therefore a felt need for a new approach to liberalisation.

One outcome of dissatisfaction with item-by-item bargaining was the preparation of a document entitled *The Problem of the Disparity of European Tariffs* in March 1951. This was sponsored by the principal Western European nations (excluding the United Kingdom) and the USA. The document was eventually developed in 1953 into a *GATT Plan for Tariff Reduction*. This plan met the problems generated by the item-by-item approach with two specific proposals. It was suggested that tariffs be lowered on a linear (across-the-board) basis, and that the reductions should be planned and staged. Further-more, there were provisions for the harmonisation of European tariffs. In fact the plan was never endorsed by the USA or the United Kingdom, and the Western European nations channelled their energies into the possibility of achieving the same ends through economic integration. The outcome of this (and of course other pressures) was the creation of the EEC in 1956 and the European Free Trade Area (EFTA) in 1959.

These developments are important within the context of GATT. They were the first major discriminatory agreements to take place under Article XXIV. More important, however, from our present perspective is that preoccupation with regional liberalisation un-doubtedly resulted in less interest in multilateral liberalisation through GATT in the 1950s.

The Kennedy Round 1964-7

The Kennedy Round of negotiations stands out as something of a landmark in the Rounds system. The Round was far more ambitious than previous Rounds, in part because of the problems it addressed, in part because more contracting parties participated than in previous Rounds, and in part because the tariff-cutting procedure marked a new departure from previous practice, with the termination of item-by-item bargaining and the introduction of across-the-board cuts. Although a linear approach to tariff liberalisation had been resisted in the 1950s, the US negotiators had the necessary enabling authority to proceed with such an approach in the Kennedy Round, and re-sistance had dissipated in the United Kingdom.

The origins of the Kennedy Round were embodied in President John F. Kennedy's Trade Expansion Act of 1962. This Act conferred on the President wider ranging negotiating powers than enjoyed by previous Presidents. To President Kennedy, a further Round of trade liberalisation was an integral element of his 'grand design' for the de-velopment of the North Atlantic Treaty countries. The Act was a major commitment to free trade. As well as proposing a 50 per cent linear tariff cut, it also proposed that tariffs be reduced to zero on any products where the USA and the EEC were 'dominant suppliers', i.e. where the USA and EEC were jointly responsible for over 80 per cent of total world exports of the commodity in question. To comprehend fully the potential implications of these proposals, one must remember that in 1962 the USA anticipated that the United Kingdom and a number of other countries would be entering the EEC. This failed to materialise, and in fact reduced the number of commodities for which the USA and an enlarged EEC would have been dominant suppliers from twenty-six to two (see Curzon and Curzon-Price, 1969).

The Kennedy Round was launched by trade ministers in May 1963, although actual negotiations did not commence until 1964. The Ministerial Directive launching the Round envisaged a series of negotiations that would cover all classes of products, including agricultural and primary products, and some non-tariff barriers as well as tariff barriers.[2] In addition it was agreed that negotiations would be conducted with a view to linear reductions of tariffs, rather than item-by-item concessions.

Our concern in this chapter is the latter, i.e. tariff liberalisation. As in the subsequent Tokyo Round, there was some dispute here over the form which any across-the-board reduction should take. The USA tended to favour a linear cut which would apply to all commodities. The EEC, on the other hand, favoured some attempt at harmonisation, i.e. higher rates of reduction on high tariff items. The difference emerged simply because the dispersion of Western European tariffs was much narrower than US tariffs as a consequence of EEC and EFTA formation. Ultimately agreement was reached in May 1967 on tariff cuts which affected some $40 billion worth of world trade – about 75 per cent of total trade. Although the average tariff reduction which took place was less than the 50 per cent allowed for in the Trade Expansion Act, it still amounted to a 36–39 per cent cut. In addition, some degree of harmonisation did in fact take place. About two-thirds of the cuts were in excess of 50 per cent, with a further one-fifth in the 25–50 per cent range.

In terms of tariff liberalisation, these results were quite the most spectacular of any of the GATT Rounds to date. We should note, however, a number of qualifications:

(1)   The figures quoted above applied only to industrial goods. Despite the pious hope to make progress with respect to agricultural commodities, very little was accomplished. Industrial countries tended to protect their agricultural sectors, largely for non-economic reasons, and even after the Kennedy Round agriculture remained a highly protected sector in most industrial countries.

(2)   There were inevitably exceptions among manufactured goods. Most significant were the relatively low cuts which applied to textiles, a 'sensitive' sector which, as we shall see, did not lose this status in years to follow. As we have already noted, the precedent of conferring special status on textiles had already been effected with the conclusion of the Long Term Arrangement on Cotton Textiles. Even by the Kennedy Round, therefore, textiles were excluded from the multilateral liberalisation process.

(3)   In the pre-Kennedy Rounds, there had been a tendency on the part of the industrialised countries to reduce tariffs on primary commodities and raw materials to a greater extent than on finished goods. As we saw in Chapter 4, the outcome of such a pattern of liberalisation is to raise effective rates of protection on finished goods. Despite the increasing awareness of the phenomenon of tariff escalation by the time of the Kennedy Round, little was done by way of reversing the process. Indeed, on a wide range of goods effective rates actually increased following the Kennedy Round.

Despite these qualifications, it is widely accepted that the Kennedy Round represented a major step in the direction of freer trade on the part of the developed market economies. Although little progress was made by way of liberalising trade in agricultural goods, or by way of codifying non-tariff restraints (apart from anti-dumping procedures), it was felt that these areas were now open to more thorough scrutiny, with a view to reform at the next major Round.

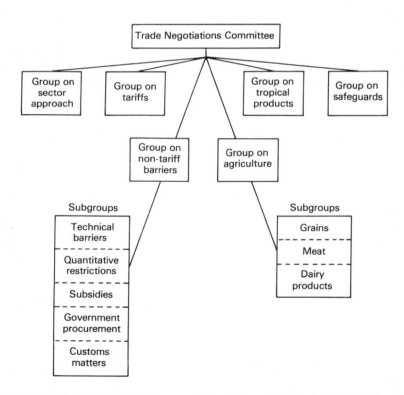

Figure 5.1 Organisational structure of the Tokyo Round of multilateral trade negotiations

The Tokyo Round, 1973-9

The Tokyo Round of trade negotiations was described by M. Olivier Long, then Director-General of GATT, as 'the most complex and far reaching ever undertaken'.[3] That this was so is indisputable. The negotiations were conducted in the most inauspicious of circumstances (the stagflation of the 1970s) and took place alongside the continued growth of the new protectionism. Indeed, many aspects of the Round were concerned with the manifestations of this phenomenon, as can be seen from the briefs of the various study groups outlined in Figure 5.1 on the previous page.

The most complicated negotiations related to non-tariff issues. However, as with our discussion of the Kennedy Round, since we are focusing specifically on tariff liberalisation, we will single out the tariff negotiations and return to non-tariff issues in Part III.

The question of tariff liberalisation proved in fact to be one of the less pressing and less controversial issues – due in part to the success of previous GATT Rounds in reducing and binding tariff rates at relatively low levels. As we can see from Table 5.2, pre-Tokyo Round averages were relatively low (by historical standards), although as is also obvious from Table 5.2, tariff escalation is clearly evident. Furthermore, as we can see from Table 5.3, low overall averages concealed quite significant country differences.

TABLE 5.2   **Tokyo Round tariff changes**

		Tariff averages		
		Pre-Tokyo	Post-Tokyo	Rate of reduction %
Total industrial products	W	7.2	4.9	33
	S	10.6	6.5	38
Raw materials	W	0.8	0.4	52
	S	2.6	1.7	36
Semi-manufactures	W	5.8	4.1	30
	S	9.7	6.2	36
Finished manufactures	W	10.3	6.9	33
	S	12.2	7.4	39

Notes: W = weighted (by MFN imports) average, S = simple average.
Source: GATT (1979) p.120.

TABLE 5.3   Tokyo Round tariff changes on industrial products: country breakdown

Country		Tariff averages		
		Pre-Tokyo	Post-Tokyo	Rate of reduction %
United States	W	6.2	4.4	30
	S	12.1	7.0	42
EEC	W	6.6	4.8	27
	S	8.1	5.6	31
Japan	W	5.2	2.6	49
	S	10.2	6.0	41
Canada	W	12.7	7.9	38
	S	12.4	7.2	42
Sweden	W	5.2	4.3	23
	S	5.9	4.8	19
Norway	W	4.2	3.2	23
	S	8.5	6.5	23
Switzerland	W	3.2	2.5	23
	S	3.8	2.8	26
New Zealand	W	22.4	17.6	21
	S	26.2	20.0	24
Austria	W	9.0	7.8	13
	S	11.6	8.1	30
Finland	W	6.0	4.8	20
	S	13.0	11.2	14

Source: Adapted from Corbet (1979a) table I, p.328.

As in the Kennedy Round, this latter pattern stimulated discussion over whether a straight linear cut should be adopted or whether some attempt at harmonisation should be made. The adoption of the so-called 'Swiss formula'[4] allowed a degree of harmonisation to take place. Although the overall depth of cut varies from 33–38 per cent, we can see the harmonisation effect at work in Table 5.3, with higher average tariff countries conceding higher average cuts. These concessions affect about $112 billion of trade in industrial products (at 1976 prices) or around 20 per cent of the value of trade in industrial products in 1976.

Again, as with the Kennedy Round, a number of qualifications are in order:

(1)   The concessions reported above again apply only to industrial

products. Agricultural commodities were treated differently, as in the Kennedy Round. Most countries operate some form of protectionism in agricultural markets, primarily for socio-political reasons. What emerged from the Tokyo Round was two agreements relating to bovine meat and dairy products. These are little more than information agreements among the major producers, and have affected access hardly at all. Thus agricultural markets in developed market economies continue to be highly protected.

(2)   The concessions did not apply to all industrial goods. 'Sensitive' items such as textiles, leather, footwear and travel goods were subject to zero or lower than average tariff reductions. Invariably these sensitive items were precisely those lines which were of interest to LDC exporters of manufactures. Furthermore, as we shall see, these are also the product lines where non-tariff protection is most in evidence.

(3)   Disappointment in general was expressed by many LDCs with the outcome of the Tokyo Round. The average tariff reduction on the exports from LDCs amounted to 25 per cent according to GATT (1979). This, however, also takes account of the concessions given on tropical products, many of which gained duty-free entry.

(4)   The tariff reductions agreed were to be implemented from 1 January 1980, and could be phased in over a period of eight years. If we take the average reduction in tariff (of 33-38 per cent) and assume that this is phased in on a linear basis, and if we further assume that the reduction is passed on in full to the consumer, crude calculations suggest that the price of imported manufactures would fall by ½ per cent per annum. This is hardly likely to have the same impact as reducing the tariff by the full amount in one fell swoop.

These remarks are simply intended as a note of caution against taking the figures on the tariff cuts at their face value. It does not mean that the reductions made are entirely worthless. It can be argued that any reductions represented a considerable achievement given the backcloth against which the negotiations were conducted. It is perhaps a measure of the extent to which the existence of GATT had demonstrated the benefits of an open and relatively orderly trading system that agreement was reached. There is, however, an equally defensible contrary view that agreement was only reached because tariffs had been superseded by non-tariff interventions. All that the Tokyo Round did, therefore, was to continue the process whereby the industrial countries encouraged increased intra-industry trade among themselves while doing little to proscribe the use of extra-legal instruments used in a discriminatory manner against LDCs. Once we have spent some time examining the new protectionism we will return to the efforts which the Tokyo Round made in this direction.

TARIFF LIBERALISATION OUTSIDE GATT

GATT has been the major instrument for multilateral tariff liberal-isation in the post-war period. We should note in passing, however, that initiatives on multilateral tariff liberalisation have not been con-fined exclusively to GATT. We mentioned earlier that Article XXIV waived the non-discrimination principle for free trade areas and customs unions. Over the post-war period a number of such regional blocs have emerged. In Western Europe there is the EEC and EFTA, but free trade areas have also existed, and in some cases still exist in Africa, Asia and Latin America.[5] Within such customs unions re-stricted liberalisation has taken place. For instance, within the EEC there is (notionally, anyway) free trade between all member countries, with all non-members facing a common external tariff. The economics of customs formation is a subject on its own, however, and the in-terested reader is encouraged to consult a text on the subject such as Robson (1980).

The United Nations Conference on Trade and Development (UNCTAD) is another organisation which, although it has not actually implemented tariff cuts itself, has influenced the pattern of tariff liberalisation. UNCTAD emerged initially as a one-off conference convened to consider the special trade problems of the LDCs. It grew out of a growing disillusionment with the gains which LDCs in general were making from the GATT system. Subsequent UNCTADs have convened on a four-yearly basis, and although the only instrument which the organisation has is exhortation, in this capacity it in-fluenced the adoption of a new Part IV by GATT in 1965 which redrafted those clauses dealing with the special trade problems of LDCs. In addition, it was instrumental in stimulating the Generalised System of Preferences (GSP).

The first UNCTAD initiated the call for a GSP which would positively discriminate in favour of LDCs. The first countries to translate the principle of preferential access into practice were the EEC, Japan and Norway in 1971. These were followed by Denmark, Finland, New Zealand, Sweden, Switzerland and Austria in 1972, Canada in 1974 and the USA in 1976. These schemes extended pref-erential access to the 'Group of 77' countries[6] (although individual members of this group can be excluded from particular schemes at the discretion of the 'donor').

Under the terms of most GSP agreements, preferential access can be extended to manufactures, semi-manufactures and a few agri-cultural commodities. Specific exclusions, however, are invariably made for textiles and clothing, leather and leather products. As we shall see in Chapter 7, these tend to be the very product lines in which the more industrialised of the LDCs have been specialising. For those commodities which do qualify for GSP access, the preference margins appear to be quite generous in nominal terms. For instance, the EEC and US schemes permit duty-free access, while the Swiss and Austrian schemes permit a 33 per cent preference margin. Against this, however, most schemes subject the preferences to a variety of restrictions. In the case of the EEC, for example, 'ceilings' are applied to GSP commodities, effectively converting the GSP into a system of 'tariff-quotas' (the economics of which we shall examine in Chapter 8). Furthermore, rules of origin and rules of consignment further restrict the impact of the GSP.

Although initially the creation of the GSP was widely hailed as a valuable and necessary compromise of the non-discrimination principle, the restrictive nature of many of the agreements has stimulated widespread disillusionment about the system among many LDCs.[7] Furthermore, the fact that GSP concessions are not 'bound' (unlike MFN concessions) means that they can be altered or even withdrawn at short notice. In 1981, for example, the EEC and the USA withdrew GSP concessions from a number of newly industrialising countries, on the grounds that they were no longer in need of such treatment.

CONCLUDING COMMENTS

Our economic analysis of Chapters 3 and 4 suggested that there were gains in economic welfare to be reaped from multilateral trade liberalisation. The GATT system provided a framework within which such gains could be realised. We also noted in Chapter 3 that unilateral action by specific countries could occasionally raise the welfare of the tariff-imposing country, where that country could influence its terms of trade. Invariably any such gains were realised at the expense of other countries, and attempts to exploit them could stimulate defensive and retaliatory action. The GATT framework initially served to make unilateral action more difficult to take with impunity, and thereby helped create an environment in which mutual trust could be fostered.

Many commentators argue that the tariff liberalisation which actually occurred under the aegis of GATT was instrumental in generating the unprecedented growth rates experienced in industrial countries in the post-war period (see Blackhurst, Marian and Tumlir, 1977). Whether GATT proves well equipped to cope with the new protectionism remains to be seen. In the meantime we will take our analysis a stage further in considering the methodological question of how one actually proceeds to evaluate the gains/losses associated with a given change in tariffs.

NOTES ON FURTHER READING

A most comprehensive account of the formation of GATT and its activities in the pre-Kennedy Round period can be found in Curzon (1965). A review of the background to, and substance of, the Kennedy Round can be found in Meier (1973) and Curzon and Curzon-Price (1969). The details of the final agreement of the Tokyo Round is contained in GATT (1979) while assessments of the Round are given in Corbet (1979a and 1979b) and Baldwin (1979).

A useful publication which gives a regular review of developments within GATT is the annual publication, *GATT Activities*.

6 Measuring the Effect of Tariff Barriers

Our analysis of tariff imposition/liberalisation has been entirely qualitative so far. We have simply indicated the effects which may follow restriction/liberalisation without giving any indication of the likely order or magnitude of such changes. This is an important question. The net welfare effects of a given liberalisation process may be positive in magnitude but may only amount to the smallest fraction of GNP. If so, one may consider the lengthy and often complicated process of reducing trade barriers simply not worth the effort. If, on the other hand, the welfare effects are not only positive but relatively large (when expressed as a proportion of GNP) then trade policy may be expected to figure prominently in the policy-makers' 'portfolio'.

In this chapter we will commence by reiterating the expected effects of trade liberalisation. Once we have identified what may happen we will outline in some detail the techniques currently available which can be used as a basis for quantifying these effects. Finally, a review of some existing studies of the liberalisation process will provide us with examples of applications of the methodology discussed.

IDENTIFYING THE EFFECTS OF TARIFF LIBERALISATION

The methodology to be outlined below will be discussed in terms of quantifying the effects of tariff liberalisation. The methodology can, however, be applied just as easily to an analysis of tariff restriction.

In Figure 6.1 we outline the now familiar partial equilibrium analysis for the 'large' country case. D_h and S_h represent home demand and supply of commodity y respectively, commodity y being the import substitute. S_{hf} represents the total market supply, i.e. home supply plus imports. S_{hf} lies everywhere below S_h because given pre-trade factor endowments, foreign producers can produce y at lower unit costs than home producers. $S_{hf}{}^t$ represents a tariff-distorted market supply curve. Thus with a nominal tariff rate of t on all imported units of y, the home market price is Pe'. At this

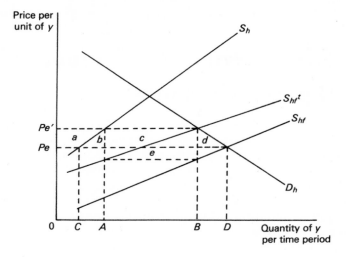

Figure 6.1

price OB is the market clearing quantity of y, of which OA is provided by domestic producers and AB imported.

When the tariff is removed, the market clearing price falls to Pe, and as a consequence quantity demanded expands to OD. In the new equilibrium domestic producers not only supply a smaller fraction of the market, but supply less in absolute terms – OC rather than OA. Import penetration increases from AB/OB to CD/OD as a result of tariff liberalisation.

These changes give rise to a number of readily identifiable effects which we now discuss.

Static effects

(1) *Production effect.* Since relatively inefficient domestic producers supply fewer units, the resource misallocation loss associated with the tariff (the triangular area b) disappears.

(2) *Consumption effect.* As existing consumers purchase y at a lower price, there is a net gain in consumer surplus equivalent to the triangular area d.

Most studies of the consequences of tariff liberalisation make some attempt at quantifying these 'deadweight gains'.

(3) *Revenue effect.* In the most elementary static analyses the revenue effect is viewed as a straight redistribution from government

to consumer, and the issue is given no further consideration. In reality, however, it is necessary to go further. If the revenue from a tariff is lost as a by-product of liberalisation, and if government expenditure is to be maintained, then revenue has to be raised from alternative sources. In terms of Figure 6.1 $e + c$ is 'lost'. The effects of any subsequent increases in income tax, expenditure taxes, etc., should be allowed for.

(4) *Balance-of-payments effect*. Again, elementary analyses tend to ignore this effect because they are implicitly barter models, within which balance-of-payments imbalance has no meaning. When trade flows are matched by opposite monetary flows, however, unilateral trade liberalisation could result in a tendency towards payments deficit. Policy action may be required to correct this deficit (e.g. devaluation or deflation) which in principle should be allowed for.

In the case of a 'small' country liberalising tariffs, this is as far as we would need to go. When, however, the country in question is a 'large' country we must make some allowance for:

(5) *Terms-of-trade effects*. Unilateral tariff reduction by a large country would generate an adverse shift in the international terms of trade. This is, of course, consistent with a fall in real income. In terms of Figure 6.1, this would be represented by the area e, and any such losses would have to be offset against the positive gains resulting from production and consumption effects.[1]

As we shall see, most empirical studies of the trade liberalisation process make some attempt to quantify some or all of these static effects. It is widely agreed that there may also be certain dynamic effects which follow the liberalisation of tariff barriers.

Dynamic effects

Dynamic effects are altogether more speculative. Possible consequences would be as follows:

(1) *Economies of scale*. It is often argued that the widening of markets which follows from trade liberalisation can result in increased opportunities for exploiting scale economies, with larger output leading to reductions in unit cost. If such reductions are passed on to consumers (as they would be in competitive markets) then there would be 'second round' gains from consumption and production effects as price falls below Pe.

(2) *Efficiency*. Another common argument is that the widening of markets results in greater competition, which in turn results in greater efficiency.[2] This too generates further falls in unit costs and/ or higher quality products. If an exhaustive investigation of the effects of a given tariff reduction were conducted, then any gains realised

here would have to be offset against deadweight gains since this would result in a rightward shift of the supply curve of import substitutes.

These dynamic consequences provide the researcher with quite intractable measurement problems, in part because of their more nebulous nature, but more so because of the difficulties of extricating such influences from other influences (whether policy-induced or otherwise). It is usually the case that researchers either have to ignore these influences or make some informed 'guesstimate' of their importance.

ESTIMATING THE STATIC CONSEQUENCES OF TARIFF LIBERALISATION

Where most policy changes are concerned, the estimation of the policy's effect(s) can be attempted prior to the policy change, or some time after, when it seems to have taken effect. If we estimate the effects of a change *ex ante*, we generally have to make certain assumptions about the behavioural relationships we are examining. If we approach the problem *ex post*, we may face difficulties in extricating the effects of the policy change we are examining from the influence of other policies and from the 'counter-factual' problem, i.e. what would have occurred if the policy was not carried out.

Empirical examination of trade policy can follow the same approaches. Thus, when a tariff is removed or reduced, we can either estimate the effects of the removal (reduction) in advance of the liberalisation, or we can wait until some time after the tariff has been removed and attempt to estimate the effects.

EX ANTE ESTIMATION

The principles of *ex ante* estimation for the small-country case can be easily elaborated by reference to Figure 6.2. In panel (a) we can see that the net effects of removing tariff *t* amount to the triangles *CDE* and *HJK*. These we will recognise as our static production and consumption gains.

Take first of all the consumption gain. Since the demand curve for importables is linear over the relevant range, we can calculate the area *HJK* as follows:

$$HJK = \tfrac{1}{2} t \, \Delta D \tag{6.1}$$

where *t* = tariff rate (= change in price) and ΔD = change in quantity demanded.

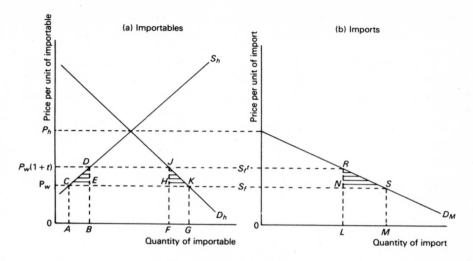

Figure 6.2

By definition we have information on the price change beforehand, since this is simply the tariff which previously prevailed. Since this is an *ex ante* estimate of the consumption gain, we do not have information on the change in quantity demanded; this we have to calculate. Clearly, the change in demand will depend on the change in price, and the slope of the demand curve over the relevant range; this we can approximate by arc elasticity of demand, which (ignoring signs) can be written as:

$$\epsilon = \frac{\Delta D}{\Delta P} \frac{P_o}{D_o} \qquad (6.2)$$

Thus,

$$\Delta D = t\epsilon \frac{D_o}{P_o} \qquad (6.3)$$

Substitution of (6.3) into (6.1) yields:

$$HJK = \tfrac{1}{2} t^2 \ \epsilon \ \frac{D_o}{P_o} \qquad (6.4)$$

If, for ease of exposition, we set the price prior to tariff liberalisation equal to one, we can write:

$$HJK = \tfrac{1}{2} t^2 \ \epsilon \ D_o \qquad (6.5)$$

By analogy we can derive a formula for estimating the production gain:

$$CDE = \tfrac{1}{2} t \, \Delta S \qquad\qquad (6.6)$$

$$\Delta S = t\lambda \frac{S_o}{P_o} \qquad\qquad (6.7)$$

where $\lambda = \dfrac{\Delta S}{\Delta P} \dfrac{P_o}{S_o}$

Again, setting P_o equal to one and substituting (6.7) into (6.6), we obtain

$$CDE = \tfrac{1}{2} t^2 \, \lambda \, S_o \qquad\qquad (6.8)$$

The total static gain (W) from tariff liberalisation therefore amounts to the sum of (6.5) and (6.8), i.e.

$$W = HJK + CDE = \tfrac{1}{2} t^2 \, (\epsilon D_o + \lambda S_o) \qquad\qquad (6.9)$$

Before we proceed to an examination of some of the technical and empirical difficulties faced in this sort of exercise, we might note that the same result can be (and usually is) obtained by a slightly different route. Rather than estimating areas below the supply and demand curves for *importables*, we could estimate the total change in one calculation if we know the total change in *imports*. This is easily elaborated by reference to Figure 6.2. Imports simply represent the difference between domestic supply of importables and demand. As long as we know what this difference is, by definition we know what the volume of imports is. With the information given in Figure 6.2(a) we can derive an import demand curve.

At a price of P_h domestic producers would supply the entire market, imports would be zero, and the import demand curve would intersect the price axis at P_h. At the tariff distorted price of $P(1 + t)$, imports amount to BF, which is equal to OL in Figure 6.2(b). By taking a series of such prices, one can derive the import demand function D_M. Thus, when we eliminate the tariff, one only calculates the area under this curve, in this case the area NRS. Thus,

$$NRS = \tfrac{1}{2} t \, \Delta M \qquad\qquad (6.10)$$

$$\Delta M = \Theta t \frac{M_o}{P_o} \qquad\qquad (6.11)$$

where $\Theta = \dfrac{\Delta M}{\Delta P}\dfrac{P_o}{M_o}$

Setting $P_o = 1$ to simplify, and substituting (6.11) into (6.10),

$$NRS = \tfrac{1}{2}t^2\ \Theta M_o \tag{6.12}$$

where Θ is the price elasticity of demand for imports, and ΔM, M_o respectively the change in, and base level of, imports.

Estimation via the import demand curve, rather than via home supply curve of importables and the domestic demand curve for importables, is relatively common. Computationally it is very much more straightforward to work from the import demand curve, since one only has to estimate a single unknown, namely Θ. Where, however, we work from domestic demand for and supply of importables, we have two unknowns, ϵ and λ.

Of course, not all tariff liberalisation takes the form of complete removal of tariffs, as Figure 6.2 implies. It is more common to find that tariffs are reduced rather than removed.

In Figure 6.3 we maintain the small-country assumption. On this occasion, however, rather than removing the tariff completely, which would reduce price from P_2 to P_0, we cut the tariff in half. As a consequence of this, price falls from P_2 to P_1. We can recognise immediately that deadweight production and consumption gains of ABC and DEF are realised. These gains can be estimated as above. In this respect the analysis is no different from the case described in Figure 6.2. Here, however, we have one important difference. Since the tariff is only reduced and not removed, any additional imports generated by tariff reduction are taxed at the new tariff rate, and thus further net gains are realised. Specifically, we have to allow for the areas $ACGH$ and $DFLK$. These areas are simply the revised tariff rate $(t_2 - t_1)$ times the additional units imported (MN and RS).

In the same way as we simplified the tariff removal case described in Figure 6.2, we can simplify the tariff reduction case of Figure 6.3 by deriving the import demand curve, thereby estimating the area below one curve rather than two. In Figure 6.3(b) we would therefore estimate the net welfare effects of tariff reduction as the sum of TUV and $TVWX$. Following from equation (6.10) TUV can be written as:

$$TUV = \tfrac{1}{2}\left(t_2 - t_1\right)\ \Delta M \tag{6.13}$$

The rectangle $TVWX$ can be approximated by:

$$TVWX = t_1\ \Delta M \tag{6.14}$$

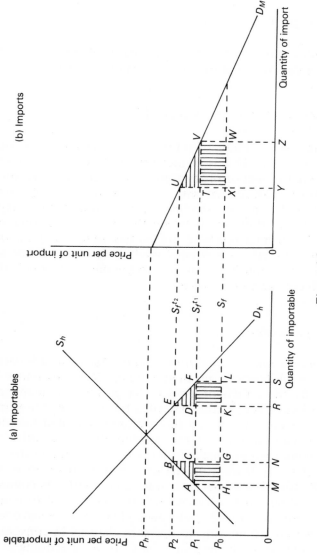

(a) Importables

(b) Imports

Figure 6.3

Thus the total welfare gain can be expressed as:

$$W = \tfrac{1}{2}(t_2 - t_1) \Delta M + t_1 \Delta M$$

$$= \Delta M \left[\tfrac{1}{2}(t_2 + t_1)\right]$$

(6.15)

ΔM we know can be estimated if we have information on the price elasticity of demand, and the initial level of imports.

PROBLEMS WITH *EX ANTE* ESTIMATION

We will take as our point of reference the elasticity approach as outlined in Figure 6.2. This is in fact the most commonly used method of estimating the cost of protection/gains from liberalisation.

The problems associated with this type of *ex ante* estimation procedure can be grouped into technical problems and practical problems. Although the dividing line between the two may to some extent be arbitrary, the former relate to difficulties which are inherent characteristics of the methodology employed, while the latter are difficulties related to the application of the technique, and which it may be possible to correct to some extent.

Technical problems

(1) *Income and substitution effects*. As most students of economics learn quite early in their studies, it is possible to separate conceptually the effects of a price change into an income effect and a substitution effect. In the case of a fall in price, the former is the result of the consumer's real income increasing and may lead to an increase in consumption of the commodity whose price has fallen and/or an increase in consumption of other commodities. The substitution effect follows from the change in relative prices which the price fall stimulates. Because one commodity becomes cheaper relative to others, the consumer will normally substitute units of the cheaper commodity for the now relatively more expensive commodity.

When we are attempting to measure changes in consumer surplus which follow from changes in prices (as we are doing in the tariff liberalisation case) we are only interested in the pure substitution effect, i.e. the substitution away from import substitutes towards imports which is stimulated by the change in relative prices. If one wished to focus unequivocally on this effect, one would have to derive a *compensated demand curve*, i.e. a demand curve for which the consumer's real income was held constant and which traced out the relationship between changes in relative prices and quantity consumed.[3]

Information on compensated demand curves is not, however, readily available; thus one simply uses the import demand curve D_M in Figure 6.2(b). This involves making the implicit assumption that income effects are relatively unimportant. Corden (1975) does not seem to think that this is an implausible assumption to make. Commenting on the compensated demand curve problem he concludes (p. 56): 'In practice, when elasticity figures have such high margins of error and are often just guesses, and since income effects do not appear to be very large anyway, this is probably not worth worrying about.'

Although we must respect this judgement, it must be emphasised that the greater the change in the tariff in question, the higher the probability that the income effect will be significant. This suggests that when we are dealing with Rounds where substantial tariff cuts are made on a wide range of traded goods, we cannot simply assume away any income effects.

(2) *The nature of demand changes.* A second technical problem we face is again one which is shared with researchers analysing the implications of any price change. In estimating our triangle of consumer surplus we are making the implicit assumption that the tariff reduction results in a movement along an existing import demand curve rather than a shift of the initial curve. If in fact the demand curve shifts, then the methodology which we have outlined is inappropriate.

There is, of course, nothing that can be done to alleviate this problem. In the case of relatively small tariff reductions (however defined) it is probably reasonable to assume that we are observing different points on a given demand curve. Where, however, the tariff reduction is relatively large, it may be a more heroic assumption.

(3) *Linearity of the demand curve.* A third implicit assumption in this analysis is that the demand curve under consideration is linear. This is what makes application of the formula in equation (6.12) appropriate. The assumption is made because it is methodologically expedient – if the demand curve is non-linear and is not of a constant elasticity form, more sophisticated statistical techniques are necessary. If the relevant curve is non-linear, the area ABC will provide an overestimate or underestimate of the change in consumer surplus, depending on whether the demand curve is convex or concave to the origin.[4]

(4) *Second best considerations*. The final implicit assumption behind the procedure is that we are analysing the welfare effects of a tariff reduction, when all other 'first best' assumptions hold. Thus we are moving from a position of second best to a situation of Pareto optimality. This, of course, is never the case in practice. In considering one tariff reduction with all other tariff and non-tariff barriers unchanged, we are in the indeterminate world of second best. As Lipsey and Lancaster (1956-7) demonstrate, strictly speaking we cannot conclude that reduction of this or that particular tariff necessarily results in a welfare gain!

(5) *Expectations regimes*. Saidi (1980) has recently argued that the implicit assumption made about the manner in which economic agents reach decisions is sufficient not only to create a 'technical problem', but also to make the entire exercise meaningless. The foundation to Saidi's critique is the assertion that individuals form their expectations about future events 'rationally' rather than 'adaptively'. It follows from this that the decision-making process of agents in export sectors and import substitute sectors will itself be affected by changes in commercial policy. One cannot therefore estimate the effects of the policy change *ex ante* because one is using estimates of price and income elasticities which prevailed prior to the policy change, and which will themselves alter as a consequence of the policy change. This is a fundamental criticism which calls into question the entire methodological procedure of *ex ante* estimation. The seriousness with which one views the point depends on the strength of one's faith in the underlying tenets of the rational expectations hypothesis – in particular one's view on the speed with which agents in product and factor markets react to changes in economic policy.

As we indicated above, these difficulties are all inherent in the procedure, and there is little we can do to alleviate them. They must nevertheless be borne in mind when considering the results of any particular analysis. Although it is not possible to estimate the quantitative significance of these complications, it may be possible to make some quantitative assessment, e.g. by indicating whether the results on hand are likely to be an over- or underestimate. Thus, if we follow Corden's conclusion on the income and substitution problem, we would feel that this is unlikely to distort our results unduly. Where the shift/movement problem is concerned, we would be aware of the fact that this is likely to be more of a problem where tariffs are adjusted by large, discrete amounts than where they are adjusted by small and/or continuous amounts. Linearity is something we can do little about, while second best considerations may be less important when (as is often the case) we are considering across-the-board cuts in tariffs rather than tariff reductions on individual commodities.

Practical problems

1. Data. Although it is not always explicitly recognised, empirical studies in economics invariably face data difficulties. In some studies data problems can be intractable – for instance, studies examining market power and innovation have great difficulty in obtaining economically meaningful proxies of market power and measures of innovation. In the case of the analysis of tariff liberalisation, data do not create insuperable difficulties. Referring to equation (6.12), we would require data on the tariff rate, the base level of imports and the price elasticity of demand for imports. Data are easily obtainable in the case of the first two. Price elasticity, however, is more problematic. Either one has to estimate elasticities oneself (which could in itself be a major research project) or one relies on the results of other researchers. The latter convention is usually followed. Since estimates of elasticity often have a relatively large margin of error associated with them, it is not uncommon to find calculations conducted for a range of estimates.

Another data problem which one faces is that trade data are generally classified according to the Standard International Trade Classification (which we introduced in Chapter 1). We might proceed to estimate the consequences of a reduction in tariffs on the assumption that the import and the domestically produced counterpart are perfect substitutes for each other. Within the SITC groups which we are examining, however, they may be imperfect substitutes, and effectively in different sub-markets. For example, the import may be a high quality machine tool and the import substitute a low quality machine tool used in different production processes. In such circumstances, substitution effects may be weaker, and income effects stronger than in the case of perfect substitutes.

2. Discounting. Often when the costs of protection of a given tariff (or the gains from liberalising a given tariff) are calculated, the calculations are conducted on a once-and-for-all basis. Thus when a tariff is imposed, a figure may be presented representing the once-and-for-all costs of imposing a given tariff, or a once-and-for-all gain from removing a given tariff.

This is not, however, a correct procedure, and is almost certain to underestimate the gains/losses associated with tariff liberalisation/ imposition. This follows because once a tariff is levied, it imposes costs for the duration of its existence. Thus if the tariff is levied for, say, a period of ten years, then the calculation of any costs should take account of the length of time over which the tariff is in existence. Furthermore, these costs will vary as the growth of the economy varies, the costs rising in absolute terms as the level of GNP rises. Similar comments apply to tariff liberalisation.

If one takes account of the time span involved, then future gains or losses have to be discounted to the present, to take account of the fact that money accruals in the future are worth less than accruals in the present. To accomplish this, a discount rate has to be chosen which suitably represents society's preferences between present and future consumption. In other words, an appropriate 'social rate of time preference' has to be applied to future gains/losses. This is not as straightforward as it first appears. For a number of years the question of what interest rate in the economy, if any, adequately represents society's rate of time preference has been the subject of heated academic debate. In principle, one should use the rate of return which the resources would gain if released for more productive employment. This is far from obvious.

3. Non-uniform tariffs. When researchers investigate the costs of tariff imposition or the gains from liberalisation for a system of tariffs, it is, strictly speaking, necessary to make allowance for any variation which may exist between rates. Typically, analyses of the tariff structure focus on the costs of some average rate of tariff across all commodities – the uniform tariff equivalent. As Johnson (1960) pointed out some years ago, however, there may be an aggregation problem here. The cost of protection is not dependent solely on the uniform tariff equivalent but also on the dispersion of tariff rates. The responsiveness of resources into and out of different activities is never likely to be equal across all activities. Thus the dispersion of tariff rates could have an important bearing on the costs associated with the tariff system. The problem has been recognised for some time, and a few investigators have made some allowance in their calculations.

4. Balance of payments effects. If the net trade effects of a given tariff change are non-zero, then payments imbalance must result. Other things being equal, adjustment forces will be set in motion to correct the imbalance. Thus, under a fixed exchange rate regime, expenditure-reducing policies might be used to reduce import demand. A tendency towards deficit under floating exchange rates would stimulate exchange rate depreciation. The effects of tariff liberalisation/imposition-induced changes in the balance of payments, and their effects on trade flows, should be allowed for. In practice, however, the exchange rate is a notoriously difficult variable to forecast, and often researchers simply ignore such effects, or assume that the trade policy change results in a balance expansion (or contraction) of trade.

Such practical problems relate to the application of the method-ology rather than the methodology itself, and can prove soluble to some degree or other.

EX POST ESTIMATION

Ex post estimation is somewhat different from *ex ante* estimation. As the title implies, *ex post* analysis attempts to assess the impact of tariff liberalisation some time after the tariffs have been reduced or eliminated.

The principles behind *ex post* estimation can be readily understood by reference to Figure 6.4, in which we plot the growth of imports against time. Suppose tariffs are removed in time period t_4 and we are investigating the effects of tariff liberalisation in t_{12}. By first examining the trend rate of growth of imports over the period t_0 to t_4 (when tariffs were in force) and projecting this forward, we can get some idea of expected imports over the period t_4 to t_{12}. Thus we are assuming that import volume would have continued to grow along the path m_1 had tariffs remained unchanged. Upon examination of the trade data for the period t_4 to t_{12}, in t_{12} we might discover, how-ever, that in actual fact imports had grown along a path m_2 rather than m_1. The difference between what was expected to occur and what actually occurred can be attributed to the elimination of tariffs in t_4. The same principle applies to the so-called 'reduced group–non-reduced group' method. Here the growth paths m_1 and m_2 would refer to different groups of commodities, rather than the same com-

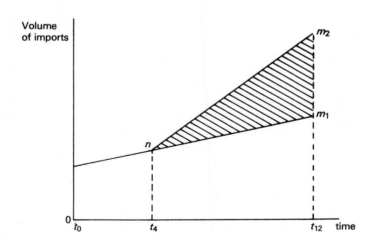

Figure 6.4

modity group. For instance, m_2 may be a group of commodities for which tariffs have been reduced, while m_1 are a similar group of commodities for which tariffs have not been reduced. On *ceteris paribus* assumptions the difference between the two in t_{12} compared with t_4 is taken as the outcome of trade or tariff liberalisation.

This is, in simplistic terms, how the *ex post* methodology operates. In practice one does not simply conduct an exercise of linear extrapolation, i.e. projecting the trend line forward. We have drawn our trends as linear for expositional convenience. In practice techniques are somewhat more sophisticated, the expected volume of imports being determined by careful perusal of income elasticities of demand for imports and detailed examination of the trade matrix. Ultimately, however, we would still end up with an area equivalent to nm_2m_1 in our diagram. On the assumption that the demand for imports is linear, we could then include this figure for ΔM in formula (6.10) above and proceed to estimate the welfare effects of the liberalisation.

This methodology has one broad advantage over the *ex ante* methods. As long as t_{12} is selected such that all of the liberalisation effects have worked themselves out, the area nm_2m_1 provides an estimate of the total static effects of liberalisation. There is no need to estimate the 'deadweight' effects, balance-of-payments effects and terms-of-trade effects separately, since we have a global figure which includes all of these. It is also possible that the impact of some of the dynamic effects is included. For instance, if the liberalisation results in a reduction of X-inefficiency and increased competitiveness of import substitutes, then this will also show up in the volume of imports demanded.

Against this, however, there are two major drawbacks to using this methodology. First, there is a technical consideration. The volume of imports observed at t_{12} may not just be the outcome of a change in tariffs which occurred in t_4. Other policy changes may have taken place between t_4 and t_{12} which influenced the demand for imports. Some changes might be obvious and it may be possible to make some allowance for them. For instance, it may be possible to make some allowance for imports of a completely new product which appears between t_4 and t_{12} and which would have been imported whether or not any tariff liberalisation took place in t_4. Even here, however, there may be an element of arbitrariness in that one has to draw a line between those which would have been imported anyway, e.g. some revolutionary petroleum substitute due perhaps to a technological breakthrough abroad, and those that are tariff-induced, e.g. new varieties of existing products. At the other extreme it may be very difficult to allow for obvious changes like a movement towards the greater use of non-tariff barriers following the liberalisation of tariffs; or less obvious policy influences like regional incentives to encourage industrial development which subsidise the production of import substitutes. In other words, one cannot 'control' for all other influences in order to extricate the effects of tariff liberalisation from other policy changes.

The second difficulty associated with *ex post* studies is more subtle, but no less important. By definition if one wishes to conduct an *ex post* analysis one has to wait until after the event. In order to ensure that the effects have worked themselves out fully, this may have to be a considerable time after the event. In the case of the Tokyo Round tariff reductions, for example, we have the introduction of the reductions on 1 January 1980, and there is then up to an eight-year phasing-in period! Presumably some further time would have to elapse before any *ex post* calculations could be made. Apart from the obvious point that the longer the time lag, the more likely it will become that other influences will play a significant role, there is the very pertinent consideration that such calculations may be of little value to the policy-maker. After all, when one is involved in negotiations on tariff reductions, one would wish to have some idea of the anticipated effects of the change. Of course, one could refer to *ex post* studies of previous cases of tariff liberalisation for guidance. Ultimately, however, the information which would be given greatest weight in the policy-makers' 'calculations' is information on the matter at hand. It is this consideration which is predominant in explaining the more general use of *ex ante* methods.

We have dwelt at some length on an examination of the principal methods used in assessing welfare changes which may follow from trade liberalisation. It is important that the uses and limitations of these techniques are clearly understood, since these provide the basis for empirical analyses of protection and liberalisation. A clear understanding of the principles involved is important since, in the last analysis, even using imperfect techniques, trade policy prescriptions should be guided by empirical findings rather than any blind faith in free trade or protectionism. We will now turn our attention to some of the results of research in this area.

EMPIRICAL STUDIES OF THE EFFECTS OF TARIFF BARRIERS

Ex ante studies

One of the earliest applications of the *ex ante* methodology discussed above was Stern's (1964) attempt to evaluate the deadweight gains which would be associated with a unilateral tariff reduction on the part of the USA.

Using a range of elasticity estimates to predict ΔM in equation (6.10), Stern reached the conclusion that a unilateral removal of tariffs by the USA would stimulate an increased demand for imports of between 2.8 and 3.9 billion dollars depending on the elasticity assumed. If, on the other hand, both tariffs and quotas were eliminated, imports would increase by 4.1 to 5.2 billion dollars. (Both of these estimates are in 1960 prices.) The higher of these estimates amount to 28 per cent and 36 per cent of 1960 imports respectively. Although this is a relatively large proportion of total imports, the fact that imports amount to such a small proportion of GNP in the USA means that even the highest figure of $5.2 billion represents only 1 per cent of 1960 GNP.

Referring to our earlier discussion, we know that from an estimate of the induced change in imports, we can estimate the total deadweight welfare gain according to equation (6.12). This Stern estimates at 0.11 per cent of GNP.

Expressed in these terms this seems a relatively insignificant effect. We must bear in mind, however, that the calculations take no account of the reciprocal benefits which may follow as a result of increased purchasing power overseas – so-called 'responding effects'. Furthermore, the calculation refers to a unilateral action on the part of the USA. Since tariff liberalisation in the post-war period has been multilateral rather than unilateral, this would undoubtedly be a source of understatement. Against this, no account is taken of possible terms-of-trade effects. In the case of a *unilateral* tariff reduction, in the USA one would expect these to be adverse, and indeed this has subsequently been confirmed by Basevi (1968).

If these effects were more or less to cancel each other out, two concluding comments could be made on the figure of 0.11 per cent of GNP. First, the impact of many non-macroeconomic policies often appears small when expressed as a proportion of GNP. Even so, the sums involved may be significant in terms of their opportunity cost. In this study, 0.11 per cent of GNP amounts to something approaching $600 million, at 1960 prices. One might argue that the alternative forgone associated with this type of saving is well worth having. Second, we are of course looking at a once-and-for-all effect rather than an ongoing benefit which tariff elimination represents. Also, we are only considering the static consequences of the action – it may be that the dynamic consequences are more significant. As we indicated earlier, imputing a value for improvements in X-efficiency or a widening of consumer choice is far from straightforward. The gains may nevertheless be significant if domestic market concentration is relatively high (in the case of X-efficiency gains), and if intra-industry trade forms a relatively high proportion of total trade (in the case of widening of consumer choice).

Thus, referring back to the various 'effects' introduced earlier in this chapter, Stern concerned himself only with estimating the dead-weight production and consumption changes associated with a *unilateral* action. No attempt was made to incorporate terms-of-trade, balance-of-payments or dynamic effects. Subsequent work relating to the USA has been more extensive. Basevi (1968), for example, did allow for terms-of-trade changes and exchange-rate changes, but none the less confined himself to estimating the effects of a unilateral tariff reduction. Interestingly Basevi uses a more sophisticated model than Stern and finds that efficiency losses from the presence of tariffs are greater, but these are outweighed by terms-of-trade considerations, such that the net effect of tariff reduction would be negative (coincidentally by - 0.11 per cent of GNP).

Additional studies for the USA have been completed by Magee (1972) and Baldwin (1976). The latter we will examine in detail in Chapter 11 when we consider employment consequences of trade policy. For the moment we might merely note that the trade changes predicted by Magee and Baldwin are consistent with net welfare changes of a similar order of magnitude to those identified by Stern and Basevi.

By contrast, Batchelor and Minford (1977) investigate the costs of tariff imposition in the United Kingdom – an economy which is altogether more dependent on the foreign trade sector than the USA, and one which we can reasonably safely refer to as a 'small open economy'.[5] They estimate the effects of unilateral tariff imposition.

Two interesting features of the study distinguish it from Stern's model. First, the time dimension of the problem is explicitly recognised. Thus, rather than calculating once-and-for-all deadweight losses, losses which will accrue sometime in the future are included, and discounted to obtain a present value. Second, the authors do not rely solely on the usual 'classical model' which assumes that the imported and domestically produced varieties of a given commodity are perfect substitutes. Instead, because such a large proportion of UK trade comprises manufactures, allowance is made for the possibility that in the short to medium term (up to five years) they may be imperfect substitutes, which would reduce the extent to which a given tariff encourages domestic consumers to switch away from imports to import substitutes.

Using the elasticity methodology, the authors predict the effect on import demand of a range of tariff rates. From this they estimate the cumulative deadweight production and consumption losses.

The Old Protectionism

TABLE 6.1   Welfare effects of tariff imposition in the United Kingdom

Balance of payments deficit to be eliminated (% of GDP)	Required tariff rate (%)	Cumulative total cost* (% of 1976 GDP)
0.5	8	6.4
1.0	18	20.2
1.5	30	20.9
2.0	45	21.8
2.5	65	23.2
3.0	92	25.1
3.5	132	27.8
4.0	196	31.7

* The present discounted value, applying a discount rate of 5 per cent, of future losses. The calculation assumes that real GDP grows at 2 per cent p.a.

Source: Adapted from Batchelor and Minford (1977) tables 4.5 and 4.6.

Their estimates are presented in Table 6.1. It is immediately apparent that these calculations suggest the costs of protection are considerably in excess of the figures suggested by US studies. This is in part due to the fact that the foreign trade sector is relatively more important in the United Kingdom, in part due to the fact that future costs are allowed for. Even the lowest tariff rate implies a cost of over 6 per cent of GDP, while the highest rate estimated (196 per cent) is consistent with a cumulative cost of over 30 per cent of GDP.

There is one point which the authors make to suggest that these results are possibly an overestimate. The study only allows for import controls on finished consumer goods. The authors argue that a widening of incidence to intermediate goods and raw materials might reduce the total welfare costs of controls because 'any move from a discriminatory system to one which approaches more closely the ideal uniform tariff/subsidy implicit in devaluation will be an improvement in terms of resource reallocation' (p. 71). On the basis of their estimate about elasticity of demand for producer goods, the authors feel that a reduction of about 20 per cent of the cumulative cost figures in Table 6.1 would be in order. One ought perhaps to be a little circumspect about this conclusion since we are making no allowance for differences in effective protection which would result from a given uniform, non-discriminatory, nominal tariff.

Against this the authors feel that a discount rate of 5 per cent is on the high side, and that a discount rate of 2–3 per cent would be more appropriate. Application of a lower discount rate would, of course, raise the cumulative total cost of the controls. Furthermore, the calculations apply only to static deadweight losses, making no allowances for any dynamic losses, and they apply to a unilateral action on the part of the United Kingdom and assume no retaliation.

Note that no allowance is made for induced exchange rate changes because of the way in which the analysis is conducted. The average nominal tariff necessary to remove a given payments deficit is estimated. By implication, therefore, there are no induced exchange rate changes.

One of the most ambitious and comprehensive *ex ante* studies of the effects of tariff changes is the attempt by Cline *et al.* (1978) to predict the economic effects of the outcome of the Tokyo Round negotiations. The authors estimate the effects of a *multilateral* tariff reduction implemented by the EEC and ten other industrial countries.[6] This feature alone immediately differentiates it from those studies which we have thus far reviewed. When the study was completed, final agreement on a tariff-cutting formula had not yet been reached by the participating countries. The authors had therefore to assume a particular tariff change, and in fact they estimated the welfare changes (and as we shall see in Chapter 11, employment changes also) for no less than twelve different tariff-cutting formulae. Static welfare effects were estimated for all countries, but not just on a once-and-for-all basis. The gains were projected, then discounted to obtain a present value. In addition, a 'guesstimate' of dynamic effects was included in the final summary statistics. Since the model was examining the effects of a multilateral tariff reduction, responding effects were also allowed for, as were induced exchange rate changes. Finally, there was also an attempt to estimate the effects of non-tariff barriers.

Since the study is *ex ante*, it is methodologically similar (although somewhat more sophisticated, of course) to the framework developed earlier in the chapter. Changes in imports were estimated at a highly disaggregated level, at the so-called 'tariff-line' of the Brussels Trade Nomenclature. There tend to be some 5,000 such categories for a given industrialised country. Clearly, with so many product categories and such a large number of countries in the sample, data problems are at their most intractable. Trade and tariff data can be obtained relatively easily. The same cannot be said, however, of data on the most crucial parameter in the entire exercise, namely elasticities – both of import demand and of substitution between alternative suppliers.

As we noted earlier, elasticities in general, and import demand elasticities in particular, are notoriously difficult to compute – indeed, many researchers, following Orcutt (1950), have questioned whether they can be identified in any meaningful sense. This is a sentiment which has gained even more currency with the increasingly influential presence of the rational expectations school of thought (see Saidi, 1980). Notwithstanding this 'technical' criticism, Cline *et al.* faced especially intractable problems in obtaining reliable elasticity estimates. First, although the detailed predictions of trade flows were being conducted at a highly disaggregated level, available elasticity estimates were invariably prepared for more highly aggregated product groups. Consequently, aggregate estimates were applied across more disaggregated component product groups. Second, as the study applied to some ten importing areas, elasticity estimates had to be drawn from a number of sources - in fact, five different studies. Third, where the EEC was concerned, elasticity estimates were only available for individual member countries, yet the EEC was treated as one importing area; therefore a weighted average 'composite' elasticity had to be derived for the EEC as a whole.

To many, these difficulties, and the procedures which had to be followed to overcome them, are sufficiently fundamental to render the entire exercise meaningless and incapable even of being trusted as a basis for reporting relevant orders of magnitude. The authors themselves recognise the problems inherent in the exercise and, as well as carefully selecting elasticity estimates from available sources to ensure the maximum degree of consistency, they conduct a 'sensitivity' analysis to ascertain how responsive the results are to alternative elasticity estimates.

Space constraints preclude detailed comment on the estimated welfare effects for all twelve tariff-cutting formulae, but Table 6.2 summarises the once-and-for-all static welfare effects at 1974 prices for all countries, and Table 6.3 (p.122) for the four main negotiating groups.

Before we comment on these results we might note parenthetically that most of these formulae were actually proposed during the Tokyo Round. As we saw in Chapter 5, there was some discussion over the formula to be adopted, and the degree of harmonisation acceptable - the range of formulae proposed should give some idea of the problem faced by the negotiators.

Formula 12 reported above in fact comes very close to the actual 'Swiss formula' agreed in the Tokyo Round. This yields an aggregate static welfare gain of $1.53 billion per annum. In addition, the authors also attempt to make some allowance for dynamic gains from increased X-efficiency, economies of scale and a boost to growth rates caused by a stimulus to new investment and marketing opportunities. Referring to the existing literature on these effects, they suggest that a *conservative* estimate would put them at some five times the static gains, i.e. around $7.65 billion per annum. The trade

TABLE 6.2   Static welfare effects of various multilateral tariff cuts

Formula number	Tariff formula	Static welfare effect $ millions
1	60% linear cut	1,681
2	Three iteration harmonisation $t_1 = t_0 (1 - t_0)$ 3 times	1,397
3	If $t_0 < 5\%$, $t_1 = 0$	1,601
	If $t_0 > 40\%$, $t_1 = 20\%$	
	If $5\% < t_0 < 40\%$, $t_1 = 0.5\ t_0$	
4	100% linear cut	1,991
5	30% + t_0 cut	1,603
6	60% cut plus 3%	1,330
7	43.4% linear cut	1,374
8	60% linear cut and reduce $t_1 = 0$ when t_0 5%	1,686
9	60% cut with 5% floor	1,568
10	Sector harmonisation t_1 set equal to lowest t_0	1,098
11	20% + $3t_0$	1,622
12	Six iteration harmonisation $t_1 = t_0 (1 - t_0)$ 6 times	1,530

t_0 = base tariff; t_1 = reduced tariff.

Source: Adapted from Cline *et al.* (1978) tables 3.1 and 3.2, pp. 77–8.

balance implications of these changes are explored and their effects on exchange rates estimated. The results of this exercise lead the authors to conclude that exchange-rate changes would be 'negligible', since we are dealing with a multilateral tariff cut with an allowance made for respending effects. Finally, the authors take account of the fact that these gains would accrue on a recurring basis. To take account of the time dimension it was assumed that world trade would grow at 5 per cent per annum (which is 2 per cent below the trend growth for 1948–73) and then discounted future gains at an interest rate of 10 per cent. This calculation would suggest a total welfare gain of over $150 billion, or about 15 per cent of the 1974 value of world exports.

Table 6.3 provides details of the estimated static effects of the various formulae for the principal negotiating parties. Again, taking formula 12 as our reference point, it is clear that all parties gain, the figures as a proportion of 1974 GNP amounting to 0.04 per cent for

TABLE 6.3   Static welfare gains of alternative tariff-cutting formulae

Formula number	Value $ millions 1974			
	USA	Canada	Japan	EEC
1	490.3	178.2	289.3	451.2
2	437.8	124.5	268.5	304.4
3	470.3	159.4	296.2	415.5
4	583.7	212.1	344.4	527.7
5	491.0	151.5	293.7	384.6
6	395.2	134.4	244.4	317.8
7	400.6	145.6	236.4	374.3
8	491.1	178.4	289.9	453.0
9	448.9	171.5	276.8	409.4
10	395.4	150.2	83.7	235.1
11	470.8	174.0	281.7	426.9
12	451.1	160.4	270.5	384.5

Source: Adapted from Cline *et al.* (1978) table 3.8, p. 99.

the USA, 0.11 per cent for Canada, 0.07 per cent for Japan, and 0.03 per cent for the EEC. These are only static figures, however, and a similar exercise in 'grossing up' for dynamic effects and discounting to gain a present value yields figures of $21 billion for the USA, $8 billion for Canada, $12 billion for Japan and $19 billion for the EEC, or 1.99 per cent, 6.0 per cent, 3.02 per cent and 1.40 per cent of their respective 1974 GNPs.

By any standards these are significant gains. If the assumptions which underpin the calculations are reasonable, and if the calculations themselves are accurate, then they suggest that the potential gains of multilateral trade liberalisation are considerable. The final figures rely heavily on the estimate of the dynamic gains – in particular the very reasonableness of even attempting to impute a value for such effects. The authors, however, do emphasise that the figures are deliberately conservative, and if anything are likely to understate any such gains which accrue. A more obvious source of understatement is the fact that the calculations refer only to trade liberalisation in the major industrial economies. Although these economies dominate world trade, it seems reasonable to assume that the total 'gains' would be even greater if trade with LDCs were included.

We have dwelt at length on this study because it is an excellent example of a multilateral, general equilibrium application of the *ex ante* methodology. Other multilateral studies in a similar vein have recently been concluded, and the reader is referred to Stern (1979) in particular.

Ex post studies[7]

Studies using the 'reduced group-non-reduced group' methodology date back to Krause's (1959) paper. Here Krause attempted an *ex post* assessment of the effect of tariff concessions granted by the USA in the Torquay Round in 1951. The method involved examining the post-1951 growth of imports for one group of commodities which had experienced tariff reductions, and comparing these with a similar group of commodities for which no tariff reductions were made.

Referring to our discussion of methodologies earlier in this chapter, Krause does avoid the difficulty of having to apply income elasticities of demand. There is, however, bound to be an element of arbitrariness in selecting comparable groups. In principle, the 'reduced' group and 'non-reduced' group should be matched according to cross elasticities of demand. In fact, Krause merely matched commodities from tariff lines. As we have already stressed, there is always a difficulty in interpreting *ex post* results since we can never be certain of what would have happened anyway. This is likely to have been particularly important in Krause's case as the analysis was conducted for the immediate post-war period. From his comparison Krause concluded that 'no significant difference' could be found between the reduced and non-reduced group.

Krause's paper was quickly followed by a study conducted by Kreinin (1961) who employed the same methodology to investigate the impact of the 1956 Geneva Round of tariff cuts. Kreinin finds clearer evidence to suggest that the tariff reductions had a significant impact. He finds, for example, that the growth in the volume of manufactures in the reduced group was a full percentage point more than imports of finished manufactures in the non-reduced group. He suggests a number of reasons why his results differ markedly from Krause's; he found in particular that many of the tariff concessions promoted in 1951 were simply 'dissipated in the elimination of excess protection', while those granted in 1956 genuinely served to encourage import growth.

This in fact is what we found in our discussion of GATT liberalisation in the previous chapter. Furthermore, the main suppliers (i.e. Western Europe) were in a better position by the later 1950s to penetrate the US market to any significant degree. Kreinin translates his findings into an assessment of the gain in welfare which amounts to $31.5 billion (1955 prices).

The most sophisticated recent applications of the reduced group-non-reduced group technique are Finger's (1974, 1977) attempts to estimate the effects of the Dillon Round and Kennedy Round tariff reductions. With respect to the former, he estimates that some five years after the implementation of the concessions, imports were $700 million higher than they would have otherwise been.

Finger's (1977) analysis of the effects of the Kennedy Round is worth examining in more detail, much as we did with the Cline study, in order to bring out a little more fully the difficulties one faces in *ex post* analysis.

The study is firmly in the 'reduced group-non-reduced group' mould. Finger took a random sample of products on which large tariff reductions were made by the principal industrial countries (the USA, the EEC and Japan). He then prepared a sample of similar products on which smaller tariff reductions were made. The changes in trade volume which occurred in the two groups between the conclusion of the Kennedy Round (1967) and 1970 were compared, and this provided the basic material for estimating the effects of the tariff reductions.

Finger recognised at the outset that this methodology involved three crucial assumptions. First, he assumed that over the control period, any other policy changes affect the product groups being examined with equal intensity. Second, he assumed that there is no substitutability between the products in the small reduction group and the large reduction group. Finally, he assumed that the elasticities of import demand for, and supply of, the products in one group are equal to their counterparts in the other group.

The first assumption is clearly made in order to avoid the general problem of *ex post* studies which we identified above, namely that we can never be certain that any changes which take place are solely due to tariff alterations. Finger selected his sample period in order to minimise the effects of exogenous shocks – for instance, 1970 was selected as the end year in order to avoid distortions associated with the 'Nixon shock' of 1971 (which included a 10 per cent import surcharge).

The second assumption is crucial. Clearly, if there is any substitutability between the two groups then the estimate of the effects of tariff reduction is likely to be an overstatement. Since the two groups are chosen such that there are similar products in each group, then there must by definition be some degree of substitutability between the products in the two groups. In recognising this difficulty, Finger points out that although it might lead us to be somewhat cautious about the precise magnitude of estimated effects, it does not invalidate using the technique to establish direction of magnitude. In other words, the method cannot indicate a response to tariff reduction when there is none, and therefore it can still be used to comment on whether tariffs matter or not.

With respect to the final assumption, Finger was assuming that his sample was genuinely 'random' in the sense that products with particularly high elasticities were not systematically omitted. Without very detailed data on elasticities, there is no way of checking this.

With these caveats in mind, Finger examined the response of imports at the tariff line level, for a sample of some 200 product groups, which comprised about 15 per cent of the items on which concessions were made in the Kennedy Round for the USA, Japan and the EEC. Upon comparing the changes which took place in imports into these three areas of commodities in the 'large' reduced group with commodities in the 'small' reduced group, Finger reached two conclusions. First of all, there was evidence to indicate that tariffs do matter in restricting trade flows, i.e. there was a greater responsiveness of imports to tariff reduction in the large reduced group than the small reduced group in all three areas. Second, his findings indicated that developing countries gained significantly from the concessions.

Although precise figures are not furnished to facilitate comparison with the other studies mentioned, this particular study is worthy of note. As the Cline study served to provide a practical example of the problem of *ex ante* estimation, this study did likewise for *ex post* methods.

SUMMARY AND CONCLUSIONS

We have seen that there are a number of established methods of providing quantitative estimates of the effects of tariff liberalisation/imposition. Although there are a number of difficulties associated with the use of *ex ante* and *ex post* methods, there have been a large number of studies applying these techniques. We have only really considered a fraction of this literature by selecting a few studies for detailed comment. Notwithstanding this, a number of concluding comments can be made:

(1) Available *ex ante* and *ex post* studies provide overwhelming support that tariffs 'matter' in the sense that they influence trade flows. The majority of studies seem to point to the general conclusion that there tend to be net gains associated with tariff liberalisation and net costs associated with tariff imposition.

(2) The estimated importance of tariff liberalisation/protection varies directly with the 'openness' of the economy. Thus we find that some studies relating to the USA report the welfare changes as being relatively small. In the case of the United Kingdom, however, potential changes seem altogether more significant, and this conclusion can be

supported by research on other small open economies (e.g. MacAleese, 1977, Cline *et al.*, 1978).

(3)   The results of empirical analyses are markedly influenced by whether or not one discounts future costs/benefits, and if so, the rate used. As we have seen, some studies calculate the net benefits on a once-and-for-all basis, with the consequences that they appear to be relatively unimportant. The essence of trade restriction or liberalisation is that although initial effects may appear to be limited, their long-term effects are a good deal more significant, and there is a good deal of empirical evidence to support this supposition.

(4)   A complete analysis of the welfare implications of tariff liberalisation would involve an assessment of multilateral rather than unilateral tariff reduction. Not all studies are so comprehensive. Those that are indicate, as we would expect, that the benefits of bilateral or multilateral liberalisation exceed those associated with unilateral action.

(5)   Few studies have made an allowance for induced exchange rate changes. Those that have indicate that, as we would expect, these reduce the magnitude of the welfare changes. The extent of the reduction will be greater with a unilateral action (Baldwin and Lewis, 1978) than with a multilateral action (Cline *et al.*, 1978; Stern, 1979).

It could be argued, however, that this type of exercise does not tell the full story about the effects of tariff liberalisation, because by taking an aggregate view it fails to focus on the most important feature of the repercussions of tariff changes, namely that their effects are concentrated. The fact that certain sectors contract following liberalisation often means that the employment displacement effects are geographically concentrated. If so, one may find that adjustment pressures build up which not only resist liberalisation efforts, but actually press for protection to maintain employment.

The relationship between changes in trade policy and employment change is something which we have yet to consider. It is a fundamentally important issue, but we will defer a review of empirical work in this area until we have spent some time examining the new protectionism.

NOTES ON FURTHER READING

A rigorous appraisal of the mechanics of the estimation process can be found in Leamer and Stern (1971) chapter 9. A more intuitive treatment is given in Cline *et al.* (1978) chapter 3. Useful papers which provide surveys of the literature relating to the question are Corden (1975), Kreinin and Officer (1979) and

Mayes (1978). The latter deals particularly with *ex post* studies of regional liberalisation.

Additional empirical studies not mentioned above are Balassa and Kreinin (1967), Lowinger (1976) and Pelzman and Bradberry (1980), all of which cover the USA.

PART III

The New Protectionism: Aspects of Non-Tariff Interventions

7 The Economic Effects of Non-Tariff Interventions

We have already introduced non-tariff interventions in Chapter 3 in connection with our analysis of the theory of optimal intervention. There we identified the criteria by which we could rank one policy instrument relative to another. In this chapter we will consider the economic effects of some non-tariff interventions in rather more detail. One important difference between this chapter and Chapter 3 is that we will not spend a great deal of time considering arguments for non-tariff barriers. The material we introduced in connection with tariffs can largely be replicated here, although as we shall see in the following chapter, the predominant motive where the new protectionism is concerned has been employment protection. Although we will not spend as much time formally evaluating 'arguments' as we did in connection with tariffs in Chapter 3, it is important to remember that prescriptions about non-tariff interventions are subject to the same sort of analysis, and can be ranked relative to tariffs.

Clearly, given space constraints it is not feasible to offer a formal analysis of all non-tariff barriers (assuming we could identify a definitive list). Anyway, not all non-tariff interventions lend themselves readily to analysis within a partial economic framework. Consequently, we will focus our attention on those non-tariff barriers (NTBs) which have been used predominantly. In terms of the classification outlined in Table 7.1, we will concentrate mainly on those instruments grouped under the heading of 'direct' interventions.

DIRECT QUANTITATIVE NON-TARIFF BARRIERS

The most common trade-restricting, non-tariff barriers are quantitative restrictions of some form or another. These are instruments employed to limit the amount of imports over a given period, either in terms of the number of physical units, or in terms of the value of imports. The mechanism by which this is accomplished may be a direct quantitative restriction (or quota), a voluntary export restraint, or some kind of split system like the tariff quota. We will examine each

TABLE 7.1   Non-tariff instruments of intervention

Direct	*Quantitative*
(i.e. explicitly designed and implemented for purposes of restricting trade)	Quantitative restriction Tariff quota Voluntary export restraint Orderly marketing agreement
	Fiscal Export subsidy Export credit subsidy Government procurement
	Administrative Import licensing
Indirect	*Fiscal*
(i.e. notionally implemented to meet some other policy target but affecting trade flows in the process)	Regional subsidisation Subsidisation of public enterprises Tied aid
	Administrative Health and safety regulations Environmental controls Customs valuation procedures Marks of origin

Note: The list is neither exhaustive nor definitive, but rather intended as illustrative.

of these in turn, emphasising the contrasts which can be drawn with the tariff.

Motives for quantitative restrictions

Regulation of imports by direct quantitative controls is often viewed as an alternative to regulation through the price system, i.e. via a tariff. Motives for quantitative restriction are similar to those invoked to justify tariff imposition, i.e. broadly speaking protective or fiscal. The protective motive is entirely analogous to the tariff case, i.e. one physically restricts the volume (or value) of imports in order to enlarge the potential market for domestic suppliers. The fiscal motive in the case of tariff imposition refers to the use of import tariffs to raise revenue.[1] The fiscal motive in the case of quantitative restrictions is qualitatively different. As we shall see below, it is possible for the authorities to raise revenue via a quota - if the licences to import are auctioned off in a competitive market. Often, however, licences are distributed by some alternative means, with the result that no revenue is directly raised. A value quota, however, may have a different fiscal purpose; it may be imposed in order to economise on foreign exchange. If a fixed limit is placed on the *value* of imports in a given commodity group, then the authorities can predict, with some degree of certainty, the foreign exchange requirements for that sector. Note that we are deliberately associating this fiscal motive with a value quota. A quota which limited the number of physical units need not have the same implications. In fact it is not unusual to find that the foreign exchange necessary for a given number of units *increases* after a physical quota is imposed because foreign exporters respond to the quantitative restriction by specialising more in products within the restricted category which have a higher unit value.[2]

Economic effects of quotas[3]

Figure 7.1 outlines the effects of a quota for a given small open economy. In the world economy, the home country is a price taker. All of the assumptions which underpinned the analysis of tariffs in Chapter 3 continue to hold - in summary we are in the world of the two-country, two-commodity, two-factor Heckscher-Ohlin-Samuelson

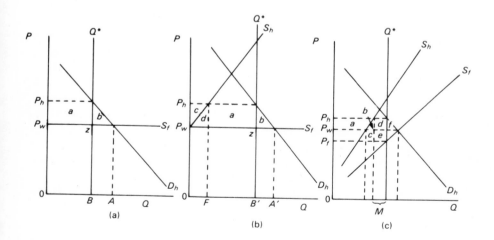

Figure 7.1

model, where countries specialise in accordance with relative factor endowments.

In panel (a) of Figure 7.1 we examine the simplest possible case – quota imposition with no domestic production capability. D_h represents the domestic demand for, and S_f the foreign supply of, imports. In free trade equilibrium, OA units are imported and sell on the home market for a unit price of P_w. Suppose now that, for whatever reason, the volume of imports is to be restricted to a physical maximum of OB. We can see immediately that the foreign supply curve becomes totally inelastic at point z and is now represented by $P_w ZQ^*$. The quota-restricted volume of imports must now be less than the unrestricted market clearing volume. In order to eliminate excess demand, the home price of imports rises above the world price, settling at P_h. Reapplying our surplus analysis of Chapter 3, it should be obvious that consumers' surplus has contracted by the areas $a + b$. Area a, however, represents a redistribution from domestic consumers to importers. The area is found by taking the difference between the fixed world price, i.e. the price which importers actually pay for the commodity, and the price at which the commodity sells on the home market. The holders of import licences therefore earn super-normal profits and the net loss to consumers is equivalent to the triangular area b.

In panel (b) we introduce the possibility of domestic producers being able to supply units of the importable which are assumed to be perfect substitutes for the imported commodity. To simplify the analysis we have drawn the domestic supply curve (S_h) as intersecting the vertical axis at P_w. Thus in conditions of free trade, domestic supply is zero. If, however, price rises above P_w, resources will be attracted from other sectors into the import substitute sector.

Again, assume that a physical maximum volume of imports is imposed. As in panel (a), the foreign supply curve becomes $P_w zQ^*$, imports are restricted to FB' and the welfare effects are again obvious. Consumers' surplus falls by $c + d + a + b$. As before, a represents a redistribution to importers. Because domestic price rises to P_h and domestic suppliers of import substitutes have entered the market, there is also a redistribution from consumers to domestic producers. Specifically, producers' surplus increases by area c. The net welfare effects in this case amount, therefore, to the triangles $d + b$, the former being a production loss, the latter a consumption loss.

The analysis for a country which can influence its terms of trade is similar. In panel (c) of Figure 7.1, S_f is now positively sloped, indicating that the foreign supply elasticity is now less than infinite. The main difference in the analysis here is that as the quota becomes effective, not only does the home price of imports rise (from P_w to P_h) but the foreign export price falls (from P_w to P_f). Thus the quota profit *per unit* of import is greater ($d + e$) than it would be if foreign supply were infinitely elastic (d), and the deadweight loss is also greater ($b + c + f$). There is a terms-of-trade gain (approximated by the area e) which goes to the holders of import licences.

A comparison of quotas and tariffs

As we suggested at the beginning of this section, tariffs and quotas are often viewed as substitutes for each other. It is therefore worthwhile comparing briefly the economic effects of each.

If we compare Figure 7.1(b) with Figure 3.1, we can see immediately certain similarities between the analysis of a nominal tariff on imports and a given quota. Indeed, in terms of surplus analysis the same areas of change appear common to both diagrams. The initial effects are in fact identical in all respects but one. The area c in Figure 3.1 we recognised as being a redistribution from consumer to the tariff-levying authority, i.e. tariff revenue. In the case of a quota this area represents, as we have seen, quota profits to importers, i.e. the holders of import licences. The only way in which the authorities could appropriate this surplus is if they auctioned off the licences in advance, rather than allocating them administratively. As Corden (1971) points out, the surplus is an economic rent which accrues to the licences due to their scarcity value. If the licences are allocated administratively, their holders gain the rent; if the authorities can auction them off in a competitive market, their selling price would equal the discounted value of the rents, and the authorities thereby appropriate the gain.

This question of how the licences are allocated and whether there is any subsequent trade in licences is an interesting and important one. The possibility of trade in licences, for example, makes it conceivable that monopoly control of licences could result, in which case price may be even higher and imports lower. Unfortunately space constraints forbid detailed considerations of such issues. The interested reader is encouraged to consult Corden (1971) chapter 9. For our part we will maintain the assumption that licences are distributed administratively (which is the most usual form of allocation) and that no trade takes place in licences following the initial distribution.

This 'revenue effect' is frequently viewed as being the principal difference between tariffs and quotas. In so far as this amounts to an income transfer in both cases, there may be little to choose between the two instruments in terms of their effect on *static* efficiency (although equity considerations might lead us to prefer one instrument relative to the other, e.g. if the holders of import licences are in a high income group).

One can then proceed to ascertain the tariff equivalent of a given quota.[4] We should, however, note a number of further contrasts:

(1)   The mechanism of control in the case of a tariff is the price mechanism. In the case of quotas, the action of the price mechanism is effectively negated. If one is instinctively of the view that the invisible hand of the market is the most efficacious signalling mechanism for resource reallocation, then, *ceteris paribus*, tariffs are likely to be preferred. If, on the other hand, one feels that planning of markets is not only necessary but desirable, then quotas are likely to be preferred.

(2)   The effect of quantitative restrictions on the market mechanism can be most clearly illustrated by moving to a more dynamic context and considering the implications of an increase in the demand for importables. This case is illustrated in Figure 7.2.

In panel (a) a nominal tariff of t per unit restricts imports to CD by pushing the domestic price of the importable from P_1 to P_2 (i.e. the world price plus the tariff). In panel (b) we see that the same volume and price effect can be achieved by a quota restricting imports to $C'D'$. Suppose now that an increase in disposable income shifts the domestic demand curve for importables from D_1 to D_2. In the tariff case domestic price must remain at P_2 and the increased demand is

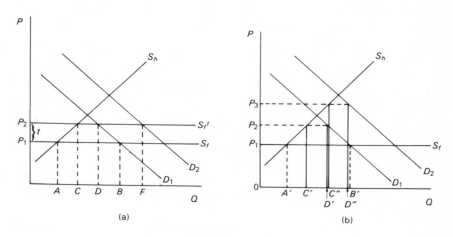

Figure 7.2

met by an expansion of imports from *CD* to *CF*. We have constructed D_1 and D_2 in order to ensure that the deadweight triangles remain unchanged. By contrast, the existence of a quota in case (b) means that imports must continue to be limited to $C''D''$ (= $C'D'$) even following the demand expansion. Thus domestic price is pushed further above the world price, eventually reaching P_3. Here imports continue to be limited and the additional demand must be met by an expansion of supply in the import substitute sector. Consequently, the deadweight triangles increase in size, as should be apparent from inspection. When the domestic market is growing, then, it seems that a tariff regime directs production to (relatively efficient) foreign producers, while a quota regime concentrates supplies increasingly on relatively inefficient domestic producers.

(3) Following from the above, it can be argued that quotas are likely to inhibit the growth process to a greater extent than tariffs. An important element in generating growth is resource reallocation, the rundown of relatively inefficient sectors to make resources available for relatively efficient sectors to expand. A given fixed quota, by raising the price of the importable in a growing market, raises the effective protection given to the important substitute sector. This could frustrate, rather than encourage, resource reallocation.[5]

(4) One final resource allocation effect that we might mention also follows from point (2) above. We noted that quotas tend to concentrate supplies on domestic sources, while tariffs concentrate supplies on overseas sources. Since quotas tend to discriminate between overseas suppliers, then a further outcome of their imposition may very well be that those imports which do enter are not concentrated on least cost supplies. As we shall see in Chapter 9, this has become one of the more striking characteristics of the new protectionism - controls on imports from some suppliers but not others.

These, then, are some of the contrasts which can be drawn between quotas and tariffs that may influence the decision as to which is levied at any point in time. These economic considerations are likely to lead us to rank consistently the tariff above the quota as an instrument of intervention. In practice, however, economic criteria may be secondary to administrative considerations. It seems that quotas are administratively more straightforward to operate than tariffs, but there is more scope for abuse (through allocation and possible transfer of licences). Given, however, the revenue yield associated with tariffs, any higher administrative costs can be offset by revenue accruals. Ideally, when comparing tariffs and quotas a full cost-benefit appraisal ought to be conducted in order to evaluate the net benefits of both instruments.[6]

Voluntary export restraints and orderly marketing agreements

As we saw in Chapter 5, Article XIX of GATT permits emergency action against imports to safeguard domestic industry. Recently, however, for reasons we will elaborate on in subsequent chapters, rather than imposing controls under the conditions of GATT Article XIX, many actions have taken the form of voluntary export restraint agreements (VERs) or orderly marketing agreements (OMAs). We will treat the VER and OMA as identical, and simply refer to the VER in our analysis.[7]

The welfare effects of a VER can be analysed within the same framework as that developed for the analysis of quotas. Thus, Figure 7.1 could be used to examine the implications of a VER which restricted the volume of imports to Q^*. The effects on price and output would be the same as in the case of the quantitative restriction. The fundamental difference between the formal quota and the VER is in the area a. We saw that in the case of a quota this area represented an accrual of quota profits to importers (unless the authorities auctioned off the licences). A VER, however, is by definition administered by the exporting country (or countries). In this case, therefore, the quota revenue unequivocally accrues to overseas exporters. Thus the reduction in consumers' surplus of area a is not offset by a redistribution to domestic importers or the authorities, but rather is redistributed abroad. If one takes a global perspective this may be viewed as irrelevant. In the more usual case where one adopts a 'national' perspective, it might be viewed as a further loss associated with the restriction.

The terms-of-trade and balance-of-payments implications of VERs also differ from quotas. From the home country's viewpoint a VER stimulates a rise in unit import prices and, *ceteris paribus*, an adverse movement in the international terms of trade.

With respect to the balance of payments, a quota should reduce foreign exchange requirements, as long as the international price ratio remains unchanged or moves in favour of the importing country, and as long as the volume of imports is actually reduced. In the case of a VER, however, foreign exchange requirements may very well increase. Whether they do or do not depends on the elasticity of the demand curve over the relevant range. If price elasticity of demand is less than one, then foreign exchange requirements will increase as unit export prices increase. Other things being equal, this implies a movement into balance-of-payments deficit and subsequent exchange-rate depreciation (where exchange rates are free to float) or income-reducing policies (where exchange rates are fixed).

There is one other important possibility which Murray, Schmidt and Walter (1978) consider. This is the case of monopolisation of export supply, either because only one firm supplies the relevant commodity or because cartelisation is an outcome of a VER. The essential features of this case can easily be comprehended by reference to Figure 7.3.

Given a perfectly elastic foreign supply curve for imports, and a domestic demand curve given by D_M, free trade equilibrium would result in OA units being imported at a price of OP_1. Suppose now a VER were negotiated whereby imports were to be voluntarily limited to OB per time period. If exports were competitively supplied, OB would in fact be imported and this would generate VER 'profit' of P_1FGP_2. If, however, the VER were negotiated with a single supplier, or if it were negotiated with a group of suppliers who were in a position to exploit collectively their latent market power, the final equilibrium may in fact be different. Specifically the monopoly (or cartel) may follow a profit-maximising (joint profit-maximising) policy. This would necessitate marginal cost and marginal revenue being equated and a price of P_3 being set. VER profits would be maximised at P_1JKP_3.

In this case, therefore, the use of a VER rather than a quota not only results in the transfer of any quota revenue abroad (in the form of VER profit) but results in the volume of imports being lower and price being higher. Furthermore, other things being equal, this is consistent with a greater degree of effective protection being given to the import substitute sector (by virtue of the home price of the import being higher).

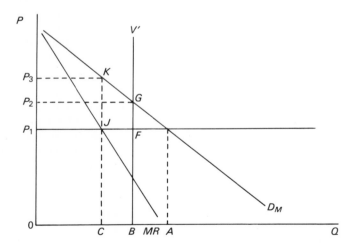

Figure 7.3

Quotas and voluntary export restraints

From the foregoing discussion we can make a number of concluding comments on the contrasts which can be drawn between quotas and voluntary export restraints.

Although, given second best considerations, it is not always possible to rank formally alternative trade policy instruments, there does appear to be good ground for regarding a formal quota as being superior to a VER. This conclusion is reached on the grounds that there is a greater likelihood of adverse terms-of-trade and balance-of-payments effects with a VER than with a quota. In addition, there might be a greater degree of uncertainty associated with the use of VERs.

Despite this the use of VERs has become increasingly popular – in many cases in preference to formal quantitative restrictions. As we have seen, this has more to do with political expediency than any rational evaluation of alternative instruments. Because VERs are 'voluntary' and exist outside the GATT framework, they are not subject to reciprocity obligations, and they can be applied in a discriminatory manner. Such considerations can make their use seem attractive. (For a more formal comparison, see Takacs, 1978.)

Tariff quotas

Tariff quotas are another instrument of trade policy, the incidence of which has become more common in recent years. As with quotas and VERs, this is in part a response to protectionist pressures in the 1970s.

The tariff quota (TQ), as the name suggests, is a hybrid of the tariff and the quota. In an exhaustive analysis of tariff quotas, Michael Rom (1979) defines a tariff quota as follows:

A tariff quota . . . sets no absolute maximum to the total amount of imports of a product or products permitted into a customs area during a given period. Instead, it provides that a specified quantity, value or share of this import may enter during a given period into all or part of the area free of duty or at a lower rate of duty than imports in excess of that limit. (p. 2)

In other words, imports are subject to tariffs, but a variety of tariff rates may be set with quotas imposed on the volume (or value) of imports subject to each tariff rate. Thus the initial x units imported would be subject to a tariff of Z per cent (where $Z \geqslant 0$). Anything in excess of x is subject to a tariff rate of $(Z + w)$ per cent (where $w > 0$).

The TQ may be confined to one threshold with two rates or it may have n thresholds with $n + 1$ rates (where $n > 1$).

Since quantitative limits are set for different rates, we can see immediately some of the administrative difficulties which are raised. For example, will the TQ be 'allocated' or 'unallocated'? If the latter were to apply, exporting countries would benefit from the lower rates of duty on a first come, first served basis. If, however, the TQ is allocated, specific countries or geographic regions might be given shares of the lower duty quotas. Similarly, the TQ could be discriminatory or non-discriminatory, that is to say it may explicitly exclude certain exporting countries to the benefit of others. TQs can be specified in absolute or relative terms, i.e. differential duties are either applied up to some physical limit, or up to when the commodity reaches a given proportion of total dutiable imports. The tariff rates applied can be specific, *ad valorem*, or a combination of both.

When we bear these and other administrative problems in mind, the relevance of Curzon's (1979) remark that a necessary condition for the proliferation of tariff quotas is computerisation becomes clear! Tariff quotas not only combine the technical characteristics of tariffs and quotas, but they also serve to combine (and compound) the administrative difficulties of both.

Having said this, however, the tariff quota is viewed by many as a useful instrument of trade policy, primarily because it is regarded as being more liberal than either the quota or the tariff. We can review the basic principles of the TQ by reference to Figure 7.4.

Given demand and supply conditions for imports, in an unrestricted

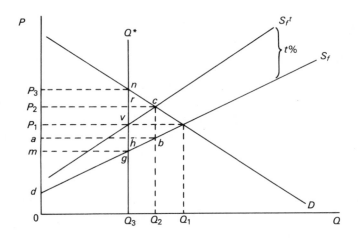

Figure 7.4

market, OQ_1 would be traded at a market clearing price of OP_1. Suppose now that an *ad valorem* tariff is imposed on imports which displaces the foreign supply curve from S_f to $S_f{}^t$. In the absence of any further intervention, the market would contract to OQ_2, with consumers paying the tariff-distorted price of OP_2. The tariff yields revenue of $abcP_2$, the burden of which is shared between domestic consumer and foreign producer by dint of S_f having an elasticity of less than infinity.

It may be felt desirable, however, to permit some imports to enter duty free (or at a lower rate of duty than t per cent). A common situation is that imports from some countries are allowed preferential access to the home market. These may, for example, be higher cost developing countries which are allocated quotas for certain imports. Imports up to the quota limit enter duty free, while any in excess of this are liable to duty.

In terms of Figure 7.4, a quota of Q^* may be set, such that OQ_3 units enter duty free and any imports in excess of this pay t per cent. Once the quota is imposed, the effective supply curve of imports becomes $dgvS_f{}^t$. The market clearing price and quantity are again established at OP_2 and OQ_2 respectively. The gains and losses compared with free trade equilibrium differ, however, from both the quota and tariff cases. If a quota were used in isolation, domestic price would rise to P_3, and importers would enjoy quota profits of P_3ngm. In the pure tariff case, as we have already seen, the market clearing price and quantity are as in the tariff quota case. With the latter, however, because only imports in excess of OQ_3 are subject to duty, tariff revenue is less than in the pure tariff case ($cbhr < P_2cba$). There is an element of quota profit for importers, but, due to the fact that market clearing price is less than in the pure quota case, we find that quota profits are also lower than in the pure quota case ($P_2rgm < P_3ngm$).

What we seem to have, then, is some kind of half-way house. The net welfare effect of all three instruments (tariff, quota and tariff quota) is the same (the deadweight triangles) but the redistributions differ. Even in an extremely simplified analysis, such as the one we have here, it is quite obvious that the TQ is a more complicated instrument than either of its progenitors used in isolation. One incurs the administrative costs of operating a quota, and the machinery for enforcing the tariff still has to be set up. Add to this inevitable complications which result from precisely defining and monitoring those countries and commodities which are subject to tariff exemption, and one can see the substance of Curzon's point about computerisation being a necessary condition for the proliferation of TQs.

Despite relatively high administrative costs, the TQ has become increasingly common. One very important reason for this has been the development of the Generalised System of Preferences (GSP). As we noted in Chapter 5, although details of GSP arrangements differ from country to country, what GSP treatment often amounts to is a tariff quota, i.e. a limit is set whereby a certain volume of imports from designated countries enters duty free, anything in excess of this being subject to MFN duty.

Thus tariff quotas have become a convenient method whereby DMEs can apparently provide some kind of preferential access to their markets for LDCs. We might note, however, that there is considerable debate over the extent to which tariff quotas under the GSP have benefited LDCs (see Baldwin and Murray, 1977; Murray, 1977). It is even argued by some that they have served to increase the protectionism against LDCs.

FISCAL NON-TARIFF INTERVENTIONS

There are a number of fiscal, non-tariff instruments which can influence the pattern of international exchanges. The most important class of such instruments is subsidies of one form or another. A few examples of this class of instruments will occupy our attention for most of the remainder of this chapter.

Production subsidies

When we examined the use of tariffs to meet certain domestic production objectives in Chapter 3, we noted that production subsidies could be used for such purposes by altering the price faced by domestic producers, while leaving the price which domestic consumers face unchanged. The effects are outlined in Figure 7.5.

In free trade equilibrium imports amount to AB. A tariff, we will recall, acted by vertically displacing the foreign supply curve, the extent of the displacement depending on the rate of tariff. A subsidy is in fact a negative tax. Thus, whereas a tariff (or positive tax) displaces the relevant supply curve upwards, a subsidy has the effect of displacing it vertically downwards. Again, the extent of the displacement depends on the rate of subsidy given.

A production subsidy would, of course, be given to domestic producers with the result that S_h in Figure 7.5 shifts down to S_h^s. For any given output, the price which producers receive exceeds the price which consumers pay by the amount of the subsidy. At a world price of P_1, therefore, domestic producers are now able to supply OC

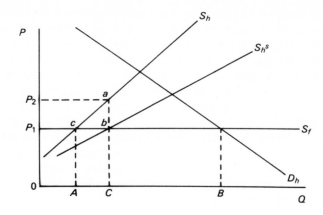

Figure 7.5

rather than OA. Consumers continue to pay OP_1 per unit, but domestic producers receive OP_2, that is $OP_1(=Cb)$ plus a subsidy of ab per unit. The outcome of this subsidy is that imports fall from AB to CB.

Use of this framework for analysis of the production subsidy facilitates straightforward comparison with the tariff. We have already noted that there is an import-reducing effect. Whereas this is achieved by influencing both consumption and production in the case of a tariff, the subsidy achieves the same impact by influencing production only. The subsidy has, of course, to be financed by the Exchequer. Thus there is a redistribution from the Exchequer to domestic producers equivalent to the area P_1baP_2. This also contrasts with the tariff, where the redistribution was from domestic consumers to the Exchequer and domestic producers. Finally, in net welfare terms we can note the presence of a production loss equivalent to abc. This, however, is the only loss. Because the price faced by consumers remains unaffected by the subsidy, there is no consumption deadweight loss.

It is this latter effect which led us to rank production subsidies above import tariffs in Chapter 3. *Ceteris paribus* the former only creates one distortion (by changing the price received by producers) while use of the latter creates two distortions (by altering the prices received by producers and consumers).

In Chapter 3 we also emphasised that there is the question of how the subsidy is financed. In Paretian terms, we concluded that if one can show that consumers would be willing and able to pay the production subsidy, and still remain better off than with an equivalent tariff, then intervention via a production subsidy is preferable.

The production subsidy need not be viewed strictly as an alternative to the tariff. It may indeed be implemented in conjunction with a given import tariff – the end product being a self-financing production subsidy. In other words an import tariff is levied, the revenue from which is used to finance a production subsidy. One would naturally expect the protective impact of such a policy to be greater than that associated with the production subsidy in isolation.

Most developed market economies employ production subsidies which encourage import substitution and influence international exchanges. Regional policy in the United Kingdom has relied heavily on a variety of subsidies designed to influence supply – cash grants for investment, employment subsidies, and so on. A policy of underwriting the losses of public corporations amounts to a *de facto* subsidy, since otherwise the companies concerned would have to charge higher prices. If the commodities concerned are tradables – as are, for instance, coal, steel and shipbuilding, then the effect of underwriting losses is to encourage import substitution. These industries were deliberately chosen for illustrative purposes because such traditional industries were, as we have seen, under considerable pressure in the 1970s and were in the vanguard of the movement for protectionist intervention – not only in the United Kingdom but elsewhere in the Western world.

Discriminatory government procurement

In most developed market economies, government agencies and authorities are significant purchasers of goods and services. At the very least most governments provide pure public goods such as defence, judiciary and public administration. In addition, however, many governments actually provide (as opposed to simply financing) certain 'merit goods' (Musgrave, 1959) such as health, education and housing.

Many of the inputs into the production process are traded goods. As a buyer, therefore, the government through its agencies is in a position to exert a significant effect on trade flows, and it is not unusual to find that governments discriminate between domestic and foreign firms in the award of contracts. Such a procedure may be formalised on the statute books. Thus the Buy American Act of 1933 compelled government agencies to give a preference margin of 50 per cent to domestic firms in the award of defence contracts, and a margin of 14 per cent in non-defence contracts. This is the exception rather than the rule, however. It is more common to find that such arrangements are not formalised but that *de facto* preference is given. Arrangements may also take the form of pressure exerted on one public corporation to purchase the output of another in preference to purchasing imports.

Whatever form this discrimination takes, the end result basically amounts to a subsidy being given to the domestic firm, since if the firm were forced to compete openly with overseas firms, its prices would have to be lower than otherwise. As in the case outlined in Figure 7.5, the cost of such a policy would be borne by the Exchequer, and taxes would be higher than otherwise (in the case of goods or services provided free at the point of consumption), or the prices of final goods would be higher to consumers (in the case where public corporations are obliged to purchase their inputs from other public corporations).[8]

Export subsidies

A further policy option might involve the subsidisation of exports rather than (or as well as) the protection of imports. The rationale here may be that rather than maintain a sector which is at a comparative disadvantage, either by the use of import tariffs or production subsidies, one may instead encourage the use of resources displaced from the import substitute sector by encouraging exports. Such a strategy of export orientation has been recommended as being more likely to promote economic development in LDCs than inward-oriented policies of import substitution (Balassa and Sharpston, 1977).

In Figure 7.6 home supply and demand intersect below the ruling world price of OP_1, indicating that the commodity concerned is an exportable. In a situation of unrestricted trade, OB would be produced, OA of which is consumed by domestic residents while the remaining AB is exported. One way of raising exports (and employment if total output increases as a result) would be by providing an export subsidy. A subsidy of S per cent has the effect of shifting the supply curve from S_h to S_h^s, thereby inducing an increase in exports from AB to AC. This, however, is not the only effect of the subsidy. Clearly, if the domestic price continues to be OP_1, all production would be exported. In order for the home market to gain a share of the production, therefore, domestic prices have to rise from OP_1 to OP_2, with domestic consumption contracting from OA to OD. Thus the net effect on exports is an increase from AB to DC.

The effects of an export subsidy are in fact equivalent but opposite to those associated with an import tariff. A wedge is driven between domestic and international prices in both cases: with an import tariff the home price of importables rises above the world price,

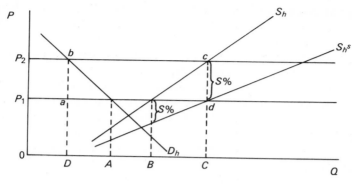

Figure 7.6

while with an export subsidy the home price of exportables rises above the world price. With the tariff there is a net revenue gain to the Exchequer, with an export subsidy there is a net revenue loss (equivalent to *adcb*).

Export subsidies may take a number of forms. They may be a direct production subsidy on those units exported or they may be less obvious. For instance, export credit may be given at interest rates which are below market rates, or 'tax holidays' may be given to firms which produce predominantly for export. The former is a particularly common method of providing a subsidy. One of the functions of the Export Credit and Guarantee Fund in the United Kingdom is to provide such a facility (as well as acting as guarantor to loans). Strictly speaking this is not necessarily an export subsidy of the form described in Figure 7.6, since the finance raised is generally for purposes of setting up plant, extending marketing organisations, and so on. As such, however, they do operate to shift the intercept of the supply curve, although we cannot be certain about the implications for slope. As with quantitative interventions, the use of subsidies has also increased in recent years.

ADMINISTRATIVE AND TECHNICAL BARRIERS

We have concentrated at length on the issues of quantitative restrictions and subsidies. This is not meant to imply that these instruments are necessarily the most common or indeed the most effective restraints on international exchange. We concentrated on these instruments for two reasons. First, their economic implications can be considered using the partial equilibrium tools which we have developed as the core of our analysis. Second, it is likely that since there is a greater measure of agreement on the economic effects of such instruments, there is greater scope for negotiation on the circumstances under which their use is permissible/prohibited.

The same cannot be said of administrative and technical barriers to trade, however. It is probable that this group of interventions has a greater impact on international exchanges than either subsidies or quotas. From an economic point of view there is unfortunately little we can say here, since there is a basic problem in identifying those regulations which influence international exchanges.

This section on administrative and technical barriers covers a multitude of possible influences, from customs valuation procedures and rules of origin to regulations relating to environmental control, public health and safety. In the case of customs valuation procedures, for instance, we may find that these are deliberately complicated in order to create uncertainty for the importers concerned – as many businessmen would readily testify, uncertainty can be an extremely effective non-tariff barrier to trade. Environmental regulations may be drafted in order to constrain the extent to which individual exchanges impose external costs on others. Legislation at home which forces motorists to drive cars with lead-free petrol only means that any overseas car manufacturer whose assembly line is geared to producing cars propelled by petrol with lead added is then placed in a position whereby it has to incur re-tooling costs if it wishes to export. One might regard this as being perfectly legitimate, but the motive and its implementation may on occasions give greater grounds for suspicion – for instance, where exporters have to alter designs to make exhausts two inches shorter, or tail lights three inches closer together, or they are denied batch-testing facilities. The extent and impact of such interventions is impossible to assess.

The same can be said of health and safety regulations. Such regulations are bound to differ from country to country and are bound therefore to make certain goods non-tradable, or reduce the volume of trade. In many cases, of course, these may be felt to be unobjectionable. Thus trade in live animals in particular is subject to tight controls in order to constrain the spread of communicable diseases. Other regulations, however, may be used to raise costs deliberately to importers and distort trade flows.

We must bear in mind, then, that there exists this very important class of non-tariff barriers. As economists we are not really in a position to make the value judgement as to when a particular regulation is being abused, and when it is not.

NON-TARIFF BARRIERS AND EFFECTIVE PROTECTION

When we examined the role of tariff interventions, we took great care to emphasise that one should not simply look at the nominal rate of tariff which applies to the final value of a particular commodity; rather one should always look at the entire tariff structure, i.e. tariffs which apply to inputs as well as final goods. The tariff structure was summarised by the effective tariff rate in equation (4.4a):

$$e_j = \frac{t_j - \sum_{i=1}^{n} z_{ij} t_i^*}{1 - \sum_{i=1}^{n} z_{ij}} \qquad (4.4a)$$

The same point can be made with respect to non-tariff barriers. We have considered each of our instruments in a partial equilibrium framework, and so far considered only the implications of a given instrument in nominal terms. Implicitly we are therefore assuming either a single-stage production process or that no imported inputs are employed in the production process. As we have seen, this is rarely the case. Clearly if we are interested in the protection given to a particular domestic activity, we should then take into account the implications of any subsidies or quotas on intermediate inputs. In other words, what we ought to compute is the effective rate of protection. This is analogous to the effective tariff rate, and was summarised in equation (4.4b):

$$e_j^T = \frac{t_j + s_j(1 + t_j) - \sum_{i=1}^{n} z_{ij} t_i}{1 - \sum_{i=1}^{n} z_{ij}} \qquad (4.4b)$$

This looks very similar to equation (4.4a). There are, however, two important differences. The first is that e_j^T refers not just to the nominal rate of tariff which applies to the final value of the commodity, but represents the tariff equivalent of any quotas which apply on the final good. Thus, whereas the effective tariff rate summarises the tariff structure, the effective protective rate summarises the entire protective structure in one summary statistic. As such it is clearly of greater potential value than the effective tariff rate. As we saw in Chapter 3, by dint of its more comprehensive nature, however, it is also a good deal more complicated to compute. The effective tariff rate is relatively easy to obtain because tariff schedules can be obtained without too much difficulty. In the case of effective rate of protection, however, there may be problems in calculating the tariff equivalent of a given quota. As we saw above, the 'tariff equivalent' of a quota is far from being an unambiguous concept. Calculating the protective impact of a range of subsidies is even more intractable – even when the subsidies concerned are transparent. In many cases, however, subsidies are hidden. To gain some idea of the problems involved, consider assessing the industry-specific effective protection conferred by various subsidy instruments which formed a part of UK regional policy in the 1970s. As well as cash grants for investment, there were also employment subsidies available (in the form of the regional employment premium) and various subsidies designed to reduce fixed costs, such as property rented at less than market value. Throw in any hidden subsidies which may have applied (such as subsidised fuel costs perhaps due to price control) and make allowance for the fact that such instruments varied across regions, and one gets some idea of the exercise on hand.

This conveniently brings us to our final point. As we noted, our analysis has been almost entirely partial equilibrium. In principle we ought to be concerned also with the general equilibrium effects of tariff and non-tariff interventions. By shifting attention from nominal to effective protection we go some way along this road, but we are nevertheless still focusing primarily on the sector in which the instrument has its primary impact. The implications for all other sectors are relevant to an analysis of the efficacy of any policy instrument. Empirical analyses which are explicitly general equilibrium, although becoming more common, are still the exception rather than the rule. This perhaps applies to econometric analyses of trade interventions more than any other field of applied economics. There have been a number of notable studies in recent years which have attempted to assess the general equilibrium effects of tariff imposition/liberalisation. These we commented on in Chapter 6. All of the remarks which we made when commenting on the calculation of effective protective rates can be reiterated here with even greater force, and it is for this reason that no major general equilibrium analyses of the effects of non-tariff barriers have yet been conducted.

CONCLUDING COMMENTS

The same partial equilibrium techniques which we employed to examine the economic effects of tariff interventions can be applied to non-tariff interventions. As well as permitting us to identify the effects of a number of instruments, the analysis also facilitated a comparison of some of these instruments with the tariff. From such comparisons there is an economic case for ranking the tariff as a superior instrument to the quota and VER. Despite this, these instruments have become increasingly popular in recent years for reasons which we will discuss in the next chapter.

NOTES ON FURTHER READING

One of the most authoritative sources on the identification, effects and extent of non-tariff barriers is Baldwin's (1970) text. This is well supplemented by the much briefer and less rigorous review provided by Curzon and Curzon-Price (1970) and Hindley's (1972) review of non-tariff barriers in the United Kingdom. Krauss (1979) also provides some analysis of the economic effects of non-tariff barriers.

A more detailed review of subsidies can be found in Malmgren (1977) and Balassa and Sharpston (1977), while the most authoritative review of tariff quotas is provided by Rom (1979).

8 The Emergence of the New Protectionism

In Chapters 3 and 4 we examined the mechanics of tariff interventions. Such instruments are traditionally viewed as the principal method of intervention in international markets. In our review of post-war trade liberalisation in Chapter 5, however, we saw that where developed market economies (DMEs) are concerned, the tariff has become less important over the post-war period. Successive Rounds of GATT negotiations have resulted in average nominal tariffs being reduced to relatively low levels on manufactured goods.

This is not, of course, to argue that such instruments are unimportant *per se*. Single-figure nominal tariffs can still affect competitiveness at the margin, and since many import-competing firms often operate at the margin, even low rates can have a protective impact. Anyway, our analysis of nominal and effective tariff rates illustrated that even when nominal rates on a given commodity are relatively low, effective rates can be relatively high because of the phenomenon of tariff escalation. Thus, despite the impact of GATT Rounds of tariff liberalisation, the tariff should not be regarded as a redundant instrument in DMEs, especially in relation to agricultural products.

Recent developments in the principal DMEs, however, have resulted in the importance of the tariff as an instrument of trade policy being challenged. Employment pressures in Western markets in the 1970s have been met by widespread protectionist pressures and actions, as similar pressures were met in the 1930s. The important qualitative difference between the two periods is that recently relatively little use has been made of the tariff. Instead we have witnessed a widespread proliferation of non-tariff interventions – quantitative restrictions, subsidisation and discriminatory administrative procedures – which have collectively become known as the 'new protectionism'. 'New' applies here in both a chronological sense and to distinguish the instruments employed from those used in the 'old protectionism'. Table 7.1 outlines the instruments we will be discussing.

DYNAMIC COMPARATIVE ADVANTAGE AND STRUCTURAL UNEMPLOYMENT

The analysis of trends in aggregate trade flows is an exercise fraught with dangers. Although it enables us to paint a picture with a very broad brush, and therefore to focus on the essential general features, we must inevitably do so at the cost of ignoring the particular. In considering broad structural changes which have taken place in the exchange of goods between less developed countries (LDCs) and developed market economies (DMEs), we are inevitably taking a broad perspective, and no doubt in the process we will ignore many factors which impinge on changes in the structure of LDC-DME trade, but which are peculiar to certain countries. This is unfortunately the price we must pay for generality. The student interested in a more detailed analysis should consult Morton and Tulloch (1977) or Blackhurst *et al.* (1978).

Trends in comparative advantage in manufactures

The period from 1948 to 1973 seems to have been a period of quite unprecedented expansion for the world economy, with output and trade growing faster (and more consistently) than in any previously recorded period, and certainly by comparison with the post-1973 period. Specifically, global output expanded at an annual average rate of 5 per cent, while the growth of exports was even higher at 7 per cent per annum (Blackhurst *et al.*, 1977).

This provided an economic climate generally conducive to trade liberalisation and, as we have seen, it was against this backcloth that the 'old protectionism' was dismantled.

With the benefit of hindsight it is possible to focus on a number of fundamental structural changes which were taking place over this period, the most profound change from our point of view being the shift away from a traditional dependence on exports of primary products, to an increasing commitment to exports of manufactured goods on the part of a number of LDCs.

Although we are dealing with general trends, we can be somewhat more specific here with respect to:

(1) *Timing*. Although a small number of LDCs (e.g. India, Pakistan and Japan)[1] demonstrated an increasing propensity to export manufactures (principally textile products) in the 1950s, the developments we are referring to occurred principally in the 1960s and 1970s.

(2) *Product coverage*. By 'manufactures' we are referring to a rela-

tively limited product coverage. We are not referring to the entire range of manufactured goods (groups 5,6,7 and 8 of the Standard Industrial Trade Classification) but to a range of 'low technology' manufactures, for instance textiles, clothing, footwear, sportswear, cutlery, toys, etc. - in other words, the type of standardised manufacture which can be produced using a relatively (unskilled) labour-intensive production technology.

(3) *Country coverage*. Following World Bank conventions (World Bank, 1980) at least ninety LDCs can be identified. Of these countries the most successful exporters of manufactures have been a relatively small band of so-called newly industrialising countries (NICs). Although no definitive list of NICs exists, most commentators would agree that it includes such countries as Hong Kong, Taiwan, Korea, Singapore, Brazil, India, Mexico, Malaysia, the Philippines and the Mediterranean countries of Europe, Greece, Portugal, Spain, Yugoslavia and Turkey.

Thus in referring to the growth of exports of manufactures from LDCs we are referring primarily to the growth of exports of certain standardised manufactures from the NICs during the 1960s and 1970s.

As new suppliers enter a given market, it is not of course *inevitable* that existing suppliers are displaced: new suppliers may be marginal entrants in the sense that they supply increments to an expanding market. This to some extent has been the case where NIC supplies of manufactures are concerned, i.e. they have taken advantage of expanding markets in the DMEs and of course at home. Undoubtedly, however, NIC expansion has been associated with contraction of production capacity in many product groups. The precise implications of this latter development we will consider in due course. In the meantime we can give some quantitative meaning to these changes. Table 8.1 compares the structure of merchandise exports for the principal NICs between 1960 and 1977. As we can see, there has been a fundamental change in structure, with, broadly speaking, a shift away from primary products towards manufactures. Furthermore, this is not a change in the composition of a static basket of exports. As we can see from the first column, in all cases except Pakistan merchandise exports increased steadily (in some cases, e.g. Korea, spectacularly) over the period 1960-78.

Table 8.2 gives details of the change in LDCs' shares of total OECD imports of certain commodities between 1963 and 1977. Again we can see that growth has been concentrated in a relatively narrow range of product groups and has been dominated by the NICs.

This increasing propensity to specialise in, and export, manufactured goods is of course the outcome of the process of dynamic comparative advantage. Industries such as textiles, clothing, footwear and

TABLE 8.1 Commodity composition and growth of merchandise exports for selected NICs

Country	Average % change p.a. in exports 1970–8	Percentage shares of merchandise exports					
		Primary commodities		Textiles & clothing		Other manufactures	
		1960	1977	1960	1977	1960	1977
Spain	11.0	78	29	7	6	15	65
Singapore	9.8	74	56	5	5	21	39
Greece	13.1	90	50	1	18	9	32
Hong Kong	4.8	20	4	45	46	35	50
Brazil	6.0	95	74	0	4	5	22
Korea	28.8	86	15	8	32	8	53
Malaysia	5.2	94	83	0	2	6	15
Philippines	5.4	96	75	1	5	3	20
Pakistan	−1.3	73	41	23	44	4	15
India	6.0	55	44	35	20	10	36
Israel	10.6	39	20	8	7	63	73
Yugoslavia	4.8	63	31	4	8	33	61

Source: Adapted from World Bank (1980) tables 8 and 9.

TABLE 8.2   **OECD imports of manufactures from newly industrialising countries**

Commodity group	% of total imports of manufactures from NICs	
	1963	1977
All manufactures	2.6	8.1
Paper	0.3	2.2
Chemicals	2.1	2.5
Machinery (other than electric)	0.3	2.8
Transport equipment	1.0	2.8
Iron and steel	1.3	4.8
Non-metallic mineral manufactures	2.7	4.9
Manufactures of metal	1.5	7.4
Rubber manufactures	0.5	7.5
Textiles	5.7	10.8
Miscellaneous finished manufactures	4.2	11.2
Electrical machinery	0.8	12.0
Wood and cork manufactures	12.3	23.8
Leather, footwear and travel goods	7.2	31.3
Clothing	17.3	38.5

Source: Adapted from OECD (1979b) tables 4 and 5.

basic engineering activities were initially developed in the DMEs.
During the post-war period the technological know-how associated
with these activities has diffused from DMEs to LDCs. In consequence,
comparative advantage has shifted in the manner suggested by
Vernon's product cycle model which we met in Chapter 1. Given the
technological know-how, LDCs are in a position to benefit from their
relatively abundant factor, namely labour. We have really only
dynamised the basic Heckscher-Ohlin paradigm by introducing 'knowledge capital', in order to explain how comparative advantage can shift
from 'North' to 'South'. This shifting comparative advantage is a
crucial element in explaining the emergence of the 'new protectionism'.

Adjustment and structural unemployment

This process of shifting comparative advantage must inevitably have
employment displacement consequences in the DMEs, both as a direct
outcome of the replacement of DME supplies with LDC sources and
as an indirect effect of competitive pressures which are placed on
DME suppliers.

Direct employment displacement is quite straightforward, and
simply follows from the change in supply as marginal firms in DMEs
are forced to leave the market. 'Indirect' employment displacement is
more subtle, and frequently goes unrecognised by protectionist

pressure groups. Broadly speaking, the source of uncompetitiveness in the DME import-competing sectors is relatively expensive labour—relative, that is, to factor prices in the LDCs. (It has to be emphasised that this is not a value judgement based on any notion about what labour 'should' be paid in DMEs. It is simply the outcome of differing factor endowments.) In order to become competitive, output per unit of labour in the 'typical' DME has to increase to reduce wage costs per unit. In other words, productivity has to increase, and as this process occurs (for a given market share) employment decreases.

Such developments are, of course, an integral part of capturing the gains from trade. In terms of the model we developed in Chapter 1, these are the employment consequences of moving around the production frontier. In a smoothly operating economy, specialisation would result in resources being transferred from the contracting (import substitute) sector to the expanding (export and/or non-traded goods) sectors. If, however, the expanding sectors are growing too slowly to accommodate displaced factors, or if they demand factors in the wrong proportion (e.g. if they are capital-intensive), or if there are rigidities which frustrate the growth of export-oriented activities (e.g. occupational/geographical barriers to the mobility of labour), then some factors may become unemployed on a long-term basis. In other words, structural unemployment may emerge.

Thus the growth of manufactured exports from LDCs, structural unemployment in the DMEs and the growth of the new protectionism are all related. This is not the same thing as saying that the LDCs, or more specifically the NICs, are culpable for any structural unemployment in the DMEs.

Cyclical unemployment and protectionist pressures

We have already noted that over the period 1948–73, global output increased by 5 per cent and global exports by 7 per cent per annum. Clearly, economies in general must have been becoming more open in the process. Over this period, adjustment to imports in general, and imports of manufactures from LDCs in particular, does not seem to have been too much of a problem. Again we emphasise that this is a generalisation to which there are likely to be any number of exceptions. The point is that output and trade were growing at a sufficiently high and sustained rate to ensure that the employment-creating effects of international exchange and specialisation were outweighing any employment-displacing effects. Although we cannot equate 'labour-shedding' industries with import-competing sectors, or 'labour-absorbing' industries with export-oriented sectors, Table 8.3 broadly

TABLE 8.3   Contribution of 'labour-absorbing' and 'labour-shedding' industries
to annual average growth rates of manufacturing employment

Country	Labour-absorbing industries		Labour-shedding industries	
	1963–70	1973–7	1963–70	1973–7
Australia	2.9	0.0	−0.2	−2.9
Belgium	0.9	0.0	−0.5	−3.4
Canada	2.3	0.3	0.0	−0.9
Denmark	1.3	0.0	−0.3	−4.0
Finland	2.7	0.4	0.0	−0.9
France	1.5	0.1	−0.4	−0.9
Germany	1.2	0.1	−0.5	−2.1
Italy	1.3	1.0	−0.1	−0.2
Japan	3.1	0.2	0.0	−3.3
Norway	1.7	2.5	−0.4	−0.9
United Kingdom	0.0	0.0	−1.0	−1.6
USA	1.9	0.1	0.0	−0.7

Source: Adapted from OECD (1979b).

illustrates this tendency for the years 1963–70. The outcome of this
is that the benefits of trade were relatively obvious, and by and large
consumers and producers were willing acquiescers to the trade liberalisation process.[2] Protectionist pressures were specific rather than
general.[3]

We can also see from Table 8.3 that the period immediately following 1973 (1973–7) provides a stark contrast to the earlier period. The
connection between the upward administration of crude oil prices and
recession in the DMEs in the mid-1970s, followed by some years of
'energy-constrained growth', is well documented, and it is not something which we need to examine in any great detail. For our purposes
we may merely note that there was a dramatic rise in unemployment
in the DMEs. Although unemployment rates were already showing a
tendency to move on to a higher trend in the late 1960s and early
1970s in a number of DMEs (e.g. the United Kingdom, the USA,
France and the Netherlands), the suddenness of the increase in the
mid-1970s brought employment to the centre of political debate.

This is the final link in the story we have been trying to piece
together. The importance of recession was to focus the attention of
pressure groups on the perceived connection between foreign trade
and domestic employment. To be more accurate, the effect was to
focus attention on the link between employment displacement and

import penetration. Employment preservation by restricting entry of imports became quite widely viewed as a means of preventing unemployment from rising to 'politically unacceptable' levels (whether nationally or regionally).

Where do the LDCs as suppliers of manufactures fit in? In Tables 8.1 and 8.2 we tried to give some indication of the increasing importance of LDCs as suppliers of manufactures. These figures were deliberately chosen to highlight in the most dramatic terms the increasing importance of LDCs. It must not be assumed from this that these countries were swamping Western markets with their goods. Overall LDCs still only supplied less than 10 per cent of total OECD imports of manufactures in 1980. Furthermore, the DMEs showed a healthy surplus in trade in manufactures with LDCs: $45 billion in 1977 (exports of $75 billion, imports of $30 billion). For the 'typical' DME, LDCs were still relatively unimportant suppliers of manufactures when compared to other DMEs.

Nevertheless, LDCs became the target of a great deal of protectionist pressure in DMEs. This followed from the points we made early in this chapter relating to the commodity composition of LDC manufactured exports, and the countries concerned. Since the industrial bases of even the more advanced LDCs are relatively narrow, and since their exporting effort was concentrated in a relatively narrow range of goods, the success of particular LDCs in particular markets made them an obvious 'scapegoat' for rising unemployment. A clear connection could be drawn between employment displacement and import penetration in particular sectors, irrespective of whether the two were causally related, or if so how strongly. (As we have already noted, most empirical research suggests that productivity change is a more important influence on employment displacement than import growth.)

To summarise the argument so far, then:

1. Dynamic comparative advantage resulted in a shift of competitiveness for many low technology manufactures from DMEs to LDCs.
2. While output in the OECD countries was growing, this appeared to create relatively few adjustment difficulties.
3. Recession in the early 1970s raised cyclical unemployment to historically high levels, and made structurally unemployed resources more apparent and more difficult to absorb.
4. Increased unemployment in the West generated increased pressures for protectionism.
5. The concentration of LDC exports in particular markets focused attention on these countries.

THE NEW PROTECTIONISM

A similar combination of circumstances, i.e. high cyclical unemployment and import penetration, had obtained before and acted as a
catalyst to protectionist pressures – most dramatically in the 1930s.
After all, foreign producers are unrepresented, consumers of imports
under-represented and protectionism is frequently a politically expedient option. The 1970s is no different from the 1930s in that respect.
What characterises the 1970s, however, is the increasing use of non-
tariff instruments. We will now make some attempt to explain why
non-tariff interventions were used in preference to tariff interventions
over this period.

GATT escape clauses

The single most important factor in explaining the different protectionist instruments employed in the 1930s and 1970s is the existence
of a set of rules and regulations in the latter period. The introduction
of GATT in 1948 provided a set of rules proscribing the use of quantitative restrictions and facilitating trade liberalisation. In general,
once quantitative restrictions were removed, or tariffs reduced, they
could not be unilaterally reimposed or raised.

As we have already seen, however, the GATT Articles do provide
for the introduction of restraints under certain designated circumstances. For example, Article XII permits the imposition of import
controls to relieve *temporary* balance-of-payments pressures, and this
particular clause has been invoked on a few notable occasions – in
1964 in the United Kingdom, and President Nixon's 10 per cent surcharge in 1971. Article VI permits the use of restrictions against goods
which are 'dumped' on the home market. Most important from our
point of view, however, is Article XIX, which condones the use of
import controls for the emergency protection of domestic industry.[4]
The idea behind this clause is that if the domestic import-substitute
industry faces actual or threatened 'serious injury' due to a sudden
surge of imports, quantitative restrictions can be imposed on the imported product.

As Table 8.4 indicates, recourse to these escape clauses became increasingly prevalent in the 1970s, as the principal DMEs made more
frequent use of the protectionist option. This table understates quite
considerably, however, the extent of protectionist actions over this
period because recourse to the escape clauses, in particular Article XIX,
was rather limited. Countries taking the protectionist option found
that illegal or extra-legal alternatives suited their purposes rather better

TABLE 8.4   Actions to restrict imports, 1971-7

Country	Year and number of actions						
	1971	1972	1973	1974	1975	1976	1977
USA	6	18	12	9	5	26	16
EEC	5	9	6	4	23	13	41
Canada	5	4	7	8	17	22	35
Total	16	31	25	21	45	61	92

Source: Compiled from Nowzad (1978) tables 2, 3 and 4, pp. 28, 29, 31, 33.

than the use of Article XIX. The reason for this derives from the fundamental GATT principles of non-discrimination and reciprocity.

As we saw in Chapter 5, non-discrimination means that if a tariff concession is negotiated between any two contracting parties, the concession is automatically extended to all contracting parties. Reciprocity means that the party to whom the concession is made should reciprocate by making similar or equivalent concessions. These principles however, do not only apply to trade liberalisation, but also to trade restriction. Thus if a particular country wishes to take action under Article XIX, this action must be non-discriminatory and cannot be applied to any exporting country in particular. Following the reciprocity principle, the party facing the import controls has a right to claim compensation for any action taken.

These provisions are central to the explanation of a reluctance to use Article XIX, and a willingness to look for alternatives outside the GATT framework. In many cases the threat of 'serious injury' was perceived as emanating from a particular LDC supplier rather than suppliers in general. The negotiation of a 'voluntary export restraint' permitted action to be taken on a discriminatory basis, a facility unavailable under Article XIX. As we noted earlier, because of a somewhat narrow industrial base, many LDCs tend to concentrate their efforts in particular commodities which may make them an obvious target for protectionist pressure. More often than not, however, the use of alternatives to Article XIX is a reflection of crude bargaining power. It would be politically more complicated and there would be a greater risk of retaliation if controls were general and non-discriminatory, as opposed to particular suppliers being selected for action.

Similar remarks can be made with respect to reciprocity. The possibility of having to make compensation arrangements reduces the incentives to use Article XIX *per se*. Again, however, if non-discriminatory arrangements are made, some of the countries facing import controls might be important trading partners who do have the necessary bargaining power to secure compensation.

Alternatives to escape clause action

Thus, in order to appease pressure groups at home (an important electoral objective to the vote-maximising government) while at the same time doing little to impair export prospects (by not offending important trading partners and therefore not risking retaliation) the line of least resistance is frequently taken. If overt controls are used, then they take the form of extra-legal interventions like the voluntary export restraint. Alternatively, any intervention can be hidden. Customs valuation procedures could be made unnecessarily complicated to create uncertainty for potential importers and discourage imports. Imports could be controlled on health, safety or environmental grounds where the regulations are drafted in order to discriminate against imported commodities. Intervention could be via subsidies rather than tariffs or import controls. Use of export subsidies is proscribed by GATT, but there are many methods of providing hidden subsidies to exporters (see Malmgren, 1977). Government procurement policies could deliberately discriminate in favour of domestic suppliers (see Table 7.1).

This list is meant to be illustrative rather than exhaustive. The point to note is that the system seemed to encourage the use of such instruments, and there is a great deal of evidence to suggest that the new protectionism spread quickly, and as a result the proportion of total trade which was 'managed' in some way or other rose dramatically in the 1970s. A glance forward to Table 9.2 on p.167 gives some idea of how extensive this management became, and how its importance increased, particularly in those markets where LDCs are important suppliers of manufactured exports.

CONCLUDING REMARKS

This brief chapter has been directed at outling the circumstances under which the 'new protectionism' emerged and flourished in the 1970s. The chapter has been concerned with broad trends, which means of course that the remarks made may not apply to the particular circumstances of particular countries at particular times. It is, however, important to consider these broad trends because an appreciation of the historical background is central to considering any constrasts between the generally liberal trends in trade policy over the period 1948–70 and the more protectionist complexion of the period 1970–80. Furthermore, a historical perspective is also essential to any analysis of the dramatic change in the instruments of trade policy which took place in the 1970s. Some familiarity with the back-cloth to the emergence of the new protectionism will also prove useful when we consider reform of the GATT system in our final chapter.

NOTES ON FURTHER READING

Morton and Tulloch (1977) and Yeats (1979) provide a more detailed review of the increasing importance of LDC export of manufactures, while Balassa (1977) and the OECD (1979b) specifically investigate the economic implications of shift-ing comparative advantage. A most thorough and informative analysis of the growth of protectionist pressures in a particular sector (textiles and clothing) can be found in Keesing and Wolf (1980).

The historical background to the new protectionism can be further studied in Nowzad (1978), Greenaway and Milner (1979) and Balassa (1978), while Robertson (1977) focuses specifically on the role of GATT safeguard provisions. A collection of interesting papers relating to the general historical context can be found in Amacher, Haberler and Willett (1979).

9 The Extent and Consequences of the New Protectionism

In this chapter we shall endeavour to gain some indication of the extent to which non-tariff barriers affect international exchange. This is a somewhat challenging prospect for one very good reason, namely that the essence of the new protectionism is that many of the instruments employed are 'hidden' barriers. As we saw in Chapter 7, a desire to avoid formal recourse to Article XIX influenced the decision of a number of countries to negotiate voluntary export restraints, or to give production subsidies. By their very nature, it is difficult to gauge the proliferation of such interventions accurately, let alone their economic effects.

Nevertheless, a number of international organisations do attempt to keep an inventory of non-tariff restrictions. In addition, an increasing number of studies have attempted to estimate the economic effects of non-tariff barriers. Our task in this chapter will be to review this literature as a means of gaining some idea of the role which non-tariff interventions now play in commercial policy. We will commence by examining the evidence accumulated by various researchers on the volume of trade subject to non-tariff interventions. Following this we will comment on studies aimed at establishing the restrictiveness of non-tariff barriers. Finally, we will focus more specifically on a sector which has been subject to widespread non-tariff intervention over the post-war period, namely textiles and clothing.

THE PATTERN OF NON-TARIFF INTERVENTIONS

A number of international organisations monitor developments in commercial policy and maintain an inventory of non-tariff interventions which is updated on a regular basis. Such records, for example, are maintained by the IMF, UNCTAD, the office of the Special Trade Representative of the USA and GATT.[1] Typically these organisations rely on reports from affected parties but they also monitor trade journals, official communiqués, etc., in order to compile an inventory of protectionist measures. Clearly, any such inventory is bound to be incomplete and will inevitably understate the spread of non-tariff barriers, simply because many actions are unreported. Nevertheless, the inventories provide valuable source material on the use of non-tariff interventions. Much of the information is collected at a relatively disaggregated level, and its availability facilitates the development of a fairly detailed picture of recent developments.

Our first interest lies in ascertaining whether the available data suggest any notable pattern to the incidence of non-tariff barriers (NTBs). As we saw in Chapter 8, the spread of the 'new protectionism' appears to be associated with difficulties faced by developed market economies in adjusting to shifts in comparative advantage to LDCs during a period of surplus capacity. Without offering much in the way of corroborative evidence in Chapter 8, we suggested that non- tariff barriers are becoming increasingly more common. Furthermore, we suggested that they tend to be applied relatively more to commodities in which LDCs enjoy a comparative advantage. Proceeding from this, there are a number of interrelated questions which we can seek to answer by reference to available evidence. First, is there any apparent pattern to the commodity incidence of NTBs, and recent changes in that incidence? Second, is there any evidence to suggest that NTBs do tend to discriminate against the exports of LDCs? Finally, if one of the motive forces behind increasing recourse to NTBs is a desire to avoid Article XIX, is the use of NTBs a substitute for the use of TBs?

Commodity incidence

A number of researchers have processed the material available in the inventories in order to examine the commodity incidence of NTBs. Walter and Chung (1972), for instance, compute a 'weighted mean non-tariff factor' as a summary statistic for comparing the incidence of NTBs across product groups. Their index is given by equation (9.1):

$$NTBF_j = \frac{1}{n} \sum_{i=1}^{n} \frac{\sum\limits_{j} p_{ij} M_j}{M} \cdot 100 \qquad (9.1)$$

where n refers to the number of developed market economies under consideration, P_{ij} is the number of five-digit SITC commodities in a given two-digit division which are subject to NTBs in country i. M_j refers to OECD imports of the commodity. Thus the measure gives an indication of the proportion of five-digit commodities which are subject to NTBs in developed market economies, weighted by OECD imports, and averaged across all DMEs. It is therefore a weighted frequency measure. The results of Walter and Chung's calculations for 1970 are summarised in Table 9.1.

TABLE 9.1   Frequency of non-tariff barriers by commodity group: imports into OECD countries, 1970

SITC	Product group	NTBF	SITC	Product group	NTBF
01	Processed meat	78.9	57	Explosives	1.8
			58	Plastics	13.2
03	Processed fish	40.0	59	Miscellaneous	
04	Cereal products	32.8		chemicals	22.7
05	Prepared fruit products	55.8	61	Leather manufactures	8.6
			62	Rubber manufactures	14.9
06	Sugar confectionery	43.6	63	Wood and cork	
				manufactures	5.5
07	Processed coffee, tea and		64	Paper and paperboard	
	cocoa	27.9		manufactures	2.9
09	Miscellaneous prepared				
	foodstuffs	46.5	65	Textile manufactures	25.7
11	Beverages	79.1			
			66	Mineral manufactures	3.5
12	Processed tobacco	73.9	67	Iron and steel	
				products	22.6
23	Synthetic and recl.		68	Non-ferrous metal	
	rubber	0.2		manufactures	2.3
			69	Miscellaneous metal	
24	Sawn and shaped wood	3.6		manufactures	6.3
			71	Non-electric	
25	Pulp and waste paper	0.0		machinery	6.3
26	Textile fibres	0.0	72	Electric machinery	54.3
33	Petroleum products	33.8	73	Transport equipment	32.7
			81	Construction equip-	
34	Gas	1.8		ment	12.8
35	Electric energy	1.8	82	Furniture	0.0
			83	Travel goods and	
43	Processed oils and fats	14.5		accessories	0.0
51	Chemical elements	20.6	84	Clothing	68.7
52	Tar and crude derivatives	10.7	85	Footwear	29.1
53	Dyes	10.8	86	Precision instruments	8.6
			89	Miscellaneous	
54	Medicinal products	38.9		manufactures	6.7
55	Perfumes and toiletries	10.6			

Source: Adapted from Walter and Chung (1972) table I, pp. 127–8.

From Table 9.1 we can see that basic commodities and foodstuffs are heavily subjected to NTBs. This is very much as we would expect, given the significant protection accorded to agricultural sectors in developed market economies. The incidence for manufactured products (broadly speading, SITCs 51-89) is somewhat less. Notably, however, an above average incidence is clear in certain basic manufactures (footwear, clothing and textiles) and heavy industry (iron and steel, transport equipment).

The frequency index does have an obvious limitation, namely that it gives no indication of the volume of trade actually affected by NTBs since it focuses on an index of the number of actions taken. Using the same data, however, it is possible to compute a 'coverage index':

$$C_j = \frac{M_{Bj}}{M_j} \cdot 100 \tag{9.2}$$

where M_{Bj} refers to the value of imports of commodity j which are subject to NTBs, while M_j refers to the total value of imports of commodity j. Like $NTBF_j$, C_j is a summary statistic. On this occasion, however, affected imports as a proportion of total imports is the focus of attention. A number of studies have computed coverage ratios to ascertain the influence of NTBs. Tables 9.2 and 9.3 present some information from Page's 1981 and 1979 studies respectively.

Although the commodity groupings are more highly aggregated than in Table 9.1, a number of significant features are discernible. First of all, we might note that in those sectors where trade is traditionally 'managed'[2] (i.e. agricultural commodities and foodstuffs) a high proportion of total trade was affected by NTBs in both 1974 and 1979. In addition, however, it is clear that there was little change in the levels between 1974 and 1979.

When we separate out manufactures from 'all goods' in Table 9.2, and examine more specifically the product groups in the lower part of Table 9.3, we observe a dramatic change in the extent to which trade in manufactures is managed. From Table 9.2 we can see that for most DMEs in 1974, the proportion of trade in manufactures which was managed was extremely low, zero in many cases. By 1980, however, these shares had grown markedly to an average of 16 per cent for the EEC countries and 17 per cent for the OECD countries. If we refer to Table 9.3, we see that there are only a few manufacturing activities for which the proportion of total trade which was 'managed' in 1979 exceeded 30 per cent. Significantly, however, those that do enter this category are either standardised manufactures, where LDCs have developed a comparative advantage in recent years (footwear, clothing,

TABLE 9.2   Managed trade* by country

Country	All goods			Manufactures		
	1974	1979	1980	1974	1979	1980
Belgium/Luxembourg	27.5	33.4	34.0	0.7	9.1	10.0
Denmark	29.5	42.8	43.2	0	21.1	21.7
France	32.8	42.6	42.7	0	16.0	16.2
Germany	37.3	47.1	47.3	0	17.9	18.3
Ireland	26.8	33.5	34.0	1.5	11.0	11.7
Italy	44.1	52.2	52.3	0	16.1	16.4
Netherlands	32.5	39.8	40.1	0	12.8	14.8
United Kingdom	38.5	47.4	47.9	0.2	17.0	17.4
EEC (9)†	35.8	44.5	44.8	0.1	15.7	16.1
Australia	17.9	34.8	34.8	7.8	30.0	30.0
Austria	20.8	30.3	30.3	0	13.1	13.1
Canada	22.4	18.3	18.3	11.4	5.8	5.8
Finland	32.9	33.6	33.6	3.1	3.5	3.5
Japan	56.1	59.4	59.4	0	4.3	4.3
Norway	16.3	33.7	33.7	0	24.6	24.6
Sweden	24.7	36.3	36.3	3.1	19.4	19.4
Switzerland	16.9	18.3	18.3	2.1	3.4	3.4
USA	36.2	44.4	45.8	5.6	18.4	21.0
OECD (22)†	36.3	43.8	44.3	4.0	16.8	17.4
Oil exporters (15)†	54.0	65.3	65.3	45.8	59.8	59.8
Non-oil LDCs (81)†	49.8	46.8	46.9	25.0	22.7	22.8
World (122)†	40.1	47.5	47.8	12.9	23.0	23.6

Notes: * as a proportion of 1974 trade, † number of countries in parentheses.

Source: Adapted from Page (1981) table 1, p. 29.

textiles, etc.), or heavy industry where a combination of structural change and cyclical pressures have generated particularly acute adjustment problems (iron and steel, shipbuilding). Furthermore, it is in these sectors that the most marked increases in managed trade took place between 1974 and 1979. These appear to be the sectors which are in the vanguard of the advance of the new protectionism.

From these studies there does appear to be a non-random commodity incidence of NTBs. Levels of incidence appear to be highest in those sectors which are traditionally protected, such as agriculture; while the highest rates of growth of protectionist actions seem to be

TABLE 9.3   Commodities in which importers controlled more than 30 per cent of trade in 1979

Commodity	Share of trade controlled (%)	
	1974	1979
Live animals	64	64
Fish	30	31
Cereals	76	76
Fruit and vegetables	70	78
Confectionery	43	43
Cocoa	56	56
Chocolate	62	62
Tea	66	64
Animal feeding stuffs	69	69
Miscellaneous food	49	48
Non-alcoholic beverages	57	58
Silk fibres	6	71
Textiles	21	35
Lime and cement	32	35
Iron and steel	16	66
Aircraft	12	83
Ships	18	82
Clothing	20	48
Footwear	1	32

Source: Adapted from Page (1979) table 7.6, p. 176.

recorded in sectors where comparative advantage is shifting. The evidence presented here is highly selective, but not unrepresentative. Other work suggests a similar commodity pattern (see, for example, Walter, 1972; Murray and Walter, 1977: Yeats, 1979).

Coverage ratios are, of course, summary statistics, and as such they have a number of limitations, the most obvious and probably most important being that they tell us nothing about the restrictiveness of particular NTBs. Thus where NTBs are protective and influence measured trade, C_j will be distorted. (The restrictiveness of NTBs is something which we will comment on in greater detail shortly.)

Country incidence

We have implied that the commodity incidence identified above says something about country incidence. Specifically, it has been suggested (in Chapter 8 as well as in this chapter) that the incidence of NTBs tends to be heaviest in those markets where LDCs are becoming in-

creasingly important exporters. The implication is that NTBs differentially affect LDCs. We must, however, examine this question in
greater detail. Even if the greatest increase in NTBs did take place in
those commodities in which LDCs have an increasing export interest,
it does not automatically follow that there is differential treatment
between LDCs and non-LDCs. All imports of the sensitive product
could be subject to the NTBs, irrespective of origin.

An early study by Allen and Walter (1970) exploring this very
question suggested that LDCs bore a disproportionate burden of NTBs
for a combination of reasons. First, in the case of quotas, they frequently found that licences were allocated in favour of 'traditional'
sources, which tended to work against the interests of LDCs. Second,
with respect to government procurement, they found that the practice
of limited circulation of tender invitations, short bidding times and
tied aid all appeared to have a disproportionate impact on LDCs.
Third, they found that import deposit schemes and advance credit
requirements frequently disadvantaged exporters with weak financial
backing, i.e. LDCs. Finally, it was found that LDCs may have been
disadvantaged because they were unable fully to comply with the
'destination' principle with respect to tax incidence, i.e. they did not
have the requisite machinery to claw back taxes on exports. To this
list we can add the very obvious point that LDCs tend to be subject
to voluntary export restraints to a much greater degree than developed
market economies, simply because of their weaker bargaining power.
There is a good deal of evidence to support this proposition (see
Nowzad, 1978, for instance).

A number of studies have examined cross-country differences in the
proportion of exports affected by NTBs, the general conclusion of
which appears to be that NTBs do tend to affect LDCs to a greater
extent that they do DMEs, and furthermore they are being affected
to an increasing degree. LDCs have undoubtedly been the principal
'beneficiaries' of the spread of the 'new protectionism' (see Walter and
Chung, 1972; Murray and Walter, 1977; Nowzad, 1978; Page, 1979).
Again, summary material from Page's study can be cited to illustrate
this tendency (Table 9.4).

General features of the pattern of NTBs

By its very nature the foregoing has been a selective review of the pattern of NTBs. Nevertheless, the studies which we have reviewed (and
others which we have not) suggest that a number of general features
can be identified:

TABLE 9.4   **Shares of managed trade in world trade flows, 1970-7 (%)**

	1970	1973	1974	1977
Industrial area imports	36	38	46	44
From industrial countries	26	27	29	27
From non-oil LDCs	52	55	58	62
Share in total trade of:				
Industrial countries	54	52	40	40
Non-oil LDCs	18	17	15	17
Non-oil LDC imports	38	42	47	46
From industrial countries	24	27	29	24
From non-oil LDCs	48	40	45	47
Share in total trade of:				
Industrial countries	42	42	36	30
Non-oil LDCs	13	15	13	15

Source: Adapted from Page (1979) table 7.8, p. 178.

1.   There is a good deal of evidence suggesting a concentration of NTBs in 'sensitive' sectors.
2.   The exports of LDCs tend to bear a disproportionate share of NTBs.

These features are evident from above. A number of other features which are not evident from above but which have been identified are:

3.   Products experiencing a high incidence of NTBs also tend to be products which are subject to relatively high tariffs. Interestingly this suggests that tariff barriers and NTBs are complements rather than substitutes.
4.   The phenomenon of multi-stacking of NTBs has been frequently noted. That is to say, those commodities which are subject to NTBs often have a number of NTBs imposed concurrently, rather than simply being subject to one.

Having commented in general terms about the commodity and country pattern of NTBs, we will now address ourselves to the problem of evaluating the restrictive impact of NTBs.

THE RESTRICTIVENESS OF NON-TARIFF BARRIERS

In Chapter 6 we examined the methodology behind estimating the effect of tariff interventions/liberalisation. Although there were a number of technical and practical difficulties inherent in the technique, the fact that a tariff change was manifested in a price change permitted us to ascertain the consumption and production effects relatively easily. The same cannot unfortunately be said of NTBs. In part this is due to a point which we have repeatedly stressed, namely that many NTBs are hidden. Consequently, the very act of establishing the extent of non-tariff interventions is itself problematic. (This indeed has been the subject of the first part of this chapter.) However, even where we can accurately identify the extent of non-tariff interventions, we still face another difficulty which militates against accurate identification of their restrictiveness: it is most unlikely that the effect of a given NTB (or combination of NTBs) on price will be obvious. If it were obvious, clearly we could easily compute the *ad valorem* tariff equivalent of a given NTB and then apply the methodology of Chapter 6 to gain some idea of its welfare effects. Unfortunately, however, it is not quite so straightforward.

Price differentials approach to NTBs

The Haberler Report (1958) suggested that a rough approximation of the price-distorting effect of NTBs could be gauged by examination of international price differentials. It was suggested that the degree of protection could be estimated as the difference between the price paid to domestic producers and the world price for the comparable commodity. For commodity x, therefore, the effect of all trade distortions on price would be defined as:

$$D_p = P_w - P_D \qquad (9.3)$$

where P_w refers to the world price of the commodity and P_D the price received by domestic producers. Now, it is of course possible that imports of this commodity are also subject to tariffs. This being so, the price which domestic producers receive will be affected by the degree of protection accorded by the tariff structure. If we assumed that domestic price increased to the full extent permitted by the nominal tariff, we could write:

$$P_D = P_w (1 + t) \qquad (9.4)$$

where t is the nominal rate of protection. If we substitute (9.4) into (9.3) we find that the effect of trade distortions on price is equal to the nominal rate of tariff protection. The rationale behind the Haberler suggestion is straightforward, therefore. If $N_T > t$ (and therefore $P_D > P_w (1 + t)$), then the difference is due to non-tariff interventions. If N_T happened to be less than t, it would simply indicate that domestic producers did not fully adjust domestic price to the extent permitted by the tariff on imports. If this procedure is legitimate, then one can compute the *ad valorem* equivalent of NTBs and apply the methodology of Chapter 6 to ascertain the welfare effects.

There are a number of obvious difficulties associated with such an aggregative approach. Once we have adjusted for nominal tariffs, we are left with a residual which is itself likely to be a compound mixture of a number of elements. Non-tariff interventions will, of course, influence its value. So too, however, will quality differences. If the domestic import substitute is a higher quality product that its imported competitors, then a premium may be levied for this. Furthermore, differing tax regimes may influence the residual. If the import substitute sector is only subject to direct taxes (some of which are passed on) while overseas competitors follow the destination principle of taxation and levy indirect taxes which are then rebated to exporters, then this too will influence the residual. Finally, there is the matter of the 'world price' and how this is identified. The simple answer might be that this is equated with the lowest price, and indeed there is a certain amount of good sense in this. It may be, however, that the lowest price is lowest due to the impact of export subsidies, or domestic production subsidies. In this event, the net effect of domestic NTBs could be overestimated.[3]

One of the most comprehensive studies in this tradition is that conducted by Roningen and Yeats (1976). They computed price relatives for a wide range of commodities in which LDCs have an export interest, in fifteen developed market economies. They made some allowances for differences in tax regimes, as well as making an adjustment for transportation charges and nominal tariffs. Using the lowest price for each commodity in the fifteen developed countries covered by the study as a proxy for the world price, the authors estimated that the highest average price differentials occurred in Japan, Sweden, France and the USA. Specifically they concluded that the *average* 'pure NTB residual' was in the range of 50-60 per cent for Japan and Sweden, and 20-25 per cent for France and the USA. A glance back to Tables 5.2 and 5.3 confirms that these rates are considerably in excess of average tariff rates. If, therefore, these estimates come close to the likely order of magnitude, it would serve to confirm the suspicions of many commentators that NTBs are a far more important source of intervention than tariff barriers.

Analysis of specific NTBs

Many researchers have been somewhat less ambitious in their objectives, and have endeavoured to identify the restrictiveness of specific NTBs.

1. *Subsidies.* Subsidies are one of the more intractable NTBs to investigate, primarily because of their heterogeneity. Invariably subsidies come in a variety of opaque forms, ranging from tax concessions to public equity, to loans at 'preferential interest rates'. In practice it is extremely difficult to translate expenditure or disbursement data into a level of subsidy equivalent, i.e. the extent to which various subsidy instruments reduce price. Consequently most studies attempt to establish the effects of subsidisation *ex post*, using various indirect methods. This is essential where a variety of instruments is employed simultaneously. Where a particular subsidy is conferred on a particular sector, it is very much easier to analyse the effects *ex ante* by estimating its effect on price.

One of the indirect methods often employed is to use estimates of effective protection rates. This in fact is what Oulton (1976) did in the study which we reported in Chapter 4. In order to proceed from nominal to effective rates, Oulton estimated the net subsidy accorded to each industry in his sample (i.e. indirect taxes less subsidies). We then gain some idea of the policy-induced changes in value added by sector. A disadvantage with this method is that the calculated effective rate is also bound to be affected by other NTBs. Furthermore, although it does focus on resource allocation effects, it fails to highlight the implications for the export sector.

A more direct method of identifying the trade effects of subsidies is to adopt a more case-study-oriented approach, whereby one attempts first to identify changes in the composition of international trade, and then to establish whether these changes are influenced by the presence of subsidies. A good example of this approach is the study by Denton, O'Cleiricain and Ash (1975), which interestingly found that where the United Kingdon was concerned, there was little evidence to suggest that the pattern of subsidisation affected trade to any significant degree in the early 1970s.

2. *Government procurement.* Estimation of the effects of discriminatory government procurement policies it also problematic. Again, this is in part due to the variety of forms which the instrument can take, and in part due to its hidden nature. There is evidence to suggest that discrimination in the award of government contracts in favour of domestic suppliers is practised in all developed market economies (and

no doubt in LDCs also). It seems, however, that only one government makes the margin of its discrimination clear, namely the USA under the Buy American Act of 1933.

Denton, O'Cleiricain and Ash (1975) examined in some detail the extent of public procurement in the United Kingdom with particular reference to selected industrial sectors. Studies by Baldwin (1970) and Lowinger (1976) actually attempted to evaluate the significance of discriminatory government procurement as a non-tariff barrier in a number of DMEs. Both studies employ a deceptively simple approach to the problem. This involves first of all examining government purchases on a sector-by-sector basis. Second, the average import penetration for each sector is calculated (i.e. the ratio of imports to total supply). Finally, the value of government imports which would exist if the government import penetration ratio were the same as the economy import penetration ratio is calculated, and compared with the actual level of government imports. Any deficiency of the latter over the former is viewed as being due to discriminatory government procurement.

The approach does have some difficulties, not least the assumption that the government propensity to import can be regarded as equal to the propensity to import in the rest of the economy. This is unlikely, given the large proportion on non-tradables consumed by government. In addition, we clearly cannot allow for imports used as intermediate inputs into domestically produced final goods which are purchased by government.

The studies do, however, give some indication of possible orders of magnitude. Particularly significant discrimination is found in the USA, France and the United Kingdom in both studies. Baldwin found that for the USA 'actual' imports were one-sixth of 'predicted' imports in 1958, while Lowinger found that actual amounted to only one-seventh in 1963. Cline *et al.* (1978) estimated that if a 60 per cent reduction in government procurement 'protection'[4] were implemented, the effect on imports would be about one-sixth as large as the increase in imports which could be expected from a corresponding 60 per cent cut in US tariffs. For France and the United Kingdom, it was estimated that a similar liberalisation would increase imports by about one-twelfth of the amount which would follow a 60 per cent tariff cut.

3. *Quantitative restrictions.*   In principle it is more straightforward to calculate the effect of quantitative restrictions (QRs) than either subsidies or government procurement. The most common method in the case of QRs is the price differential approach. Thus the price differential stimulated by a particular QR or group of QRs is computed (in similar fashion to the procedure outlined above). An *ad valorem*

tariff equivalent is then calculated and, using the methodology developed in Chapter 6, one can then estimate import diversion, employment effects, welfare effects, and so on. More work has been completed on QRs than on other NTBs. However, rather than comment on particular studies here, we shall discuss QRs in connection with a more detailed examination of NTBs in a specific sector, namely textiles and clothing.

NON-TARIFF PROTECTION IN THE TEXTILE AND CLOTHING SECTORS

The process of intervention

Production of textiles and clothing is invariably one of the first routes to industrialisation. Consequently it is often the first manufacturing product line in which many LDCs find themselves exporting. In many respects international management of trade in textiles provides a model pattern for the proliferation of NTBs.

Trade in textiles has been actively managed for more than twenty years now. In the 1950s, falling demand generated excess capacity in the textile sectors of the developed market economies, while simultaneously supply increased as the result of developing countries entering the market. Thus, over the period 1953–60, textile exports from DMEs fell by 5 per cent, while exports from LDCs increased by 88 per cent, and from Japan by 155 per cent. Faced with increased import penetration and classic structural adjustment problems, the response of some countries (most notably the United Kingdom) was to negotiate voluntary export restraints with the new suppliers (Japan, Hong Kong and India).

In 1961, however, unilateral action was replaced by a multilateral arrangement designed to deal with 'short-run' problems in the textile sector. This was the Short Term Arrangement on Cotton Textiles (STA) which was negotiated under the auspices of GATT. The objective of the nineteen parties to the Agreement was 'to maintain orderly access' to Western markets while acting 'to secure from exporting countries, where necessary, a measure of restraint in their export policy so as to avoid disruptive effects in import markets'. Market disruption was to be identified by the presence of 'a sharp and substantial increase or potential increase of imports of particular products from particular sources [which results in] serious damage to domestic producers or threat thereof'. Where the latter resulted, the participating importing country could unilaterally impose quota restrictions which contained imports to a level not lower than that which applied to the previous twelve month period.

This short-term arrangement therefore incorporated some important departures from GATT principles. Unilateral action was sanctioned, and this action could take the form of quantitative restraints. Furthermore, the action could be discriminatory. This might not have been viewed with undue alarm had the Short Term Arrangement been truly short term. It did only last for one year but it was immediately 'superseded' by a Long Term Arrangement Regarding International Trade in Cotton Textiles (LTA). The LTA crystallised many of the provisional arrangements of the STA and extended the scope for 'management' by including provisions for control over the growth of imports. In cases where restrictions were to be maintained for more than one year, the quota should be permitted to grow by at least 5 per cent per annum. The LTA was endorsed by some twenty-nine participating countries. Its provisions were altogether more elaborate than those of the STA, not least because some notional measure of 'supervision' was introduced, namely that those countries invoking the market disruption clause were obliged to report annually to the Cotton Textiles Committee. Although the LTA was negotiated for five years and was viewed as an exceptional and transitional measure', it was renewed in 1967 and 1970, ultimately expiring in September 1973.

During the period in which the LTA was in force, a number of significant structural changes took place in the world textile market. First, production of textiles and clothing continued to expand more quickly in LDCs than in DMEs (for the decade 1963-72, 58 per cent for textiles in LDCs, 46 per cent in DMEs; for clothing 66 per cent and 24 per cent respectively). Thus despite the restrictive arrangements, comparative advantage continued to shift. There was also a shift in consumption, however, with increasing substitution of man-made for natural fibres. Thus, when the LTA expired, it was replaced by the Multifibre Arrangement (MFA), which came into force in 1974. This Arrangement has forty-two signatories (with the EEC counting as one) and it extended the arrangements for managing trade to man-made fibres as well as natural fibres.

The MFA again endorsed recourse to quantitative restriction in response to market disruption. However, it also offered clearer guidance on the identification of market disruption, as well as more stringent conditions for the use of QRs. Once imposed, they were to be removed after one year, unless a growth rate of 6 per cent per annum were permitted, or unless they were phased out within three years. A Textiles Surveillance Body was created as a surveillance mechanism and a forum for the settlement of disputes. The Arrangement was extended in January 1978 to remain in force until December 1981. One significant addition to the Arrangement when it was extended was a 'reasonable departures' clause introduced by the EEC which permitted more restrictive measures than those sanctioned by the original MFA.

Some implications of the arrangements

The first thing we may note is the effect of taking an entire sector out of the GATT arrangements. Effectively, special-case status has been accorded to a specific sector, and the principles of GATT which proscribe non-discrimination and which forbid recourse to quantitative restrictions removed. It may be argued that there are sound socio-politico-economic reasons for according special status to textiles, on the grounds perhaps that the industry tends to be geographically concentrated. However, even if such an argument were accepted, one must question whether quota restrictions are conducive to encouraging adjustment. Arguably, by exempting textiles from GATT rules, the conditions for atrophy were created: the transitional arrangements became permanent. Despite the permanence of the arrangements, it is notable that the trend in comparative advantage has continued inexorably. This in turn has contributed to a gradual tightening of the arrangements (notwithstanding the creation of the Textiles Surveillance Board) with product coverage and country coverage widening. As the arrangements have become more restrictive, it seems as if the market has 'kicked-back', as Curzon (1981) puts it. There is, for example, a good deal of evidence of diversification into non-controlled product lines, and/or a reorientation to higher unit value product lines. Furthermore, the possibility of channelling exports through non-controlled third countries has not escaped the attention of LDCs. The pattern seems to accord with experience in other sectors.

What have been the costs and benefits of this elaborate system of arrangements? A recent exhaustive examination of the global textiles market conducted by Keesing and Wolf (1980) sought to provide some answers to these questions. In assessing the implications of quota restrictions in the developed economies (i.e. the quota imposers), they reached the following conclusions:

1. There was widespread evidence of the price-raising effects of quotas. Specifically they concluded that 'There is apparently room to argue that the prices of clothing may be raised by quotas on average by 5 per cent to 10 per cent whenever demand is strong, and much more on low cost items, compared with the price that would prevail with the same tariff but no quota' (p. 107).

2. Higher prices can be translated into an estimate of deadweight loss, using methodology similar to that applied to tariffs in Chapter 6.

A study by the US Council on Wage and Price Stability estimated that for quotas which grew at 6 per cent p.a., the cost to US consumers would be $369.4 million in the first year, rising to $790.6 million in the fifth year. For quotas growing at 3 per cent p.a., the equivalent costs would be $427.2 million and $1,062.6 million – the latter representing a value equivalent to 10 per cent of total consumption.[5]

3. The purpose of protectionism in this sector has, of course, been the preservation of employment. Despite increasing rates of import penetration in the textile and clothing markets of the LDCs, output in the DMEs did continue to grow in the 1970s. Admittedly these activities did not grow as fast as manufacturing in general (which was itself under cyclical pressure). Nevertheless, they continued to expand. One of the reasons why output continued to grow, however, was that productivity grew quite rapidly over the period. This is an important point, which is frequently ignored. Employment change can be associated with changes in net trade positions. The principal source of the change, however, is induced productivity change rather than direct import replacement. This is no more than part of the process of specialisation which we outlined in Chapter 1 when we investigated the opening of trade. In order to compete with exporters with relatively low labour costs, productivity has to rise. Consequently, although output has been maintained over this period, employment has declined.

Since the purpose of the MFA and its predecessors is to smooth the adjustment process and preserve employment, we might be tempted to ask how much of the employment decline is directly due to trade and, by implication, how many jobs have been preserved by restricting imports. Table 9.5 reports the results of a study by Apan *et al.* which suggests that, in all countries apart from the Netherlands, changes in net trade position are relatively unimportant sources of job displacement – relative, that is, to productivity change. Note also that this applies to all trade, *not* just trade with LDCs. This conclusion is supported by a number of other studies which apply to employment change in DMEs.[6] Although it may remain true that rapid import penetration in a particular market at a particular time could generate immediate employment pressure directly, it appears that over the medium to long term, net changes in trade balances are relatively unimportant. The implication, therefore, is that the number of jobs saved by the MFA restrictions has been rather limited. Furthermore, it suggests that any jobs saved may have been preserved at a relatively high cost. Indeed, the Council on Wages and Prices Stability study cited above go so far as actually to place a figure on this of $81,000 per job in the USA.

This is perhaps a convenient point at which to leave textiles for

TABLE 9.5 Effects of changes in demand, productivity and trade balance on apparel employment in seven leading industrial countries, 1970–6

	Number employed in 1970 (thousands)	Net job losses (thousands)	% changes in employment number due to			Job losses from changes in net trade (thousands)
			Domestic demand	Labour productivity	Net trade	
USA	1,376	53	+23.1	−22.1	−4.9	67
West Germany	374	98	+0.5	−19.0	−7.8	29
United Kingdom	333	42	+20.6	−23.7	−9.5	32
France	322	42	+8.0	−18.7	−2.2	7
Italy	207	1	+7.3	−18.7	+10.9	−23
Belgium	77	7	+38.6	−33.2	−15.1	12
Netherlands	49	28	+17.6	−37.0	−38.3	19
Total	2,678	271	+17.1	−21.8	−5.2	143

Source: Apan *et al.* (1978) exhibits 10 and 11.

the present. The whole issue of trade and employment change, and the efficacy of trade policy as an instrument of employment preservation has been thrust to the centre of debate in recent years, and a more general discussion of the issues is warranted.

CONCLUDING COMMENTS

We set out to gain a clearer impression of the features of the new protectionism. In particular, we were interested in the extent to which it influences international exchange, the commodities with which it is most frequently associated, and the countries to which it is most frequently applied. There is no systematic method of accomplishing this, and a good deal of evidence which applies to the proliferation of the new protectionism is qualitative rather than quantitative.

Nevertheless, from the studies which we consulted, there seems to be a consensus that the use of non-tariff interventions is increasing and that developing country exporters of manufactures tend to be more susceptible to NTBs than other developed market economies.

One sector where NTBs are more transparent is the textile and clothing sector. Our brief review of recent commercial policy in this sector served to highlight further a number of features of the new protectionism, as well as giving us further opportunity to consider some of its effects. The issue on which we concluded our review of textiles and clothing, namely employment change, is perhaps the most sensitive and controversial theme of recent trade policy in developed market economies, and it is to a more general consideration of this question in the context of adjustment policy that we turn in Chapter 10.

NOTES ON FURTHER READING

Useful, regular sources of developments in commercial policy can be found in the IMF's *Annual Report on Exchange Restrictions* and GATT's *Developments in Commercial Policy*. Reviews of recent actions which have been taken under the auspices of GATT are provided by Nowzad (1978) and Gard and Reidel (1980). Walter and Chung (1972), Murray and Walter (1977) and Page (1979) all make an attempt to comment on the extent of NTBs. The latter is especially useful. An increasing number of studies evaluating restrictiveness are available. A number which have been conducted by reference to trade with LDCs are noted in Yeats (1979). Cline *et al*. (1978) also consider this issue, with particular reference to the protection of agricultural markets. A growing literature looks specifically at the textile and clothing sectors. Here, however, one is best advised to commence with Keesing and Wolf's (1980) thorough review.

PART IV

Adjustment to Trade Expansion

10 The Economics of Adjustment

Adjustment implies change. Consumers change consumption bundles in response to alterations in real income and relative prices; changes in consumer demand require producers to alter production techniques and vary their demand for productive factors.

Our focus in these final chapters will be on trade-related adjustment problems. This is not to imply that trade is the only, or indeed the most important, source of pressure for adjustment. In fact trade *per se* cannot be regarded as the source of any pressure for adjustment. Rather it is the underlying determinants of changes in comparative advantage - whether these be related to differential factor endowments, differential productivity change, product cycles or preference diversity - which generate pressure for adjustment. The foreign trade sector merely acts as a channel through which the impulses are transmitted.

TRADE-RELATED ADJUSTMENT PRESSURES

The essential characteristics of the 'adjustment problem' can be brought out by reference to a simple trade model. Consider again our basic 2 x 2 x 2 Heckscher-Ohlin-Samuelson model. We will refer to our two countries, A and B, which are differentially endowed with capital and labour. Thus,

$$\left(\frac{K}{L}\right)_A > \left(\frac{K}{L}\right)_B \Rightarrow \left(\frac{P_k}{P_l}\right)_A < \left(\frac{P_k}{P_l}\right)_B$$

Commodity y is relatively labour-intensive, and commodity x relatively capital-intensive:

$$\left(\frac{l}{k}\right)_y > \left(\frac{l}{k}\right)_x \Rightarrow \left(\frac{P_x}{P_y}\right)_A < \left(\frac{P_x}{P_y}\right)_B$$

185

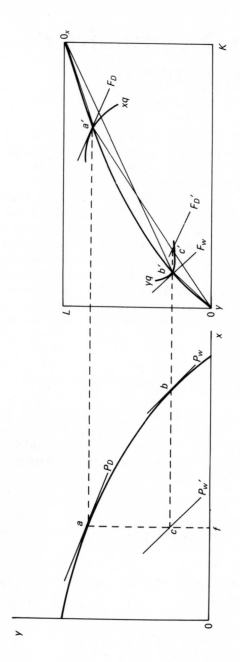

Figure 10.1

In autarky, faced with a relative price ratio of P_D in Figure 10.1, country A produces the output combination denoted by point a on the production frontier. This is consistent with point a' on the contract curve of the Edgeworth Box in the right-hand segment. F_D denotes (pre-trade) relative factor prices. As we would anticipate, capital (labour) is relatively cheap (expensive).

Given the opportunity to trade with B at the world price ratio of P_w, according to the H-O-S theorem, country A would specialise in the production of that commodity which uses its abundant factor intensively, i.e. commodity x. When full adjustment to the altered relative prices had taken place, production would settle at b, on the production frontier, b' in the Edgeworth Box. We are familiar with the characteristics of this equilibrium from Chapter 1. The real rewards of the scarce factor (labour) have fallen, while the real rewards of the abundant factor (capital) have increased. This is clear from the factor price line F_w. Furthermore, although production of y remains more labour-intensive than production of x, in the post-trade equilibrium production of both commodities is *relatively* more labour-intensive. This merely reflects the response of producers to the change in relative factor prices. As capital becomes more expensive to employ, and labour relatively cheaper, there is an incentive to use production methods which employ relatively more of the latter factor, in both sectors. The changes in factor intensities are reflected in the Edgeworth Box by the change in slope from Oxa' and Oya' to Oxb' and Oyb'.

Let us suppose that, for reasons which we will elaborate on in due course, adjustment is resisted. Specifically, let us assume that consumers can exchange at world prices, but producers are unwilling or unable to adjust factor prices. Consumers (at the margin) will switch consumption expenditure away from domestically produced y towards y imported from country B. Similarly, producers of x in country A will take advantage of more profitable export opportunities. Some international exchange will take place therefore as a result of adjustments in product markets.

If factor prices do not alter, however, this will have important implications for output. Output will contract in the y sector. Since exchange takes place at the relative price ratio P_w $(= P_w')$ output contracts from fa to fc. Because factor prices are fixed, however, no expansion of output takes place in the x sector. All that occurs here is a reallocation of output, with a proportion being exported (to pay for imports of y). Producers of x continue to face the factor price ratio of F_D and remain on isoquant xq, which is consistent with a level of output which would result given full adjustment in both sectors, but since y producers face a factor price ratio of F_D' $(=\!|FD)$ rather than F_w, the output mix does not coincide with a point on the contract curve.

In this model, the failure of relative factor prices to respond to changes in demand is the source of the 'adjustment problem'. The lack of flexibility in factor rewards prevents factor intensities from changing; this in turn prevents the export sector from expanding to absorb factors displaced in the import substitute sector. An underemployment 'equilibrium' is reached, with a contracted import substitute sector and a 'locked in' export sector. There is underemployment of both labour and capital, and a reliance on relatively inefficient production methods because factor intensities remain at pre-trade levels. (Oya' and $Oxa' = Oyc'$ rather than Oyb' and Oxb').

Factor immobility and adjustment

There are other possible sources of adjustment pressure in addition to inflexible factor prices. The most obvious, perhaps, is that there may be a mismatch of factor requirements between sectors. For example, the export sector may require an entirely different set of labour skills from the contracting import substitute sector. Clearly it takes time to retrain labour, and the more dissimilar the skills demanded by the two sectors, the greater any potential mismatch.

This could be an important barrier to occupational mobility of labour. In fact, the argument is frequently advanced in connection not only with trade-related adjustment difficulties, but in connection with adjustment to technological change. It could be argued that this is no more than a transitional difficulty and not a barrier to adjustment *per se*. In principle, this would be correct. In practice, however, there may be significant private costs associated with retraining which serve to restrict mobility.

Where resources are relatively easily transferable between sectors, adjustment will be very much easier. It is for this reason that some commentators have asserted that adjustment to trade expansion is likely to be easier when that expansion is predominantly of an intra-industry rather than an inter-industry type. If the labour skills required for employment in the expanding export sector are similar to those acquired during employment in the import substitute sector, then it follows that resource transfer will be easier. There are sound reasons for believing that *one* of the influences which has affected widespread acceptance of tariff liberalisation over the post-war period has been the growth of intra-industry exchange (see Hufbauer and Chilas, 1974). We should note that this is not the same thing as saying that all we require is similar factor intensities across the two sectors. The probability of labour skills being suited to the expanding activity will be greater when factor intensities are similar, but it does not follow that they *must* be similar. Clearly, quite different production processes can have similar factor intensities, if by factor intensity we mean simple capital:labour ratios. The erroneous equating of factor intensity with intra-industry trade lies behind the equally erroneous asertions of a number of commentators that intra-industry trade is little more than a statistical artefact (see Finger, 1975).

A related aspect of resource transfer which may also have a bearing on adjustment is a geographical mismatch of employment opportunities. The contracting import substitute sector may be concentrated in a specific region, the expanding export sector being entirely based in a different region. If factors of production are geographically immobile, then this will doubtless serve to frustrate the expansion of the export sector. This is a phenomenon which is not at all uncommon. The regional problems' of a number of developed market economies can be viewed, at least in part, as the outcome of slow adjustment to changing comparative advantage. In the United Kingdom, for example, the process of structural decline of the staple industries in the early twentieth century, which were predominantly concentrated in the peripheral regions, and the concurrent emergence of light engineering industry in central regions, is widely accepted as being a source of adjustment pressure.

ADJUSTMENT AND THE NEW PROTECTIONISM

The growth of the new protectionism is viewed by many as essentially a defensive reaction to adjustment pressures. Although we have already devoted a chapter to considering the emergence of the new protectionism, we shall now briefly examine the phenomenon with a view to relating it directly to adjustment.

When examining the emergence of the new protectionism we summarised our thoughts on its development as follows:

1. Dynamic comparative advantage resulted in a shift of competitiveness for many low technology manufactures from DMEs to LDCs.
2. While output in the OECD countries was growing, this appeared to create relatively few adjustment difficulties.
3. Recession in the early 1970s raised cyclical unemployment to historically high levels and made structurally unemployed resources more apparent and more difficult to absorb.
4. Increased unemployment in the West generated increased pressures for protectionism.
5. The concentration of LDC exports in particular markets focused attention on these countries.

In Chapter 8 we therefore highlighted the role of shifting comparative advantage against a background of recession. This is really the counterpart of the model which we analysed earlier in this chapter. The picture is, however, a little more complex. A corollary of changing comparative advantage has been the process of tertiarisation in the developed market economies – a phenomenon which is often labelled, in rather more emotive terms, as 'de-industrialisation'. Basically this involves a transfer of resources from manufacturing into (traded and non-traded) services. It has also generated adjustment resistance. As Curzon-Price (1980) argues, increased productivity in manufacturing, combined with shifting comparative advantage, tends to increase real income and reduce the demand for labour in the manufacturing sector. As the demand for 'services' is income elastic, an increased demand for services should follow. Since, in general terms, service production tends to be more labour-intensive than manufacturing production, in a smoothly functioning system, the service sector should expand to absorb the resources released by the contracting manufacturing sector.

This sounds very much like the process we described in our simple model earlier. In this case, however, we could very well be dealing with two non-traded goods. Even if we were, we could still observe a similar resistance to adjustment. Relative factor price inflexibility could be a problem; occupational immobility could again serve as a barrier (although as Curzon-Price argues, on *a priori* grounds, this is less likely to occur with a manufactures-services shift); and geographical immobility of factors could again be a constraint. (McEnery, 1981, provides an interesting review of the way in which the manufacturing bias of government regional policies in the United Kingdom has served to frustrate the development of services in the 'regions' and actually slowed up the adjustment process.)

The point is that it would be quite wrong to regard adjustment problems as being exclusively trade-related. As we shall see in Chapter 11, trade tends to be a relatively unimportant source of employment change when compared to productivity growth and shifts in demand. It can be extremely important at the margin, however, given the tendency of some countries to specialise in relatively narrow product lines, and it is this fact which is largely responsible for the defensive reaction via trade controls. However, as we are examining adjustment policies, we will do well to keep at the forefront of our mind the fact that adjustment is not a problem exclusively associated with trade expansion. As the authors of a recent GATT report note, 'Adjustment to change is a necessary condition of economic growth – indeed the growth process is little more than a sequence of adjustments of this kind' (Blackhurst, Marian and Tumlir, 1978, p.1).

RESPONSES TO ADJUSTMENT DIFFICULTIES

Is there a case for responding to adjustment problems (or more accurately, the manifestation of such problems in the form of a rise in the natural rate of unemployment)[1] with some kind of government intervention, or should we simply view such difficulties as essentially transitional, and ignore them? If there is a case for intervention, what form should that intervention take, and who should benefit?

Following the theory of optimal intervention developed in Chapter 3, our initial response to the first question might be that the case for intervention depends on whether resistance to adjustment is caused by a market distortion or not. If it is, then there is an economic case for intervention, and policy should be directed at the source of the distortion. If adjustment resistance is not generated by a distortion, then there may be no economic arguments for intervention (although non-economic justifications may, of course, be invoked).

In recent years there has been a great deal of debate over the efficacy and form of adjustment assistance, with much controversy deriving from disagreement over the actual barriers to adjustment. We shall examine three qualitatively different views on the subject which can be described as the 'market-freeing view', the 'market-augmenting view' and the 'market-replacing view'.

Market-freeing view

This view of the problem can be summarised by the following statement: 'In a competitive market economy, adjustment would proceed rapidly. Its present inadequacy is largely the result of policy which in this case takes the form of micro-interventions, measures implemented by the government on behalf of particular industries, regions or groups of income recipients' (Blackhurst, Marian and Tumlir, 1978, p. 71). Implicit in this diagnosis is the judgement that adjustment is not specifically a trade-related problem. Furthermore, when adjustment problems arise they are created by distortions which prevent the market performing its allocative function. What distinguishes this diagnosis is the view that these distortions have largely been induced by inappropriate government legislation at both the macro and the micro level. At the macro level, an undue attachment to Keynesian demand-management policies has resulted in steadily rising rates of inflation, which, other things being equal, creates uncertainty and reduces output. Furthermore, it has been asserted that higher levels of inflation are associated with a greater variability in the actual rate of inflation. This creates a greater degree of unanticipated inflation, reduces the efficiency of exchange, and also serves to raise the natural rate of unemployment (see Friedman, 1977).

At the microeconomic level, government intervention has created a battery of distortions which affect both factor and product markets. It would be argued that specific policies like minimum wage legislation and legislation which gives labour unions certain legal immunities simply reduce the flexibility of factor prices and ultimately raise, rather than lower, unemployment. The provision of 'generous' welfare support systems serves to reduce incentives to retrain, and raises unemployment. Housing policies designed to provide subsidised housing only serve to restrict geographical mobility and raise the natural rate of unemployment. Costs of complying with government regulations raise average unit costs and lower output. All of these interventions serve to reduce the costs of unemployment, and remove incentives to adjust. One version of this view regards the entire phenomenon of the new protectionism as being the 'natural' extension of the welfare state to markets for traded goods (Krauss, 1979).

The prescription which follows this diagnosis suggests that first there is no role whatever for defensive measures, designed to protect a given pattern of employment. Included in such 'defensive' measures would be instruments directed at restricting imports, whether these be tariff or non-tariff instruments. The objective of policy should quite simply be to allow markets to work. At the macro level, this would ascribe a particular role to stabilisation policies based on rules. At the micro level, most policy prescriptions would be by way of freeing markets and removing distortions – de-regulation in a general sense. The only 'positive' policy would take the form of intervention designed to increase competition[2] in both product and factor markets. If such a package were promoted, it is argued, factor prices would be very much more sensitive to changes in demand and supply and would therefore be able to perform their vital signalling function. The absence of barriers to mobility would ensure that resources would be able to respond to relative price signals.

Even if one accepts the underlying postulates of the market-freeing view, namely that decentralised decision-taking through markets is likely to result in a more efficient allocation of resources than central-ised decision-taking (the micro postulate), and that systematic counter-cyclical demand management policies can raise the natural rate of unemployment through time (the macro postulate), then there are still at least three criteria on which we could question such a programme. First, the implicit assumption that all distortions are government-induced, and that therefore no economic arguments for intervention exist. Second, some of the dynamic implications of adjustment pressures are ignored. Third, the political aspects of adjustment policy are not given sufficient emphasis. Although the market-augmenting view of adjustment is a rather broad church, most exponents emphasise these factors while accepting the desirability of decentralised decision-taking. Its prognosis therefore is somewhat more interventionist.

Market-augmenting view

The first notable difference between the market-freeing and market-augmenting views is that the latter would recognise the presence of distortions which are not necessarily government-induced.

Take, for instance, costs of adjustment. Both views would of course recognise that when factors have to adjust to changed economic conditions, there are costs involved. For example, in the case of trade expansion, factors of production in the import substitute sector will bear certain costs. Owners of physical and human capital will find that the present value of their services falls. The extent of such a loss depends on the earning differential between present and future employment, the costs of changing employment, and the level of transfers from the authorities. The first of these will depend on the nature of the expanding sector, the second on the mobility of the factor concerned. The market-freeing attitude here would be that such costs are only income transfers and do not affect aggregate welfare which will be at a higher level once adjustment has taken place.

By contrast, the market-augmenting view would highlight the role of market imperfections. In the context of the present example, there could be a divergence between private and social costs of adjustment. To take an extreme example, scrapping an item of specific capital (or labour) would have a zero social cost, on the principle that bygones are bygones. Private cost in both cases is likely to be somewhat greater. Similarly, the social benefits of having a coal miner retrain as a computer programmer might be quite apparent from a social standpoint. From the individual's viewpoint, however, the benefits of the change might not be quite so apparent. He may discount future (apprenticeship) earnings at a relatively high rate, and/or leisure might enter his utility function with a relatively heavy weighting, the combined effect being that he fails to retrain.

Where there does seem to be a divergence between private and social costs, there may be a case for positive intervention. In the example above, this might take the form of retraining grants coupled with some form of lump-sum compensation to the factors concerned. Similarly, where physical capital is concerned, grants may be made available for the scrapping of capital equipment in order to accelerate

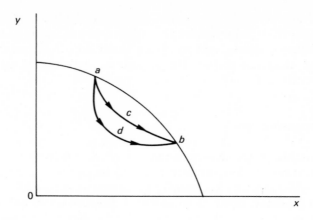

Figure 10.2

the retirement of redundant assets. The distinctive characteristic of such intervention is that it is 'positive' and directed at accelerating change.

The attractions of positive intervention may appear even more magnetic when allowance is made for so-called 'hysteresis' effects (Phelps, 1972). We have already noted that costs of adjustment are essentially transitional. Within the context of Figure 10.2, they are the costs of shifting from *a* to *b* along a path which takes us inside the production frontier. Clearly the farther into the production block we go (*ceteris paribus*) the longer the adjustment process takes, and the more costly it turns out to be. It is likely, some would say inevitable, that adjustment problems are cumulative. Once we have moved inside the production frontier, we have a certain amount of unemployed labour. If the adjustment process is relatively slow and labour finds itself unemployed for a relatively long period of time, decomposition of human capital takes place. Even as the demand for labour expands, there may be supply constraints because unemployed labour has no recent 'on the job' experience and is less adaptable than labour with recent work experience. Consequently, unemployment remains higher than it would otherwise have been. This is the so-called 'hysteresis' process.

Suitable invervention to improve the efficiency of the adjustment process – by way of training subsidies, perhaps employment subsidies – could mean that the adjustment path is *a → c → b* in Figure 10.2 rather than *a → d → b*. As long as the costs of the subsidies used were less than the difference between the areas *adb* and *acb*, society would show a net gain. This point is especially important if there is a regional concentration of unemployment, since in these circumstances a depreciation of social capital also tends to be observed. There is some evidence to suggest that this in turn can act as a deterrent to investment.

Typically, the market-augmenting view places some emphasis on the political dimension of adjustment assistance. Even if the economic case is less than watertight, it might be argued that adjustment assistance is desirable in order to encourage change, rather than risking defensive action. The market-freeing response to such an argument would be that this amounts to little more than buying off sectional interests and should be avoided. There is another, more acceptable way of interpreting it, however: namely in Paretian terms. The 'losers' are being compensated (or if one prefers it, 'bribed') by the 'gainers' to accept change. In the case of trade-related change, this invariably amounts to the majority compensating a minority to accept a change which works to the benefit of the majority. Arguably this is preferable to defensive action in the form of import protection, where potential losers are again 'compensated' yet gainers realise no benefit; indeed, they incur a hidden cost.

Market-replacing view

In general terms, the market-replacing view proceeds from the premise that unrestricted markets will be unable to accommodate the adjustment process. The market-augmenting view begins from a similar position. There are, however, important qualitative differences between the two. Although the market-augmenting view prescribes intervention to accelerate the adjustment process, it is implicit in the analysis that adjustments will take place even in the absence of intervention, albeit only slowly. The market-replacing view, on the other hand, comes closer to preaching a gospel of complete market failure than one of partial market failure. If one takes this view, one would tend to argue that no adjustment will take place, and/or the adjustment problem becomes cumulatively worse. This more radical diagnosis gives rise to a more radical prescription regarding the appropriate responses to adjustment difficulties. The policies recommended amount to more widespread intervention than that prescribed under the market-augmenting view, as well as being more selective.

It seems that UNCTAD has some sympathy with this line of thought (see UNCTAD, 1978). The UNCTAD diagnosis is directed at altering industrial structures in developed market economies to permit them to accommodate the 'graduation' of developing market economies. The emphasis is on anticipatory adjustment following detailed examination of trends in trade, and sectoral industrial studies. Policies of financial assistance and compensation should be designed according to the specific requirements of individual sectors. In sum, 'It seems . . . that those who desire this approach wish the developed countries to adopt more closely the sort of centralised planning characteristic of the Eastern European countries or the plethora of product and industry specific policies of many developing countries' (Wolf, 1979, p. 215).

In the United Kingdom a market-replacing adjustment programme has been proposed, apparently geared to the specific requirements of the UK economy. This is the so-called 'alternative strategy' propounded by the Cambridge Economic Policy Group. It is argued that the United Kingdom, as a 'relatively unsuccessful'[3] industrial country, faces long-term adjustment difficulties which the market is incapable of resolving. An interesting feature of this prognosis is that the principal source of adjustment pressure is viewed as being other 'relatively successful' industrialised countries rather than the emerging NICs. If left to themselves, the free interplay of market forces will ensure that the UK economy is constrained within a straightjacket of balance-of-payments difficulties which will ensure relatively slow growth, a contraction of the manufacturing base, and a rising natural rate of unemployment.

In order to avert this de-industrialisation, general controls would be applied to imports of manufactures into the United Kingdom. Widespread industrial restructuring could then take place behind the import barrier. This in turn would be accelerated by the use of widespread 'adjustment measures' which would rely heavily on industrial planning agreements and labour subsidies.

The efficacy of such a strategy for the UK economy has been questioned widely on a great many points of detail and principle (see Greenaway and Milner, 1979; Scott, Corden and Little, 1980). It is not our task to review this debate here; we are simply interested in looking at the CEPG strategy as representative of a market-replacing view of adjustment.

Common problem, contrasting views

The distinctive differences between these differing views of the adjustment process can be summarised by reference to Figure 10.1. The essence of the market-freeing view is that adjustment from *a* to *b* (and a' to b') can and will take place in any economic system if markets are permitted to work. The only thing which is likely to prevent full adjustment from taking place is government intervention which impedes the process. The market-augmenting view, on the other hand, argues that adjustment may be incomplete due to elements of market imperfection, and/or the process of adjustment may be extremely slow. It follows, therefore, that intervention may be necessary to remove any impediments to adjustment and to expedite the process. Finally, the market-replacing view perceives the prospect of a long-term tendency towards an underemployment equilibrium at a and c (and a', c') as being a realistic possibility for certain countries, if markets are permitted to function unhindered. Therefore the general prescription is that the nervous system be anaesthetised for a suitable period of time while major surgery on the body politic and economic is conducted.

INSTRUMENTS OF ADJUSTMENT POLICY

If it were decided to pursue a policy of 'positive' adjustment assistance, what range of instruments is available? 'The aim of adjustment policy is to lower the social cost, redistribute the private cost, and above all make change more politically acceptable' (Wolf, 1979, p. 115).

This quote identifies the targets of adjustment policy:

1.   'to lower the social cost', i.e. to expedite change and minimise transitional costs.
2.   'redistribute the private cost', i.e. transfer at least part of the private costs of adjustment away from the factors directly concerned, towards consumers in general.
3.   'make change more politically acceptable', i.e. provide a package which will make the benefits of change clearer to the agents concerned, thereby making it more acceptable.

These targets are likely to be closely interrelated. For example, if one can redistribute the private cost of adjustment, other things being equal this will make change politically more acceptable, and this greater acceptability should lower the social costs of change. Given this interrelationship, the pivotal target is therefore the redistribution of private costs. These can be redistributed in a variety of ways which combine compensation of the affected factors via some form of income transfer, and inducements to change.

Adjustment assistance to labour

The most obvious form of assistance is some form of income compensation. In an ideal world this would take the form of lump-sum transfers, since these will have no adverse effects for efficiency. In practice, most developed market economies offer adjustment assistance of this type through the social security system. This assistance, however, is of a general form in that it applies to all change irrespective of the source of adjustment pressure. Income compensation is an instrument which affects the private costs of adjustment. In general, there is no economic case for additional assistance for trade-related change, although one might feel that there is a political argument for additional compensation, namely that resistance to trade-related change is greater than resistance to non-trade-induced change, and therefore necessitates additional compensation.

Although we would anticipate that income compensation would make change more acceptable, reliance on this instrument is likely to affect incentives. Other things being equal, the more generous the programme of compensation, the less the incentive of the affected labour to engage in job search and/or retrain. Thus there are difficulties in deciding on the optimum amount of any transfer and the length of time over which it should apply.

Also, policies which influence the occupational and geographical mobility of labour will affect the social costs of adjustment. A number of possible instruments are available here:

(1) Job search costs could be reduced through direct subsidisation of the search process via reimbursement of search expenses, for instance.

(2) Occupational mobility could be improved by retraining schemes. This could take a variety of forms: for instance, retraining centres, income supplements to lower the private costs of retraining, or wage subsidies to increase the demand for labour and provide immediate on-the-job experience.

(3) Geographical mobility can be influenced by the availability of relocation grants which subsidise relocation. More important, perhaps, certainly in the UK context, geographical mobility could be influenced significantly by reform of housing policy. It is widely accepted that the presence of a local authority sector which accounts far in excess of 40 per cent of the housing stock has a direct impact on immobility. The presence of area-specific waiting lists stimulated by rents set below the market level makes mobility between areas extremely difficult for local authority residents.

Adjustment assistance to firms and industry

Again, we can identify a number of instruments which could be employed here to compensate affected firms and/or promote new industry:

(1) In much the same way that labour is compensated, one might argue that capital can also be compensated. This could be accomplished in a variety of ways. Incentives may be given to encourage firms to scrap assets of which the present social value is close to zero, but the present private value is positive. Alternatively, one could permit a firm to write off the costs of withdrawal from one activity against profits earned in any new activity. This might be viewed as preferable to the first option, since the provision of compensation is conditional. As Wolf (1979) points out, a frequently used method of compensating capital (and labour) is nationalisation.

(2) There are a number of fiscal and monetary instruments which could be used to improve adaptability and/or encourage development in new lines of activity. For example, one could subsidise research and development activity, perhaps with a 'small firm' bias. This does not involve the same kind of problems as 'picking winners' in that one is ultimately relying on 'market forces' to push forward those activities where a relative advantage can be fostered. Subsidisation of research and development effectively influences risk, and if successful encourages 'entrepreneurship'. Other aspects of providing a climate in which entrepreneurship could be expected to flourish might relate to the provision of 'information' services, perhaps through technical assistance and subsidising recourse to consultancy services.

Adjustment assistance to communities

We have noted that adjustment pressures are frequently area- or region-specific. In such circumstances, hysteresis effects can push a region into structural decline. There may, therefore, be a case for regional policy which provides region-specific incentives to adjust, for instance investment incentives, employment subsidies and infra-structural improvement.

CONCLUDING COMMENTS

The preceding paragraphs have outlined some of the instruments which can be used to give adjustment assistance to labour, capital and perhaps regions. Which, if any, are employed depends in part on the ideology adopted, and in part on the overall macro climate. The different ideologies adumbrated above would have differing recommendations to make about the appropriate mix of these policies. Note also, however, that pressures for their use will be inversely related to the overall level of macroeconomic activity. In a period of sustained growth, the creation of new investment and employment opportunities will make adjustment altogether easier and more acceptable than in a period of relatively slow growth.

NOTES ON FURTHER READING

Detailed expositions of the market-freeing, market-augmenting and market-replacing views of adjustment can be found in Blackhurst, Marian and Tumlir (1978), OECD (1979a) and UNCTAD (1978) respectively. A summary of each is given by Wolf (1980). O'Cleiricain (1972) outlines the economic case for adjustment assistance, while Wolf (1979) provides the most thorough review of the principles of adjustment policy.

11 Trade Policy and Employment

In Chapter 10 we outlined the process of adjustment and summarised differing views on whether adjustment policy should be activist or passivist. Before we conclude by attempting to deduce some broad policy implications, we ought to ponder the employment implications of trade expansion/contraction a little more fully. Although we concluded Chapters 6 and 10 by suggesting that there were aggregate net benefits (losses) from trade liberalisation (restriction), the essence of an adjustment problem is that some agents are more directly affected than others. In this chapter we will explore empirical work on the employment displacement/creating effects of trade policy, since this is likely to condition policy prescription to a large extent.

IDENTIFYING EMPLOYMENT CHANGES: METHODOLOGY

When we focused on empirical aspects of the aggregate effect of tariff changes, we identified two contrasting methodologies, *ex ante* and *ex post* examination. The same distinction can be made with respect to analyses of employment changes. Indeed, estimating the effects of trade interventions on employment is basically an extension of identifying aggregate welfare effects. In order to estimate aggregate welfare effects, one first has to predict or extricate (depending on whether one adopts an *ex ante* or an *ex post* approach) the effect of a given policy change on net imports.

The first point we might note, then, is that those 'technical' and 'practical' problems associated with empirical analyses of the aggregate effects of trade liberalisation/restriction also apply to studies of employment effects. For example, if one is endeavouring to make an *ex ante* estimate of employment change following a unilateral reduction in tariffs, one would first have to predict the effects of the change on demand for imports. This would inevitably involve assumptions about import demand elasticities, assumptions about income effects, and so on. Likewise, if one followed an *ex post* approach, one would be confronted with the task of separating the effect of the reduction in tariffs on the actual change in imports from other factors. In addition, however, to these methodological difficulties, one faces additional problems.

Ex ante methods

Assume that one is interested in the effects of a given unilateral reduction in tariffs on employment. From Chapter 6 we know that we can estimate the change in imports as:

$$\Delta M = \Theta t \ \frac{M_o}{P_o} \qquad\qquad (11.1)$$

To ascertain the effect which this increased demand for imports has on employment, we could assume that increased expenditure on imports displaces an equivalent amount of expenditure on import substitutes, ΔEs. If we knew what labour requirements in the import substitute activity were, we could then estimate labour displacement as:

$$L_i = \frac{L_i}{Q_i} \ \Delta Q_i \ (\ \Delta L_i < 0 \ ) \qquad\qquad (11.2)$$

Where L_i refers to total labour requirements in activity i, Q_i refers to the value of output in this sector, and ΔQ_i the change in the value of output as a consequence of trade liberalisation. If one were applying the methodology to a bilateral/multilateral tariff reduction rather than simply a unilateral reduction, then a similar equation would be estimated for export activities. Given the necessary information, these equations could then be estimated for a range of activities.

This is really the most basic *ex ante* methodology, and there are a number of difficulties which can be noted. First of all, ΔQ_i is derived by assuming that a given increase in imports displaces an equivalent value of import substitutes, which is tantamount to assuming that imports are perfect substitutes for the domestic counterpart. The reasonableness of this assumption depends, of course, on the nature of the product; as intra-industry trade increases in importance, the assumption becomes less satisfactory.

A second drawback with this approach is the assumption that any change in employment is directly attributable to increased import demand (in the case of tariff reduction). In Chapter 9 we noted in passing that an increasing number of *ex post* studies have revealed that the principal source of employment change in import-competing sectors is not changes in imports *per se*, but rather the impact which changes in imports have on productivity, and in turn the effect which productivity change has on employment. Clearly, equation (11.2) does not take account of this. Productivity change is more usually incorporated as a source of employment change in *ex post* analyses.

This point is related (but not identical) to another problem, namely the labour:output coefficient L_i/Q_i. Clearly, what we have here is an *average* labour:output coefficient. In fact what is relevant is *marginal* labour:output coefficients, since it is the effects of marginal changes which we are implicitly examining. This difficulty is almost a constraint, since data on marginal labour:output coefficients are rarely available.[1]

The final shortcoming we must note of the crude methodology of equation (11.2) is that it focuses only on *direct* employment effects. When the production process is single-stage (or perhaps fully integrated) this may be a legitimate assumption. In the more usual case, however, it fails to account accurately for the employment changes which actually take place. Contraction of a given final good sector must have implications for supplying sectors. Thus a crude application of equation (11.2) would tend to underestimate employment displacement where supplying sectors are domestically based. (The same would apply *mutatis mutandis* to export activities.) This problem can be overcome by using input–output tables to estimate both direct and indirect employment changes. An increasing number of studies have done precisely this (e.g. De Grauwe *et al.*, 1979; Deardorff *et al.*, 1977). This allows one to take account of linkage effects in employment displacement/creation. Unfortunately the input–output framework is not the ideal method of taking linkage effects into account, as it suffers from a number of drawbacks itself, not least its essentially static framework, which serves to impose fixed production coefficients.

Even when one takes account of indirect employment effects, the analysis need not be fully general equilibrium. If a tariff change results in aggregate payments imbalance, then one should allow for the effects of payments adjustment. Many studies simply assume fixed exchange rates or assume a balanced increase in trade. A few recent studies permit the exchange rate to change in response to any payment imbalance, thereby capturing the feedback impact on employment.

In general terms, these are the principal difficulties faced by researchers when exploring the effects of trade policy in an *ex ante* setting. We will discuss these further below in the context of a number of specific studies.

Ex post methods

Ex post analyses basically commence from a given employment change over a particular period of time, and attempt to ascertain the proportion of the change in employment due to changes in trade flows. At its crudest, this methodology could be expressed in a form analogous to the basic *ex ante* expression of equation (11.2):

$$\Delta L_{im} = \left(\frac{L_i^t}{1 - M_i^t} \right) 1 - M_i^{t-1} \tag{11.3}$$

ΔL_{im} refers to the change in employment in activity i which is attributable to increased imports between t and $t-1$. M_i^t and M_i^{t-1} refer to the value of imports as a proportion of domestic purchases of commodity i in t and $t-1$ respectively. (The same exercise could be conducted *mutatis mutandis* for exportables.)

Clearly, this is a rather unsophisticated procedure. All one is doing is extrapolating the ratio of purchases on imports to domestic output in $t-1$ forward to t, on the assumption that expenditure on the 'composite commodity', and labour requirements in the import substitute sector, both remain unchanged. As with *ex ante* methods, we are again implicitly assuming that imports and the domestic counterpart are perfect substitutes for each other. In addition, we are again using average labour:output coefficients, assuming that these have remained fixed over the period of study. Since imports frequently induce productivity change, this is a highly implausible assumption. Anyway, it is possible that other extraneous factors, such as changes in tastes, could have affected the demand for import substitutes over the intervening period, as indeed could other policy changes. In other words, we face the ubiquitous problem of *ex post* analysis, namely that we can never know what the situation would have been anyway.

We can ameliorate these difficulties to some extent by employing a more sophisticated framework than that suggested by equation (11.3), to decompose the determinants of total employment change into the contribution made by imports, changes in demand and productivity change. We will now turn to a consideration of empirical analyses of employment change, and comment on the manner in which various researchers have faced these problems, and the results which they have generated.

EMPIRICAL ANALYSES OF THE EMPLOYMENT CONSE- QUENCES OF TRADE EXPANSION/CONTRACTION

The new protectionism has served to stimulate much recent research effort in this direction. Consequently there exists a considerable literature covering a relatively large number of countries. Most studies confine themselves to single-country analyses, although a few recent projects have examined the employment implications of trade, given liberalisation, in a number of countries simultaneously. Some studies are partial equilibrium, others general equilibrium; some identify employment changes at the aggregate level only, others at a highly disaggregated level; some examine the implications of unilateral tariff reduction, others multilateral reduction; finally some employ *ex ante* methods, others *ex post* methods. There are therefore a number of criteria which we could use to categorise empirical work. However, we shall use a different basis for our categorisation by distinguishing between those studies that explore the employment implications of trade in general, and those that focus specifically on the employment implications of trade with LDCs. By first reviewing a few representative general studies, we extend the analyses of Chapters 6 and 9; by focusing on the employment implications of DME–LDC trade we might place ourselves in a position to define more clearly the nature of the adjustment problem.

Empirical studies of employment and trade in general

Luttrell (1978) is an example of an *ex post* study of a fairly rudi- mentary type. He sets out to ascertain the effect of trade on employ- ment in a number of industries in the USA where imports or exports had grown significantly between 1964–5 and 1975–6. Luttrell takes the average number of employees in each of the industries in his sample for the years 1964–5 as his base. From this he predicts what the level of employment in each industry would have been had the ratio of imports to domestic purchases remained constant between 1964-5 and 1975-6. The difference between the predicted figure and the actual figure is taken to be the result of increased imports. The same procedure is applied to those sectors where exports are important.

Luttrell estimates that job losses from imports amounted to 250,100, while job gains from exports amounted to 369,500. As a proportion of an average of base-year and end-year employment, these figures amount to about 6.5 per cent and 4.1 per cent respect- ively. This would amount to an annual average loss of jobs in the import-exposed sectors of 0.54 per cent and an annual average gain in employment in export sectors of 0.34 per cent per annum.

Luttrell's results have to be treated with a great deal of caution, however. As the author himself concedes, the exercise is only directed at establishing 'orders of magnitude'. The methodology used suffers from all of the problems identified above. It is assumed, for example, that expenditure on imports displaces expenditure on the domestic counterpart on a one-to-one basis. Even where the imported commodity and the domestic product are perfect substitutes, this assumption may be invalid if the intervening period is characterised by growth of income (as indeed it was). Anyway, the fact that four out of the seven import-competing sectors examined were finished consumer goods where product differentiation can be expected to be important would lead us immediately to question the assumption about substitutability.

Labour:output ratios are also assumed to be constant over the period, which is tantamount to assuming that labour is a quasi-fixed factor of production. Such an assumption *may* be valid in the very short run, but it is certainly invalid when the interval in question is twelve years, and when those twelve years were a period of rapid technological change. Without a doubt, productivity change would have influenced employment over this period – especially in the import-competing sectors.

This particular study seems, then, to be subject to a number of major drawbacks. It is interesting to note, however, *en passant* that if these shortcomings were allowed for, the impact of trade on employment would turn out to have been even more marginal. This conclusion is endorsed by work completed by Salant (1978), which although *ex ante* in character, bears similarities to Luttrell's approach.

By contrast Baldwin's (1976) study is altogether more ambitious and methodologically more sophisticated. The study is *ex ante*, and aims to predict the effects of a 50 per cent multilateral tariff reduction on employment in the USA. Thus the expressions above in (11.1) and (11.2) are relevant to establishing the effect of the tariff reduction on net imports, and the associated employment change.

One interesting feature of the Baldwin study is that he explicitly assumes that imports and domestic production are *not* perfect substitutes for each other. Since Baldwin excludes from his study those sectors where quantitative restrictions are important (agricultural products, oil and textiles), manufactures figure heavily in his sample and justify the assumption. This therefore overcomes one of the difficulties that we identified above.

In estimating the effects of a change in import demand and export supply on employment, a sample of 367 industries is taken from the

US input–output table of 1967. If we recall the problems discussed earlier, we will remember that this tends to constrain the study to average labour-output ratios, and it also assumes that they are fixed. Against this, however, Baldwin goes some way towards proxying marginal changes by breaking down aggregate employment into some fourteen different skill groups. This allows him to gain some indication of the distribution of employment changes across occupational groups.

Baldwin also disaggregates his sample on a regional basis in order to explore the possible pattern of employment change across the fifty States of the USA.

As we know from Chapter 6, the elasticity estimate used crucially affects the prediction of the final change in imports. Rather than relying on one set of import and export demand elasticities, Baldwin employs five sets and simulates the effects of a 50 per cent multilateral tariff reduction using all five sets. The predictions that emerge are reported in Table 11.1.

It is clear from Table 11.1 that in almost all cases the net employment effects in manufacturing are negative, while in three out of the five cases for the 'all industries' group, the net effects are negative. The only occasion where net effects for all industries and manufacturing show up as positive is in set IV, which combines a 'low' import demand with a 'high' export demand elasticity. In all cases the proportionate changes are relatively small, the greatest change being that which follows using elasticity set V, i.e. a 'high' import demand and 'low' export demand set. To ascertain whether these ostensibly negligible aggregate effects masked severe adjustment difficulties for

TABLE 11.1   Employment effects of a 50 per cent tariff cut in the USA

Net employment effect (in man-years)	I*	II*	III*	IV*	V*
All industries	−15,200 (0.0)†	900 (0.0)	−37,300 (0.0)	113,300 (0.1)	−226,400 (0.3)
Manufacturing	−31,700 (0.2)	−15,600 (0.1)	−40,900 (0.2)	93,100 (0.5)	−251,200 (1.3)

* I, II, III, IV and V refer to the sets of elasticity estimates included. The use of such a wide range of sets covers the spectrum of relatively high and relatively low elasticities.

† Figures in parentheses express the employment change as a fraction of total employment.

Source: Baldwin (1976) table 2, p. 146.

particular industries, Baldwin chose one half of one per cent of an industry's labour force as being 'significant'. He found that in fifty-four import-sensitive and nineteen export-oriented industries, the order of magnitude exceeded 0.5 per cent. Although this might suggest that more than fifty import-competing sectors could face adjustment problems, Baldwin suggested that this would probably be offset to some extent by the trend increase in labour demand, and would certainly be offset to some extent by the impact of induced exchange-rate changes. In fact, a subsequent study by Baldwin and Lewis (1978) went on to estimate the net employment effects in the flexible-exchange-rate model and found that the employment changes were even less.

Baldwin (1976) and Baldwin and Lewis (1978) therefore represent fairly sophisticated attempts to predict the impact of a significant tariff change on employment. Some of the inherent problems we alluded to above are accommodated (such as the perfect substitut-ability assumption and fixed exchange rates) and a range of elasticity estimates is employed. The most serious drawback, perhaps, is the implied constancy of labour-output coefficients and therefore the inability to allow for the effects of productivity change.

In Chapter 6 we commented in some detail on the Cline *et al.* (1978) study. There we were concerned with reporting on the net welfare effects of trade policy. This particular study went further, however, and analysed the employment implications for the principal economies concerned, i.e. the USA, Canada, the EEC and Japan. To obtain estimates of employment change it was assumed that increased imports displaced domestic production by an equivalent amount, and that increased exports caused an increase in output in the export sector by a corresponding amount. As we have noted in connection with other studies, there are good reasons for doubting these assumptions, since estimates based on them tend to overstate employment changes. Estimates of import and export change were multiplied by sectoral 'job coefficients', i.e. labour requirements per unit of output. This yielded a figure for 'direct labour' change. In addition, 'total job coefficients', which made allowance for labour inputs in the inter-mediate stage, were used to gain an estimate of indirect labour requirements. This exercise was completed for all twelve of the tariff formulae which Cline *et al.* estimated. If we take the formula which is closest to the outcome of the Tokyo Round, it would seem that the employment implications are very small. If we take job loss from increased imports as a proportion of total employment, we find fig-ures of 0.10 per cent for the USA, 0.68 per cent for Canada, 0.60 per cent for Japan and 0.07 per cent for the EEC. If we allow for em-ployment-creating effects of increased exports, then the *net* changes are even smaller, of course. Cline *et al.* compute net changes on the basis of the most unfavourable formula for each area and find job changes of +0.01 per cent for the USA, -0.57 per cent for Canada, -0.16 per cent for Japan and -0.11 per cent for the EEC.[2] Furthermore, the authors stress that these are likely to overstate the extent of employment change, not only because the most unfavourable formula is taken for each area, but also because no account is taken of respending effects on employment in export sectors.

In aggregate terms, therefore, it would appear that none of the areas considered would experience dramatic employment changes as a result of tariff liberalisation. As we saw in Chapter 10, however, the essence of adjustment problems is that they are sector-specific. From the sector-by-sector analysis concluded by the authors, it seems that relatively few sectors experience a net change in excess of $\frac{1}{2}$ per cent of sectoral employment.

From this selective review, it would appear that changes in the volume of trade are unlikely to stimulate significant changes in employment for the DMEs considered. It might nevertheless be objected that in the case of the studies covered so far, we have focused largely on trade between industrialised economies, where intra-industry trade is known to account for a large proportion of total trade and therefore where we might *a priori* anticipate that net employment changes would be of a relatively small order of magnitude. In the case of trade with LDCs, however, net employment change might be greater.

Empirical studies of employment change and trade with LDCs

De Grauwe *et al.* (1979) recently completed an *ex ante* estimate of the effects on employment in Belgium of a balanced expansion of trade with LDCs. The authors used input–output data to calculate the direct and indirect labour content of one billion Belgian francs of exports to LDCs and one billion Belgian francs of domestic products which compete with imports from LDCs. In estimating the employment effect of the increase in imports, it was assumed that import-competing products were perfect substitutes for each other.

The loss in job potential from an increase in LDC imports of one billion Belgian francs was estimated at 2,084 man-years in 1970, or 0.2 per cent of total employment. If one makes allowance for the employment-creating effects of export expansion, the net loss in employment falls to 334 man-years, a mere 0.01 per cent of total employment. Although this figure is some five times the change which would follow from a similar expansion of trade with other members of the EEC, and twice that which would be associated with a similar expansion with other DMEs, it is nevertheless a very small aggregate net change. Furthermore, it should be noted that in 1970 an expansion of one billion francs would have been equivalent to a 34 per cent increase in imports from LDCs – a significant expansion by any standards.

Although the aggregate effect on the demand for labour seemed to be relatively small, examination of predicted sectoral changes revealed significant possible shifts in the demand for labour. This follows because Belgium exports to LDCs were found to have a relatively high physical and human capital content, whereas imports from LDCs embodied a relatively low physical and human capital content. Thus the total number of workers that would have to move was found to be 2.7 times greater for trade with LDCs than for trade with DMEs, with particularly marked changes being found in low technology activities (footwear, textiles, toys). Thus De Grauwe *et al.* offer some support for the proposition that trade expansion with LDCs may be more likely to create adjustment difficulties than trade expansion between DMEs. Having said this, however, we must bear in mind that the aggregate change in the demand for labour is still of a very small order of magnitude.

Cable (1977, 1979) has examined the impact of imports from LDCs on employment in the United Kingdom. The earlier of the two studies concentrates on employment displacement in only four sectors, whereas the latter study focuses on some thirty-four industry groups. It is this study which we shall review.

Cable's 1977 study is an application of the *ex post* methodology in that he attempts to decompose the actual employment change which took place in his sample of thirty-four industry groups between 1970 and 1975. All industries where the LDC share of UK consumption exceeded 2 per cent were included. Cable estimated the components of employment change between 1970 and 1975 from the identity:

$$L_i = \frac{1}{P_i^t} [\Delta D_i + \Delta X_i - \Delta M_i - \Delta PL_i^{t+1}] \tag{11.4}$$

In other words, changes in employment in each sector are the outcome of changes in demand (ΔD_i), changes in exports (ΔX_i), changes in imports (ΔM_i) and changes in productivity (ΔPL_i). Using this methodology, Cable estimated that productivity change was responsible for 16.6 per cent of the change in employment which occurred in the industries concerned between 1970 and 1975. This compared with 10.4 per cent attributable to changes in consumption, 2.4 per cent attributable to trade shifts with all areas, and a mere 0.5 per cent due to trade shifts with LDCs. As with the De Grauwe *et al.* study, this seems to indicate that in aggregate terms LDCs have a marginal impact on employment change. Again, however, we might enquire further about the effect on particular sectors, since an aggregate figure of 0.5 per cent will very likely mask significant inter-sectoral shifts in the demand for labour. Further investigation in fact reveals that textiles and clothing, footwear, leather goods and wood and furniture experience more significant declines. In addition, as we would expect, certain engineering sectors experience a larger than average increase in labour demand. Subsequent work by Cable (1982) suggests, in sympathy with De Grauwe *et al.*, that UK exports are relatively intensive in human and physical capital, while imports are relatively intensive in unskilled labour. Such a finding is consistent with adjustment difficulties being faced by certain sectors.

Methodologically there are one or two difficulties with the Cable studies which we ought to note (and which the author himself ac-knowledges). First, expression (11.4) does not make allowances for 'interaction effects'. This would not matter if we were dealing with small changes over a very short period of time. Where, however, we are exploring larger changes over a longer time period, it is likely that some of the variables in (11.4) will be interrelated – we have noted on several occasions, for instance, the way in which productivity change is affected by imports. Second, it is assumed that imports and the domestic counterpart are perfect substitutes for each other. Third, average labour:output coefficients are used. And finally, only direct employment effects are estimated. It is impossible to say what the net effect of these omissions is. We might note, however, that despite them, Cable's results are not inconsistent with the findings of other researchers. As well as the De Grauwe study, we might note that Kierzkowski (1980) examined five categories of goods in Sweden where imports were important and looked at employment change over the years 1963–77. He reached the conclusion that imports from LDCs had a 'negligible' impact on employment change in Sweden. Wolter's (1976) study of the impact of LDC imports into West Germany and Frank's (1977) study of the impact of LDC imports on employment in the USA both suggest that, as a source of employment displacement, imports from LDCs pale into insignifi-cance alongside productivity change.

CONCLUDING COMMENTS

We have reviewed a number of studies of trade expansion and em-ployment in order to examine the methodological pitfalls associated with the exercise, and in order to gain some idea of the effect which trade has on employment change. Bearing in mind the caveats made with respect to methodological difficulties, a number of conclusions can be reached. First, trade in general does not appear to be a major source of employment displacement in industrialised countries. Second, although trade between LDCs and DMEs appears to be responsible for a greater degree of employment displacement in the latter than trade between DMEs, employment displacement by LDCs is far less important than the effects of productivity change. Having said this, however, although aggregate effects may be negligible, it is clear that certain sectors have experienced adjustment difficulties, and what is more, are likely to do so as comparative advantage in low technology manufactures continues to shift towards the LDCs. The problem from a policy viewpoint is how one should respond to such adjustment problems. The work which we have reviewed in this chapter, as with those studies introduced in Chapter 6, points to the conclusion that defensive trade policy is unlikely to cause significant changes in employment.

NOTES ON FURTHER READING

The continuing process of multilateral trade liberalisation, and the concurrent emergence of the NICs as major exporters of manufactures, has ensured a steady flow of empirical work on the relationship between trade expansion and employment. Surveys of the literature can be found in Hsieh (1973), Lydall (1975) and OECD (1979b). In addition, Kreinin and Officer (1979) contrast the results of a more selective range of studies which concentrate specifically on the effects of the Tokyo Round. The studies that we have mentioned in the chapter are representative of general studies and studies of the effects of trade with LDCs. In addition, there are a few studies which are industry-specific, for instance Miles (1968) and McDowall and Draper (1978).

12 Trade Policy and Adjustment

It would be quite impossible to design a 'model' adjustment programme which would be well suited to any system facing adjustment pressures. Economic systems are sufficiently diverse, and the relative importance of the traded goods sector sufficiently different, to make such an exercise meaningless. What we can do, however, is conclude by identifying the specific role that trade policy may be able to play.

TRADE POLICY AND DEFENSIVE ADJUSTMENT

We are now familiar with the role that trade policy has played recently with respect to adjustment. Specifically, it has been used in an essentially defensive fashion, to resist rather than encourage adjustment. Furthermore, the instruments which have been employed have tended to be discriminatory in intent and frequently hidden. This combination of characteristics we referred to as the 'new protectionism'.

It will be recalled from our discussion of the GATT framework in Chapter 5 that there exist 'escape clauses' in the GATT Articles. There is in fact an escape clause which is fashioned for adjustment purposes. Article XIX outlines the conditions under which 'emergency action' can be taken in response to sudden increases in imports which may 'cause or threaten serious injury to domestic producers'. In principle, therefore, the GATT Charter actually makes provision for safeguard action to be taken if a particular industry or sector is placed in a situation where it may have to adjust relatively quickly to import competition. In such circumstances, to cite Article XIX, paragraph 1(b) in full:

> If any product, which is the subject of a concession with respect to a preference is being imported into the territory of a contracting party in the circumstances set forth . . . so as to cause or threaten serious injury to domestic producers of like or directly competitive

213

products in the territory of a contracting party which receives or received such preferences, the importing contracting party shall be free . . . to suspend the relevant obligation in whole or in part or to withdraw or modify the concession in respect of the product, to the extent and for such time as may be necessary to prevent or remedy such injury.

Thus, action can be taken by way of withdrawal of concessions previously given, but any action taken should be essentially of a temporary nature. Paragraph 2 of Article XIX states that prior to any such action being taken, GATT and the exporting countries concerned should be consulted in writing about the importing country's intention. If no such consultation procedure is followed, then the exporting countries can, after ninety days, take retaliatory action on a discriminatory basis, according to paragraph 3 of Article XIX – the nature and extent of this action being determined by the extent to which they lose by the initial safeguard controls. Finally, any action taken under Article XIX should conform with the principles of Article II, namely the most favoured nation provisions.

In sum, Article XIX provides for emergency action to be taken where a rapid increase in imports threatens serious injury to domestic producers. If any action is taken, it should be non-discriminatory and in principle should be temporary. The provisions are, however, entirely defensive in that no commitment to positive adjustment action is required.

As we saw in Chapter 5, however, the provisions in this Article were entirely unsuited to the major trade-related structural change which was occurring in the late 1960s and early 1970s, namely the emergence of a number of NICs as significant exporters of manufactures. Although the importance of NICs as exporters of manufactures is dwarfed by the major industrialised countries, these countries were significant exporters in particular product lines. This concentration of export effort resulted in relatively rapid rates of increase in import penetration in specific markets in many DMEs. Rather than petitioning for emergency protection under Article XIX, many countries took illegal or extra-legal action. The principal reason behind the reluctance to use Article XIX appears to be the MFN requirement, i.e. the necessity that any action taken be non-discriminatory. In many instances this would have meant taking action against established trading partners whose rates of growth of imports may have been rather more stable, and where the probability of retaliation would have been relatively high. (Where the EEC countries were concerned, non-discriminatory action would have been contrary to the Treaty of Rome, if any of the affected parties were member countries.)

Thus, instead of using Article XIX, it was avoided by the creation of an alternative set of rules (as with textiles), or it was simply by-passed by the use of discriminatory controls whether illegal (as with many import quotas) or extra-legal (as with voluntary export restraints).

We have reviewed again the role of Article XIX in order to gain some clue as to the part which trade policy could play in encouraging positive adjustment, rather than simply being an instrument of defensive adjustment. From the above review, it seems clear that, in very general terms, if trade policy is to become an instrument for encouraging positive adjustment, greater inducement has to be provided to entice more widespread use of Article XIX for emergency protection. This would then provide a basis for greater reliance on transparent instruments of intervention. Second, the Article should be redrafted to ensure that action is genuinely of a temporary nature. Third, emergency action could perhaps be made conditional, by linking it to positive adjustment policies.

REFORMING THE SAFEGUARDS CLAUSE

If greater recourse to 'official' emergency action through Article XIX could be encouraged, there would be reduced scope for recourse to non-tariff interventions, whether legal, illegal or extra-legal. There can be little doubt that there would be net benefits associated with such a transformation. Because any emergency action taken would be done so 'officially', it could be monitored and, if Article XIX were redrafted in a suitable way, supervised. One of the most deleterious features of the 'new protectionism' has been that so many interventions are hidden. As we saw in Chapter 9, this creates major difficulties when we attempt to gauge the economic consequences of such action. Where action is taken 'officially' it can at least be monitored – which countries are taking what sort of action in which product lines is apparent and observable. Indeed, one might argue that such transparency may serve to act as a constraint on the misuse of emergency protection. Furthermore, it may make the provision of special treatment more obvious to domestic economic agents, notably consumer groups. Of course, such transparency may be regarded as a potential disadvantage from the standpoint of the vote-maximising government. Thus, in order to be encouraged to make greater use of official escape clause provision, some inducement would have to be offered. To accomplish this, some revision would have to be made to the reciprocity and MFN provisions.

Reciprocity is not formally drafted into Article XIX. In practice, however, action which has been taken under Article XIX has conformed with this principle in that those parties subject to the withdrawal of concessions, or imposition of new controls, have sought compensation in some form. This could amount to their withdrawing equivalent concessions themselves. Relinquishment of the right of reciprocity might act as an inducement to greater use of Article XIX. Reciprocity is, of course, a fundamental tenet of the GATT Charter, but in this context its relaxation is likely to be beneficial rather than harmful.

More problematic, however, is the related issue of MFN treatment. Clearly, if this requirement were relaxed, it would provide a major inducement to countries contemplating emergency action, to use official channels. After all, it seems as though many actions are 'hidden' simply because they are discriminatory. Many DMEs contend that this is the single most important reform necessary to Article XIX – a contention based on the argument that the source of adjustment difficulties (or threats of 'serious injury') are invariably individual NICs. The right to take discriminatory action simply recognises this reality.

However, less developed countries in general, and NICs in particular (including the first NIC to 'graduate' into the DME 'club', Japan) are understandably suspicious of such a proposal. On the one hand many have indicated that they see a reformed safeguards clause as being in their interests, since it would represent some form of basis for multilateral supervision and control – the only protection which they feel they enjoy against the potential excesses of the larger DMEs. On the other hand, however, they have watched for some years many DMEs take discriminatory extra-legal action with impunity. If the right to discriminatory action were legalised, they see themselves as being in a very exposed position and likely to be subject to emergency action even in cases where they may not be the source of 'serious injury', i.e. when other DMEs are the principal source of adjustment pressure. Furthermore, there is a feeling that 'threat' of serious injury could be somewhat loosely interpreted such that controls could be imposed in product lines where comparative advantage is potential rather than actual, and new product development stifled at birth.

There are other, more general objections to the relaxation of the MFN principle. It could be argued that it is the presence of this principle that was instrumental in the success of the post-war liberalisation process. Countries were more willing to accept (and give) concessions in the knowledge that they would not be nullified by separate bilateral deals. By the same token it could be argued that compromising the principle is simply the first step towards either complete disintegration of the GATT system, or its fragmentation into two sets of rules, one for the DMEs and another for the LDCs. This follows from possible secondary effects. Once one DME takes discriminatory action against a particular LDC, the latter is likely to intensify its exporting effort in the remaining $n-1$ 'open' DME markets. This increases the pressure on the more exposed DMEs to take discriminatory action. Clearly, if a second country closes its markets, pressure intensifies on the remaining $n-2$, and so on. There is evidence to suggest that this type of process is experienced in connection with the Multifibre Arrangement and would inevitably be a feature of a reformed safeguards system. It might be objected that it would follow whether safeguard provisions were discriminatory or non-discriminatory. This might be so, but there is clearly a much greater likelihood of it occurring when protection is discriminatory.

In recognising such shortcomings of Article XIX, a number of researchers have made specific proposals with respect to the form which a revised safeguards clause could take (see, for instance, Tumlir, 1974; and Robertson, 1977) and indeed the issue was formally examined as part of the Tokyo Round. No agreement was reached on the issue in the Tokyo Round due to the intractable problems associated with drafting a provision which struck the appropriate balance between rights and obligations on the part of the country initiating any emergency action, while simultaneously offering adequate protection against abuse to gain the confidence of the LDCs.

Tumlir (1974) suggests that such a balance was far from unattainable. He proposed that countries contemplating emergency action could be induced to take any action 'officially' by giving them the right to take discriminatory action. In return for that 'right', the country initiating the action would accept certain obligations. First of all, the action would only be approved for a finite period, and furthermore would be degressive over this period. For example, if emergency action were taken by imposing an import quota and the maximum period for which this quota were to operate was five years, there might be a zero growth of imports in year one, 5 per cent in year two, 10 per cent in year three, and so on, until at the end of year five all restrictions would be removed. This would provide an incentive for the industry concerned to take adjustment action of some form. In order to ensure that this actually happened, however, a second feature of the system would be the requirement that any emergency protection be accompanied by some form of proposal for adjustment on the part of the industry concerned. This could take the form of undertakings to the effect that no further resources would be invested in the activity, or a commitment to develop new product lines. Either way, emergency protection would be conditional.

Of course, 'official' action could be taken and undertakings given in order to secure emergency protection. Once the protection was approved it could be made tighter, and/or undertakings could be ignored. Thus a third feature would be that all emergency action would be subject to multilateral surveillance. Prior to approval of safeguard protection, a standing body would determine whether 'injury' had been suffered by the petitioning party. The proceedings of such an inquiry could be public to ensure that all interested parties had the opportunity to make representations. Once emergency action was approved, the 'progress' of the protected industry could be monitored regularly.

It might be argued that such a programme would be open to abuse, and the small LDCs in particular are likely to suffer to an even greater extent than under the 'new protectionism'. Against this, however, Tumlir argues that such countries would be given guarantees that they do not at present enjoy. In particular, the conditional nature of safeguard action and the procedure of multilateral approval/surveillance would operate to their advantage.

Clearly, this is the single most important issue, and indeed proved the sticking point in the Tokyo Round negotiations. Quite how the issue of discrimination/non-discrimination will be resolved is a matter for conjecture. Without any reformed safeguards clause, protectionist pressures will continue to find an outlet in the form of voluntary export restraints, orderly marketing agreements, and formal quotas, with obvious debilitating effects on the GATT framework. It is difficult to see how countries might be induced to accept constraints on the use of emergency action without being given the incentive of discriminatory action. Equally, however, the anxieties of the LDCs over potential abuse are understandable. The unknown in the equation is the success with which any surveillance procedure would operate and the penalties which could be applied in the event of abuse. Here the withdrawal of bilateral concessions has been proposed as one candidate. In cases where bargaining power is manifestly asymmetrical, it is difficult to see this as being an adequate policing mechanism. Multilateral action would clearly be more effective, as well as more difficult to administer. If, however, the political will existed to operate a multilateral surveillance system, a multilateral policing system might not be entirely fanciful.

THE GATT CODES: DISMANTLING THE NEW PROTECTIONISM?

If it were possible to redesign Article XIX in such a way that protectionist pressures were channelled within the system, and if it operated effectively, this would slow down the growth of the 'new protection-ism'. Although it might therefore affect the flow of extra-legal and illegal protectionist measures, it would not directly affect the stock of such measures. One could argue that provisions made for the conversion of existing restraints (in whatever form) into official safe-guard measures would accomplish this. This is certainly feasible (subject to the usual caveats regarding political will and free riders). Nevertheless, it would still not affect the stock of subsidies, procure-ment practices, administrative barriers, and so on.

To make any impact on these instruments, more direct action is necessary. This is rather easier said than done, however. Negotiating on non-tariff restrictions is problematic to say the least. This is in part due to the fact that there are considerable difficulties in agreeing on precisely what constitutes a non-tariff barrier. Even if such agree-ment were possible, however, the negotiation of equivalent concessions on non-tariff barriers is likely to give even the most skilled of nego-tiators nightmares.

The procedure which GATT has adopted in treating this problem, however, is not to view it as a liberalisation exercise analogous to that on tariffs. Rather, the approach adopted has been one of control. This is the purpose of the various codes agreed in the Tokyo Round. As we saw in Chapter 5, codes were agreed on subsidies, customs valuation procedures, government procurement and technical stan-dards.

The codes on customs valuation and technical standards are di-rected at generating standardisation of practice between countries. If achieved, greater standardisation should help reduce uncertainty, which in turn should stimulate trade at the margin. The government procurement code is aimed at encouraging greater transparency in the award of government contracts. The subsidies code is aimed at identifying subsidies with serious trade effects and providing a pro-cedure for affected parties to seek compensation.

The extent to which these codes achieve their end will not really be known until they have been operating for some time. Of particular interest here will be the success with which the subsidies code operates, since aspects of this are analogous to some of the features of the proposed safeguards proposal – except that the procedure operates in reverse: a contracting party which feels itself to be suffering 'ma-terial injury' from subsidised imports can petition to impose a counter-vailing duty.

End-Notes

1. We are not saying that intertemporal comparisons by value are of no interest at all. Clearly, even if trade does only increase in value terms, an increasing amount of some internationally acceptable medium of exchange would be required. If one or a few countries are charged with the responsibility of issuing these assets, then, at the very least, their susceptibility to external forces will be increased.

2. Typically 'openness' is proxied by taking exports and/or imports as a proportion of GNP. We have taken an average of both in order to avoid distortions generated by payments' imbalance. However, this may still fail accurately to reflect the extent to which the economy is influenced by the overseas sector. We are still not taking account of potentially important influences such as reserve currency status. Thus, in the case of the USA, for instance, we find an index of 'openness' as reported in Table I.2 which is relatively low. Clearly, however, the special role of the dollar in world commerce increases the susceptibility of the US economy to the influence of the overseas sector.

CHAPTER 1

1. It is usual in trade theory to employ community indifference curves as a basis for making judgements about gains and losses from exchange. These community indifference curves (CICs) exhibit similar properties to individual indifference curves, i.e. they are downward sloping, non-intersecting and convex to the origin. We should note however that whereas it is possible to make unequivocal statements about changes in welfare in the case of individual indifference curves, the same cannot be said about CICs. This follows because as we move from one CIC to a higher CIC, although the overall consumption bundle may have increased, distribution of the bundle may have changed. This difficulty is normally overcome by assuming either that income distribution is unaffected by the change, or if it is, compensation can take place, or that the tastes of the community are determined by a 'benevolent dictator'. For a more detailed analysis see Milner and Greenaway (1979) ch. 1.

2. In practice this adjustment process involves a movement inside the production frontier rather than along it, with a period of frictional unemployment. Whether this unemployment turns out to be frictional, or becomes structural, depends primarily on the flexibility of factor prices.

3. The factor price equalisation theorem was originally elaborated by Samuelson (1948, 1949) who demonstrated that if the H-O-S assumptions hold, unrestricted trade must equalise factor prices as well as commodity prices.

220

4. Leontief's failure to provide empirical support for the H–O–S postulate immediately became known as the Leontief paradox. It is difficult to understand, however, in what sense the results are paradoxical. They simply imply that the H–O–S theorem cannot explain the commodity composition of US trade at a particular point in time. Even if one accepts that the test was in every sense a valid one, this suggests no more than the fact that other, non-factor proportions influences, are more important.

5. Theoretical and empirical analysis has established that the determinants of process and product innovation are likely to differ. In particular, differing market structures are likely to be conducive to innovation in each case. However, this is an area which we cannot expand upon here. The interested student is referred to some of the better industrial economics texts such as Scherer (1980) or Hay and Morris (1978) for a review of the issues.

6. All references apply to SITC(2), revised 1978.

CHAPTER 2

1. The vertical distance which we are using to approximate levels of consumer and producer surplus may be viewed as some kind of index of the integrals of surplus areas associated with production and consumption. The level of surplus will depend *inter alia* on consumer income and the price of the commodity in question relative to other commodities.

CHAPTER 3

1. As students of public finance will be quick to realise, the distinction between a direct and indirect tax is not always clear cut. For instance, employers' social security contributions would be regarded as a direct tax if borne by the employer. If, however, they are passed on in the form of higher prices, they are more properly regarded as an indirect tax.

2. It is conceivable that even nominal value could fall. On the basis of casual empiricism, there are some grounds to suggest that in inflationary periods, physical dimensions may alter with less being offered for the same price. If this is so, the duty per unit would also fall.

3. A specific duty could be just as easily analysed. Since, however, it is relatively straightforward to ascertain the *ad valorem* equivalent of a specific duty $(t_a = t_s/P_m)$, we will take the *ad valorem* case as our general reference.

4. The rate of tax which should be levied for an optimum tariff is equal to

$$t = \frac{1}{1 - Ef}$$

where Ef is the foreign elasticity of demand for imports.

5. The infant industry case for protection tends to be thought of as a hybrid of a number of cases that may rely on imperfections in the capital market and scale economies, as well as externalities.

6. This is, of course, the familiar Stolper–Samuelson theorem and constitutes an integral part of the adjustment process. We should note parenthetically that this is not the same as saying that real incomes must fall. This depends on the expenditure pattern of scarce factors. If, for example, a large fraction of their money income is spent on imported goods, real *income* could of course rise despite a fall in real rewards.

7. We have in mind here some form of minimum wage legislation which sets a minimum *real* wage. In practice minimum wages are set in nominal terms and may or may not be index-linked.

8. It is widely accepted that expenditure taxes distort choices between goods, and that income taxes distort the choice between work and leisure.

9. This assumes that the recipients and the government have similar taste patterns.

CHAPTER 4

1. We will be considering below the effect which quotas, subsidies, multiple exchange rates, etc., have on effective protection.

2. Corden (1971) emphasises the distinction between negative effective protection and what he refers to as negative effective prices. The former, as we have seen, describes a situation where the protective structure lowers value added. The latter refers to a situation where either value added is made negative by the protective structure, or an already negative value added is made positive. (See Corden, 1971, pp. 50–5.)

3. Corden (1971) uses a simple model to elaborate this point with admirable clarity (see his ch. 4).

4. There is a practical problem of precisely delineating traded and non-traded goods. Conceptually the distinction depends on the structure of relative prices – non-tradables being those goods or services where c.i.f. prices are prohibitively high.

5. We are confining ourselves to empirical work which takes z_{ij} from input–output tables. The coefficient could, of course, be estimated directly by detailed examination of production of a particular commodity. This procedure is clearly much more expensive in research time, and rarely followed.

6. It should be pointed out that the theory of effective protection assumes that taxes and subsidies are levied and paid per unit of output. Clearly this is more appropriate for some interventions than others.

7. Voluntary export restraints and orderly marketing agreements will be examined in Chapter 8.

CHAPTER 5

1. The MFN principle was first incorporated in a commercial treaty in 1860, in the Treaty of Commerce between France and the United Kingdom.

2. The non-tariff barriers considered in the Kennedy Round were anti-dumping procedures, state trading and the American selling price method of customs valuation.

3. GATT (1979) preface.

4. The 'Swiss formula' can be expressed as:

$$Z = \frac{AX}{A + X}$$

where Z = final tariff rate, X = original tariff rate, and A = negotiated parameter. Thus, as A rises, the depth of tariff cut declines. The original Swiss proposal placed A at 14. In the final tariff offers, a value of 16 was agreed.

5. For example, the Latin American Free Trade Area (LAFTA), the Association of South East Asian Nations (ASEAN), and the Caribbean Community (CARICOM).

6. The 'Group of 77' refers to a group of LDCs, originally seventy-seven in number, which was formed in 1964. The group now numbers in excess of 100 countries, but retains its original name.

7. Murray (1977) provides a comprehensive review and analysis of the GSP.

CHAPTER 6

1. This is, of course, the obverse of the tariff imposition case. Thus, in static terms, if:

$(b + d) > |e| \rightarrow$ net gain

$(b + d) = |e| \rightarrow$ no change

$(b + d) < |e| \rightarrow$ net loss

the latter would apply for instance if the country eliminated what was an 'optimum tariff'.

2. The efficiency gains are often couched in terms of a reduction of X-inefficiency.

3. A simplified analysis of compensated demand curves can be found in most intermediate microeconomics texts. A more rigorous analysis is undertaken by Murphy, Currie and Schmitz (1971). A discussion of the problem in connection with tariff liberalisation can be found in Leamer and Stern (1971) ch. 8. See also Shone (1981) for a specific application.

4. One further technical point ought to be noted here. Strictly speaking, the assumption of a linear demand curve is incompatible with the procedure of holding price elasticity of demand constant. Elasticity varies at every point along a linear demand curve. The larger the tariff change, the more incompatible the assumptions become.

5. From Table I.2 in the Introduction we note that our index of openness for the USA amounts to 7 per cent over the period 1972-7, while for the United Kingdom we find a figure of 27 per cent.

6. Specifically, the USA, Canada, Japan, Austria, Finland, Sweden, Norway, Switzerland, Australia and New Zealand.

7. It is important to note here that the majority of *ex post* studies refer to 'restricted' trade liberalisation, i.e. trade liberalisation within free trade areas or customs unions. The question of economic integration is, of course, an important aspect of trade policy, but unfortunately it is something we cannot go into. Robson (1980) provides a readable review of the theory of economic integration, while Mayes (1978) surveys the empirical literature on the question.

CHAPTER 7

1. The revenue motive is only really of importance in LDCs (see Greenaway, 1980, 1981).

2. Keesing and Wolf (1980) give details of a number of cases where this has occurred in trade in textiles. It seems that it is not unusual for LDCs to respond to quota limits by reallocating production to lines with a higher value added per unit.

3. We will examine the effects of quotas which impose a fixed physical limit on the number of units imported, rather than value quotas. The case of the latter can be relatively easily analysed using similar techniques. All that has to be remembered is that when we have a value quota, price and quantity must vary inversely. Furthermore, since it is value which is fixed, the area below the value quota curve must, by definition, be the same for all price–output combinations. The curve will therefore be a rectangular hyperbola which is unit elastic at all points.

4. Corden (1971, pp. 213-14) argues that one should distinguish between the 'comparable tariff rate' and the 'implicit tariff rate'. The former refers to that tariff rate which would have the same effect on *volume* as a given quota; the latter refers to that tariff rate which has the same *price* effect Although these will tend to be identical, Corden notes three cases where they can differ:

   (i)   where price controls are implemented in conjunction with the quota;
   (ii) where the users of the restricted imports are also the holders of the import licences; and
   (iii) where the import substitute sector is monopolised.

5. It has been argued that quantitative import controls could be used as an instrument for encouraging growth in the United Kingdom by Cripps and Godley (1978). For a contrary view see Greenaway and Milner (1979).

6. We have provided only a brief and non-technical introduction to comparing tariffs and quotas. More technical and thorough evaluation is given in Bhagwati (1969).

7. The VER and OMA can to all intents and purposes be considered identical. The first-round economic effects of both are essentially the same. The only difference lies in their legal status. The VER is an agreement between importing and exporting country whereby the latter agrees voluntarily to restrict exports to the former. If the voluntarily agreed limit is exceeded, it need not be followed by any formal action because the authorities have no legal mandate to impose any restrictions. In practice a VER tends to be negotiated under the threat of more stringent action upon any contravention of the agreement. Any action would, however, be discretionary rather than automatic.

An OMA is negotiated in similar fashion to a VER, and the restriction is again generally administered by the exporting country. If the agreed limit is exceeded under an OMA, however, an explicit import quota can then be imposed automatically by the importing country. Thus the OMA may prove more effective in restricting imports than the VER.

8. We make no attempt to pass judgement on the justification for such a policy. It may be felt essential that a domestic defence industry or domestic energy industries are preserved without any dependence on imports, perhaps for strategic reasons. The point is, however, that there are costs associated with such policies.

CHAPTER 8

1. Japan was at this time considered to be a newly industrialising country.

2. This is something else which ought perhaps to be qualified further. Undoubtedly, producer groups did acquiesce in the liberalisation process. One could argue, however, as Hufbauer and Chilas (1974) do, that this only followed because producer groups ensured that the pattern of trade liberalisation was such that adjustment costs were minimised, i.e. they ensured that trade expansion which followed liberalisation was primarily intra- rather than inter-industry trade.

3. The obvious exception here is trade in textiles, where protectionist pressures have resulted in trade being controlled since 1962. See Keesing and Wolf (1980).

4. These articles are not the only escape clauses: others exist relating to public safety (Article XX), national security (Article XXI) and economic development (Article XVIII). These and escape clause provisions within the EEC and EFTA treaties are examined in more detail by Robertson (1977).

CHAPTER 9

1. Details can be found in the IMF's *Annual Report on Exchange Restrictions*, GATT's *Developments in Commercial Policy*, and the STR's *Foreign Trade Actions Monitoring Systems Report*.

2. 'Managed trade' is defined by Page (1979) as 'trade that is subject to some non-tariff control' (p. 166).

3. It might be argued that in fact this ought not to make any difference, except where a countervailing duty is explicitly levied against the export subsidy. In this event the two instruments cancel each other out.

4. As Cline *et al.* point out, it is far from obvious what form a 60 per cent reduction in government procurement protection would take.

5. Keesing and Wolf feel that this may in fact be an underestimate, because of the elasticity assumptions built into the model (p. 108).

6. See, for instance, Cable (1979), Frank (1977), Wolter (1976) and the summary of evidence in Blackhurst *et al.* (1978).

CHAPTER 10

1. The natural rate of unemployment is that rate which is consistent with a steady rate of inflation.

2. Quite what form this would take is unclear. 'Competition' is a concept which is notoriously difficult to operationalise. One could have in mind greater structural competition, in which case policy would take the form of increasing the number of firms in the market. Alternatively, one could have in mind greater behavioural competition and view competition as a process. In this case one would be more concerned with rules governing behaviour than with market structure.

3. This is the term used by Cripps and Godley (1978).

CHAPTER 11

1. One notable study which does estimate marginal rather than average coefficients is Pelzman and Bradberry (1980).

2. The EEC figure only applies to direct job loss. Even if it is trebled or quadrupled, however, it remains relatively small.

References

R. L. Allen and I. Walter (1970) *An Analysis of the Impact of Non-Tariff Measures Imposed by Developed Market Economy Countries on Products of Export Interest to Developing Countries* (UNCTAD Secretariat, Manufactures Division Working Paper).

R. C. Amacher, G. Haberler and T. D. Willett (eds) (1979) *Challenges to a Liberal International Economic Order* (Washington, American Enterprise Institute).

J. Apan *et al.* (1978) *The US Apparel Industry* (Georgia, World Congress Institute).

A. Aquino (1978) 'Intra-Industry Trade and Inter-Industry Specialisation as Concurrent Sources of International Trade in Manufactures', *Weltwirtschaftliches Archiv*, CXIV, 275–95.

B. Balassa (1965) 'Tariff Protection in Industrial Countries: An Evaluation', *Journal of Political Economy*, LXXIII, 579–94.

B. Balassa (1968) 'Tariff Protection in Industrial Nations and its Effects on the Exports of Processed Goods from Developing Countries', *Canadian Journal of Economics*, 1, 583–94.

B. Balassa (1971) *The Structure of Protection in Developing Countries* (Baltimore, Johns Hopkins Press).

B. Balassa (1977) 'A Stages Approach to Comparative Advantage', *World Bank Staff Working Paper*, 256.

B. Balassa (1978) 'The New Protectionism and the International Economy', *Journal of World Trade Law*, XII, 409–36.

B. Balassa and M. E. Kreinin (1967) 'Trade Liberalisation Under the Kennedy Round: The Static Effects', *Review of Economics and Statistics*, XXXXIX, 125–37.

B. Balassa and M. Sharpston (1977) *Export Subsidies by Developing Countries: Issues of Policy*, Commercial Policy Issues, No. 2 (Geneva, Graduate Institute of International Studies).

R. E. Baldwin (1952) 'The New Welfare Economics and Gains in International Trade', *Quarterly Journal of Economics*, LXVI, 91–101.

R. E. Baldwin (1970) *Non-Tariff Distortions of International Trade* (Washington, Brookings Institution).

R. E. Baldwin (1971) 'Determinants of the Commodity Structure of US Trade', *American Economic Review*, LXI, 126–46.

R. E. Baldwin (1976) 'Trade and Employment Effects in the US, Multilateral Tariff Reductions', *American Economic Review*, LVI, 142–8.

R. E. Baldwin (1979) *Beyond the Tokyo Round Negotiations*, Thames Essay 22, (London, Trade Policy Research Centre).

R. E. Baldwin and W. E. Lewis (1978) 'US Tariff Effects on Trade and Employment', in W. G. Dewald (ed.) *The Impact of International Trade and Investment on Employment* (Washington, US Government Printing Office).

R. E. Baldwin and T. Murray (1977) 'MFN, Tariff Reductions and LDC Benefits Under the GSP', *Economic Journal*, LXXXVII, 30–46.

T. Barker (1977) 'International Trade and Economic Growth: An Alternative to the Neo–Classical Approach', *Cambridge Journal of Economics*, 1, 153–72.

T. Barker and S. Han (1971) 'Effective Rates of Protection for UK Production', *Economic Journal*, LXXXI, 282–93.

G. Basevi (1966) 'The US Tariff Structure: Estimates of Effective Rates of Protection of US Industries and Industrial Labour', *Review of Economics and Statistics*, XLVIII, 147–60.

G. Basevi (1968) 'The Restrictive Effect of the US Tariff and its Welfare Value', *American Economic Review*, LVIII, 840–52.

R. Batchelor and A. P. Minford (1977) 'Import Controls and Devaluation as Medium Term Policies', in H. Corbet *et al., On How to Cope with Britain's Trade Position*, Thames Essay 8 (London, Trade Policy Research Centre).

J. Bhagwati (1969) 'On the Equivalence of Tariffs and Quotas', in *Trade Tariffs and Growth* (London, Weidenfeld and Nicholson).

J. Bhagwati (1971) 'The Pure Theory of International Trade: A Survey', in *Trade, Tariffs and Growth* (London, Weidenfeld and Nicolson).

J. Bhagwati (ed.) (1981) *International Trade: Selected Readings* (Cambridge, Massachusetts, MIT Press).

J. Bhagwati and V. K. Ramaswami (1963) 'Domestic Distortions, Tariffs and the Theory of Optimum Subsidy', *Journal of Political Economy*, LXXI, 44–50.

C. F. Bickerdike (1906) 'The Theory of Incipient Taxes', *Economic Journal*, XVI, 529–35.

R. Blackhurst, N. Marian and J. Tumlir (1977) *Trade Liberalisation, Protectionism and Interdependence*, GATT Studies in International Trade No. 5 (Geneva, GATT).

R. Blackhurst, N. Marian and J. Tumlir (1978) *Adjustment Trade and Growth in Developed and Developing Countries*, GATT Studies in International Trade No. 6 (Geneva, GATT).

W. Brandt (ed.) (1980) *North–South: A Programme for Survival* (London, Pan).

V. Cable (1977) 'British Protectionism and LDC Imports', *ODI Review*, 11, 29–48.

V. Cable (1979) *World Textile Trade and Protection*, EIU Special Report No. 63 (London, Economist Intelligence Unit).

V. Cable (1982) 'Cheap Imports and Jobs: The Impact of Competing Manufactured Imports from Low Labour Cost Countries on UK Employment', in W. P. Maunder (ed.), *Case Studies in Development Economics* (London, Heinemann).

R. Caves (1981) 'Intra-Industry Trade and Market Structure in the Industrial Countries', *Oxford Economic Papers*, XXXIII, 203–23.

R. Caves and H. G. Johnson (eds) (1968) *Readings in International Economics* (London, Allen and Unwin).

W. Cline *et al.* (1978) *Trade Negotiations in the Tokyo Round: A Quantitative Assessment* (Washington, Brookings Institution).

H. Corbet (1979a) 'Importance of Being Earnest About Further GATT Negotiations', *The World Economy*, III, 319–42.

H. Corbet (1979b) 'Tokyo Round: Twilight of a Liberal Era or a New Dawn?', *National Westminster Quarterly Review*, February.

W. M. Corden (1966) 'The Structure of a Tariff System and the Effective Protective Rate', *Journal of Political Economy*, LXXIV, 221–37.

W. M. Corden (1969) 'Effective Protective Rates in the General Equilibrium Model', *Oxford Economic Papers*, XXI, 135–41.

W. M. Corden (1971) *The Theory of Protection* (Oxford, The Clarendon Press).

W. M. Corden (1974) *Trade Policy and Economic Welfare* (Oxford, The Clarendon Press).

W. M. Corden (1975) 'The Costs and Consequences of Protection: A Survey of Empirical Work', in P. Kenen (ed.), *International Trade and Finance* (Cambridge, Cambridge University Press).

F. Cripps and W. Godley (1978) 'Control of Imports as a Means of Full Employment and the Expansion of World Trade: the UK Case', *Cambridge Journal of Economics*, 11, 237–54.

G. Curzon (1965) *Multilateral Commercial Diplomacy: the General Agreement on Tariffs and Trade and its Impact on National Commercial Policies and Techniques* (London, Michael Joseph).

G. Curzon (1979) 'Introduction', in M. Rom, *The Role of Tariff Quotas in Commercial Policy* (London, Macmillan).

G. Curzon (1981) 'Neo-Protectionism, the MFA and the European Community', *The World Economy*, IV, 251–62.

G. Curzon and V. Curzon-Price (1969) 'Options After the Kennedy Round', in H. G. Johnson (ed.), *New Trade Strategy for the World Economy* (London, Allen and Unwin).

G. Curzon and V. Curzon-Price (1970) *Hidden Barriers to International Trade*, Thames Essay 1 (London, Trade Policy Research Centre).

V. Curzon-Price (1980) *Unemployment and Other Non Work Issues*, Thames Essay 25 (London, Trade Policy Research Centre).

P. De Grauwe, W. Kennes, T. Peeters and R. Van Straelen (1979) 'Trade Expansion with Less Developed Countries and Employment: A Case Study of Belgium', *Weltwirtschaftliches Archiv*, CXV, 99–115.

A. Deardorff, R. M. Stern and C. F. Baum (1977) 'A Multi-Country Simulation of the Employment and Exchange Rate Effects of Post-Kennedy Round Tariff Reductions', in A. Akranasee *et al.*, *Trade and Employment in Asia and the Pacific* (Honolulu, University Press of Hawaii).

G. Denton, S. O'Cleiricain and S. Ash (1975) *Trade Effects of Public Subsidies to Private Enterprise* (London, Macmillan).

J. M. Finger (1974) 'GATT Tariff Concessions and the Exports of Developing Countries: US Concessions at the Kennedy Round', *Economic Journal*, LXXXIV, 566–75.

J. M. Finger (1975) 'Trade Overlap and Intra-Industry Trade', *Economic Inquiry*, XIII, 581–9.

J. M. Finger (1977) 'Effects of the Kennedy Round Tariff Concessions', *Economic Journal*, LXXXVII, 87–95.

C. Frank (1977) *Foreign Trade and Domestic Aid* (Washington, Brookings Institution).

M. Friedman (1977) 'Nobel Lecture: Inflation and Unemployment', *Journal of Political Economy*, LXXXV, 451–72.

L. Gamir (1971) 'The Calculation of Effective Rates of Protection in Spain', in H. G. Grubel and H. G. Johnson, *Effective Tariff Protection* (Geneva, Graduate Institute of International Studies).

L. M. Gard and J. Reidel (1980) 'Safeguard Protection of Industry in Developed Countries: Assessment of the Implications for Developing Countries', *Weltwirtschaftliches Archiv*, CXVI, 471–92.

GATT (1979) *The Tokyo Round of Multilateral Trade Negotiations*, Report by the Director General (Geneva, GATT).

H. Giersch (ed.) (1979) *On the Economics of Intra-Industry Trade* (Tübingen, J. C. B. Möhr).

D. Greenaway (1980) 'Trade Taxes as a Source of Government Revenue: An International Comparison', *Scottish Journal of Political Economy*, XXVII, 175–82.

D. Greenaway (1981) 'Trade Taxes and Economic Development', in A. T. Peacock and F. Forte (eds), *The Political Economy of Taxation* (Oxford, Basil Blackwell).

D. Greenaway (1982a) *Inter-Industry Trade and Intra-Industry Trade in Switzerland 1965–77*, mimeo (Buckingham, University College at Buckingham).

D. Greenaway (1982b) 'Identifying the Gains from Pure Intra-Industry Trade', *Journal of Economic Studies*, IX.

D. Greenaway (1982c) 'Optimal Revenue Tariffs and Maximum Revenue Tariffs: Concepts and Policy Issues', *Public Finance*, XXXVII, 67–79.

D. Greenaway and C. R. Milner (1979) *Protectionism Again . . . ?*, Hobart Paper 84 (London, Institute of Economic Affairs).

D. Greenaway and C. R. Milner (1982) *Inter-Industry Patterns in Intra-Industry Trade: An Econometric Analysis*, Discussion Paper No. 11 (Buckingham, University College at Buckingham).

H. G. Grubel and H. G. Johnson (eds) (1971) *Effective Tariff Protection* (Geneva, Graduate Institute of International Studies).

H. G. Grubel and P. J. Lloyd (1975) *Intra-Industry Trade* (London, Macmillan).

S. Guisinger (1971) 'The Characteristics of Protected Industries in Japan', in H. G. Grubel and H. G. Johnson (eds) (1971).

G. Haberler (1950) 'Some Problems in the Pure Theory of International Trade', *Economic Journal*, LX, 223–40.

G. Haberler (ed.) (1958) *Trends in International Trade* (Geneva, GATT).

C. Hamilton (1981) 'A New Approach to the Estimation of the Effects of Non Tariff Barriers to Trade: An Application to the Swedish Textile and Clothing Industry', *Weltwirtschaftliches Archiv*, CXVII, 298–325.

D. Hay and D. Morris (1978) *Industrial Economics: Theory and Evidence* (Oxford, Oxford University Press).

E. Heckscher (1919) 'The Effects of Foreign Trade on the Distribution of Income', *Economisc Tidskrift*, reprinted in H. Ellis and L. A. Metzler (eds) (1948) *Readings in the Theory of International Trade* (Homewood, Illinois, Irwin).

U. Hiemenz and K. Von Rabenau (1976) 'Effective Protection of German Industry', in W. M. Corden and G. Fels (eds), *Public Subsidy of Private Enterprise* (London, Macmillan).

B. V. Hindley (1972) *Britain's Position on Non-Tariff Protection*, Thames Essay 4 (London, Trade Policy Research Centre).

B. V. Hindley (1980) 'Voluntary Export Restraints and the GATT's Main Escape Clause', *The World Economy*, III, 313-42.

C. Hsieh (1973) 'Measuring the Effects of Trade Expansion on Employment', *International Labour Review*, CIX, 1-29.

G. Hufbauer and J. Chilas (1974) 'Specialisation by Industrial Countries: Extent and Consequences', in H. Giersch (ed.), *The International Division of Labour, Problems and Perspectives* (Tübingen, J. C. B. Möhr).

H. G. Johnson (1950-1) 'Optimum Welfare and Maximum Revenue Tariffs', *Review of Economic Studies*, XIX, 28-35.

H. G. Johnson (1958) 'Alternative Optimum Tariff Formulae', in H. G. Johnson, *International Trade and Economic Growth* (London, Allen and Unwin).

H. G. Johnson (1960) 'The Cost of Protection and the Scientific Tariff', *Journal of Political Economy*, LXVIII, 327-45.

H. G. Johnson (1965a) 'Optimum Tariffs and Retaliation', in *International Trade and Economic Growth* (London, Allen and Unwin).

H. G. Johnson (1965b) 'Optimal Trade Intervention in the Presence of Domestic Distortions', in R. Baldwin (ed.), *Trade, Growth and the Balance of Payments* (New York, Rand McNally).

H. G. Johnson (1965c) 'The Theory of Tariff Structure, With Special Reference to World Trade and Development', in H. G. Johnson and P. B. Kenen (eds), *Trade and Development* (Geneva, Librarie Droz).

H. G. Johnson (1971) *Aspects of the Theory of Tariffs* (London, Allen and Unwin).

D. Keesing and M. Wolf (1980) *Textile Quotas Against Developing Countries*, Thames Essay 23 (London, Trade Policy Research Centre).

H. Kierzkowski (1980) 'Displacement of Labour by Imports of Manufactures', *World Development*, VIII, 753-62.

Korean Development Association (1967) *Effective Rates of Protection for Korean Industry* (Korean Development Association).

L. B. Krause (1959) 'US Imports and the Tariff', *American Economic Review*, XLIX, 542-51.

L. B. Krause and J. Mathieson (1971) 'How Much of Current Unemployment Did We Import?', *Brookings Papers on Economic Activity*, 11.

M. B. Krauss (1979) *The New Protectionism, The Welfare State and International Trade* (Oxford, Basil Blackwell).

M. E. Kreinin (1961) 'Effects of Tariff Changes on Imports', *American Economic Review*, LI, 310-24.

M. E. Kreinin and L. Officer (1979) 'Tariff Reductions Under the Tokyo Round: A Review of Their Effects on Trade Flows, Employment and Welfare', *Weltwirtschaftliches Archiv*, CXV, 543-72.

P. Krugman (1979) 'Increasing Returns, Monopolistic Competition and International Trade', *Journal of International Economics*, IX, 469-79.

P. Krugman (1981) 'Intra-Industry Specialisation and the Gains from Trade', *Journal of Political Economy*, LXXXIX, 959-73.

K. Lancaster (1966) 'A New Approach to Consumer Theory', *Journal of Political Economy*, LXXIV, 132-57.

K. Lancaster (1980) 'Intra-Industry Trade Under Perfect Monopolistic Competition', *Journal of International Economics*, X, 151–76.

E. Leamer and R. Stern (1971) *Quantitative International Economics* (Chicago, Aldine).

W. Leontief (1953) 'Domestic Production and Foreign Trade: the American Capital Position Re-examined', *Economia Internazionale*, VII, 3–32.

W. Leontief (1956) 'Factor Proportions and the Structure of American Trade', *Review of Economics and Statistics*, XXXVIII, 386–407.

A. Lerner (1936) 'The Symmetry Between Import and Export Taxes', *Economica*, III, 306–13.

S. R. Lewis (1963) 'Government Revenue from Foreign Trade: An International Comparison', *Manchester School*, XXXI, 39–46.

W. A. Lewis (1954) 'Economic Development With Unlimited Supplies of Labour', *Manchester School*, XXII, 139–91.

S. B. Linder (1961) *An Essay on Trade and Transformation* (New York, John Wiley).

R. G. Lipsey and K. Lancaster (1956–7) 'The General Theory of Second Best', *Review of Economic Studies*, XXIV, 11–32.

T. S. Lowinger (1976) 'Discrimination in Government Procurement of Foreign Goods in the US and Western Europe', *Southern Economic Journal*, XXXII, 451–60.

C. B. Luttrell (1978) 'Imports and Jobs: The Observed and the Unobserved', *Federal Reserve Bank of St Louis Review*, LX, 2–10.

H. R. Lydall (1975) 'Employment Effects of Trade Expansion', *International Labour Review*, CXL, 219–34.

D. MacAleese (1971) *Effective Tariffs and the Structure of Industrial Protection in Ireland*, Paper No. 62 (Dublin, Economic and Social Research Institute).

D. MacAleese (1977) 'Do Tariffs Matter? Industrial Specialisation and Exchange in a Small Economy', *Oxford Economic Papers*, XXIX, 117–27.

S. McDowall and P. Draper (1978) *Trade Adjustment and the British Jute Industry: A Case Study*, Research Monographs (London, Overseas Development Institute).

P. McEnery (1981) *Manufacturing Two Nations*, Research Monograph 36 (London, Institute of Economic Affairs).

S. Magee (1972) 'Welfare Effects of Restrictions on US Trade', *Brooking Papers on Economic Activity*, III, 645–701.

H. Malmgren (1977) *International Order for Public Subsidies*, Thames Essay 11 (London, Trade Policy Research Centre).

D. Mayes (1978) 'The Effects of Economic Integration on Trade', *Journal of Common Market Studies*, XVII, 1–25.

G. Meier (1973) *Problems of Trade Policy* (Oxford, Oxford University Press).

R. Middleton (1975) *Negotiating on Non-Tariff Distortions of Trade* (London, Macmillan).

C. Miles (1968) *Lancashire Textiles: A Case Study of Industrial Change* (Cambridge, Cambridge University Press).

C. Milner and D. Greenaway (1979) *An Introduction to International Economics* (London, Longman).

K. Morton and P. Tulloch (1977) *Trade and Developing Countries* (London, Croom Helm).

A. Murphy, J. Currie and A. Schmitz (1971) 'The Concept of Consumer Surplus and Its Use in Economic Analysis', *Economic Journal*, LXXXI, 741–99.

T. Murray (1977) *Trade Preferences for Developing Countries* (London, Macmillan).

T. Murray and I. Walter (1977) 'Quantitative Restrictions, Developing Countries and the GATT', *Journal of World Trade Law*, XI, 391–421.

T. Murray, W. Schmidt and I. Walter (1978) 'Alternative Forms of Protection Against Market Disruption', *Kyklos*, XXI, 624–37.

R. Musgrave (1959) *The Theory of Public Finance* (London, McGraw-Hill).

J. H. Mutti and M. D. Bale (1981) 'Output and Employment Changes in a Trade Sensitive Sector: Adjustment in the US Footwear Industry', *Weltwirtschaftliches Archiv*, CXVII, 352–67.

B. Nowzad (1978) *The Rise in Protectionism*, Pamphlet 24 (Washington, International Monetary Fund).

S. O'Cleiricain (1972) 'Adjustment Assistance to Import Competition', in F. McFadzean (ed.), *Towards an Open World Economy* (London, Macmillan).

OECD (1979a) *The Case for Positive Adjustment Policies* (Paris, OECD).

OECD (1979b) *The Impact of the Newly Industrialising Countries* (Paris, OECD).

B. Ohlin (1933) *Interregional and International Trade* (Cambridge, Massachusetts, Harvard University Press).

G. Orcutt (1950) 'Measurement of Price Elasticities in International Trade', *Review of Economics and Statistics*, XXXII, 117–32.

N. Oulton (1976) 'Effective Protection of British Industry', in W. M. Corden and G. Fels, *Public Subsidy to Private Enterprise* (London, Macmillan).

S. B. Page (1979) 'The Management of International Trade', in R. Major (ed.), *Britain's Trade and Exchange Rate Policy* (London, Heinemann).

S. B. Page (1981) 'The Revival of Protectionism and its Consequences for Europe', *Journal of Common Market Studies*, XX, 17–40.

J. Pelzman and C. Bradberry (1980) 'The Welfare Effects of Reduced US Tariff Restrictions on Imported Textile Products', *Applied Economics*, XII, 455–75.

E. S. Phelps (1972) *Inflation Policy and Unemployment Theory: A Cost Benefit Approach to Monetary Planning* (London, Macmillan).

M. V. Posner (1961) 'Technical Change and International Trade', *Oxford Economic Papers*, XIII, 323–41.

D. Ricardo (1817) *The Principles of Political Economy and Taxation* (London, Dent edition 1973).

D. Robertson (1977) *Fail Safe Systems for Trade Liberalisation*, Thames Essay 12 (London, Trade Policy Research Centre).

P. Robson (1980) *The Economics of International Integration* (London, Allen and Unwin).

M. Rom (1979) *The Role of Tariff Quotas in Commercial Policy* (London, Macmillan).

V. Roningen and A. J. Yeats (1976) 'Non Tariff Distortions of International Trade: Some Preliminary Empirical Evidence', *Weltwirtschaftliches Archiv*, CXIII, 613–25.

N. Saidi (1980) *Rational Expectations, Adjustment Costs and the Theory of Tariffs*, mimeo (Geneva, Graduate Institute of International Studies).

W. Salant (1978) *The Effects of Increases in Imports on Domestic Employment: A Clarification of Concepts*, Special Report 18 (Washington, National Commission for Manpower Policy).

P. A. Samuelson (1939) 'The Gains from International Trade', *Canadian Journal of Economics and Political Science*, V, 195-205.

P. A. Samuelson (1948) 'International Trade and the Equalisation of Factor Prices', *Economic Journal*, LVIII, 163-84.

P. A. Samuelson (1949) 'International Factor Price Equalisation Once Again', *Economic Journal*, LVIX, 181-97.

P. A. Samuelson (1962) 'The Gains from International Trade Once Again', *Economic Journal*, LXXII, 820-9.

F. M. Scherer (1979) 'The Welfare Economics of Product Variety: An Application to the Ready to Eat Cereals Industry', *Journal of Industrial Economics*, XXVIII, 113-34.

F. M. Scherer (1980) *Industrial Market Structure and Economic Performance* (Chicago, Rand McNally, second edition).

M. Scott, W. M. Corden and I. M. D. Little (1980) *The Case Against General Import Controls*, Thames Essay 24 (London, Trade Policy Research Centre).

R. Shone (1981) *Topics in Applied Microeconomics* (Oxford, Martin Robertson).

A. Smith (1776) *The Wealth of Nations* (London, Dent edition 1975).

L. Stein (1981) 'The Growth and Implications of LDC Manufactured Exports to Advanced Countries', *Kyklos*, XXXIV, 36-59.

R. M. Stern (1964) 'The US Tariff and the Efficiency of the US Economy', *American Economic Review*, LIV, 459-70.

R. M. Stern (1975) 'Testing Trade Theories', in P. B. Kenen (ed.), *International Trade and Finance* (Cambridge, Cambridge University Press).

R. M. Stern (1979) 'Evaluating the Consequences of Alternative Policies for Trade Liberalisation in the Multilateral Trade Negotiations', in R. Baldwin, R. Stern and H. Kierzkowski, *Evaluating the Effects of Trade Liberalisation*, Commercial Policy Issues 3, 4 (Geneva, Graduate Institute of International Studies).

W. F. Stolper and P. A. Samuelson (1941) 'Protection and Real Wages', *Review of Economic Studies*, IX, 58-73.

W. Takacs (1978) 'The Nonequivalence of Tariffs, Import Quotas, and Voluntary Export Restraints', *Journal of International Economics*, VIII, 565-73.

J. Tumlir (1974) 'Emergency Protection Against Sharp Increases in Imports', in H. Corbet and R. Jackson (eds), *In Search of a New World Economic Order* (London, Croom Helm).

J. Tumlir and L. Till (1971) 'Tariff Averaging in International Comparisons', in H. G. Grubel and H. G. Johnson (eds), *Effective Tariff Protection* (Geneva, Graduate Institute of International Studies).

UNCTAD (1978) *Adjustment Assistance Measures*, TD/BC.2/198 (Geneva, UNCTAD).

J. Vanek (1971) 'Tariffs, Economic Welfare and Development Potential', *Economic Journal*, LXXXI, 904-13.

R. Vernon (1966) 'International Investment and International Trade in the Product Cycle', *Quarterly Journal of Economics*, LXXX, 190-207.

I. Walter (1972) 'Non Tariff Protection Among Industrial Countries: Some Preliminary Evidence', *Economia Internazionale*, XXV.

I. Walter and J. Chung (1972) 'The Pattern of Non-Tariff Obstacles to International Market Access', *Weltwirtschaftliches Archiv*, LVIII, 122–36.

M. Wolf (1979) *Adjustment Policies and Problems in Developed Countries*, Staff Working Paper 349 (Washington, World Bank).

M. Wolf (1980) 'Tower of Babel, Conflicting Ideologies of Adjustment', *The World Economy*, II, 481–94.

F. Wolter (1976) 'Adjusting to Imports from Developing Countries: the Evidence from a Capital Rich, Human Resource Poor Country', in H. Giersch (ed.), *Reshaping the World Economic Order* (Tübingen, J. C. B. Möhr).

World Bank (1980) *World Development Report 1980* (Washington, World Bank).

A. J. Yeats (1979) *Trade Barriers Facing Developing Countries* (London, Macmillan).

Author Index

236

Subject Index